BALTHASAR THE MAGUS

Also by Marisa Calvi with Kuthumi Lal Singh
"You Don't Have Problems, You're Just Bored!"
"Pharaoh Thutmose III (Let's Go For A Walk; Book One)"
"Pythagoras of Samos (Let's Go For A Walk; Book Two)"
available via www.newenergywriting.com

Let's Go For a Walk
Book Three

BALTHASAR
THE MAGUS

The Story of The Three Wise Men
as told by Ascended Master Kuthumi
with Marisa Calvi

First published in 2013 by
Marisa Calvi
20 Pinus Avenue
Glenorie NSW 2157
AUSTRALIA

A CIP catalogue record for this book is available
from the National Library of Australia

ISBN; 978-0-9803506-5-4 (paperback)
978-0-9803506-6-1 (e-book)

Cover artwork; "Journey of the Magi" by James Tissot (c1894)

Editor; Eva Smarda Carney
newenergyexpression@gmail.com

For Aandrah, Ahn and Chin Chin;
three of the wisest people I know.
Thank you for my Ohamah School.
It was just the beginning.

# Preface

And so it is that I have finished writing and I now write my preface for you all. This is my time to reflect on all that has happened around the writing of this story.

Balthasar's story took the longest to write of all the books so far. It proved frustrating and challenging to find time to write. It seemed I had become the master of creating distractions. Though some of the distractions were "necessary" and others were truly worthy of the time they took up.

I began a new job, just minutes from my home that allowed my abundance to flow. In return I would spend my days not working wanting to rest. I began doing private sessions with Kuthumi, which also took up what time I had away from my "normal" job.

My greatest distraction though was the joy of travelling. The first part of this was finally getting to Egypt. Since writing Thutmose's story I had ached to see all he spoke of. I stood and wept openly over his mummified body at the museum in Cairo. I gazed in awe at Hatshepsut's temple. I felt myself reach beyond time and space as we toned in the sanctuary of the Temple at Edfu. Kuthumi and I channelled as we sat on a boat on the Nile.

I walked all the places I had written about and gained an even greater connection to the story. It was magnificent and amazing.

After Egypt I made my way to Israel. I was taken to the ancient city of Jaffa and we found a sign saying that Thutmose had captured this city and used it as the base for his missions into the north of Egypt. It felt like he was making sure I knew just how grand his rule had been.

One day we embarked upon a tour of Jerusalem to walk amongst the pilgrims and dive into the web of history here. I wanted to do this for many reasons. I knew it was part of the story of the magi, and it was also my way to cross the border into Palestine to get to Bethlehem as part of a tour.

Our Israeli guide dropped us at the border, and our Palestinian guide greeted us on the other side. I tried to imagine riding into Bethlehem on a camel as our car sped along the road but nothing came to me. In fact any magic of the town seemed buried in the turmoil of the tourism and the political angst which the Palestinians were more than happy to share. There were few moments of true quiet to feel anything.

Still I stood for a few minutes in the place that Yeshua's birth took place, watching some nuns silently recite a rosary where the manger would have been. Beside me a tour group sang Christmas songs. Then we were pushed out for the next group to have their moment.

As I walked through the town, expecting to feel the magi, someone else kept making their presence known—Saint Francis. The man who is celebrated for creating the first nativity scene felt like he was everywhere. There were hotels named for him or statues wherever you looked. It was odd but amusing. I even ended up buying a figurine of him carved from local olive wood in a store there.

A few months later I was in Hawaii. I wish I could say Hawaii is all that its myths say it is. I unfortunately did not find a tropical paradise. Instead Adamus Saint-Germain helped me look deep into the choices I was making about my living ascension. Those choices surprised me, and somewhat scared me.

When I returned home I "grabbed" Kuthumi and said if I was going to stay to enjoy my enlightenment and be human then he needed to share some more of his experience in doing so. Of course he did as graciously as he ever would.

It was (and still is) a wonderful journey even deeper into myself and my soul connection. And more, it is taking me even deeper into the joy of life.

Some months later an old pattern of mine that I was truly done with made itself known once again. I decided to contact Norma "Aandrah" Delaney for one of her wonderful sessions. There is nothing like getting someone with Aandrah's wisdom to help you look into your blind spots and break some patterns. We talked for a while and I felt that pattern dissolve. Then Aandrah asked me how the book was doing. Aandrah has a deep connection to the magi so I was not surprised she would ask.

So I spoke how this one was just not flowing, even though it was the book I had most been looking forward to writing.

"Who were you in the story?" she asked.

So I spoke a little about my part in the story as Aandrah nodded. Then she took me deeper into that story and I saw my part clearer than before.

"You haven't forgiven Kuthumi for that part of your experience yet," she said and I felt how true that was. "See how clever your soul is! To write these books so you can bring home these parts of you."

So I sat and talked about this later with Kuthumi. It also helped me understand why I had resisted pushing on with writing—to not have to face this part of me again, to not have to relive this. I understood also why I had not felt the journey of the magi as I walked Bethlehem. It's amazing how far you can push something away until you are truly ready to face it.

My writing started again, but slowly.

I made another journey, this time to Vienna, Austria, where Kuthumi and I spoke at the Crimson Circle annual conference. Then afterwards I travelled to the most beautiful medieval town of Rust. There I attended one of Adamus Saint-Germain's mystery schools.

In Rust, Adamus confirmed all Kuthumi had shared with me since Hawaii; to fully have your experience, you need to set it free. The year had been a wonderful journey of letting go of stories, excuses and distractions. Living my ascension was now all about accepting and loving myself, and allowing however that would look and feel. No more expectations or goals.

My writing continued, but slowly. Messages and emails came asking about when the book would be ready. They inspired me as much as they reminded me how long it was taking.

I decided that 2013 would be a year of no travel. That would wipe out what had been my biggest distraction, and besides I needed to pay off my airfares. I cleared my space energetically and my writing gained momentum.

Each June it is my commitment to teach Adamus' Dreamwalker Ascension School of which I am a certified teacher. I book an apartment by the ocean, so I get a break away from home as well. This year not one student booked. Instead I created the ideal writing retreat.

The apartment I stayed at was nine storeys up; the highest you could get in Manly, the seaside town it was in. The wall looking out to the ocean was entirely glass and the view was breathtaking. I had this space all to myself for four days, with nothing to do but write—unless a whale might decide to play beyond the waves and I would grab the binoculars to share its delight.

This little retreat was perfect for what I needed to really get through. In this time I wrote the most challenging part of the storyline for myself. Then the writing just couldn't stop.

I wept when I wrote the last page. Not just because of the beauty of what Balthasar shared, but I simply did not want to let him go.

Saint Francis of Assisi will be our next story together and I know he will not be so patient with me! He made himself known in Bethlehem that he was ready and he has done so in many other manners this year. The most glorious way was in having the newest Pope choose his name.

The funniest was when he led me to buy some paint to restore my garden statue of him on the day (unknowingly) I would finish Balthasar's story.

I cannot wait to see what adventure he will take me on.

Marisa

Kuthumi's Introduction

I greet you today once more from my writing desk in India. It's been getting harder to hold my pen but I don't let this faze me or make me believe that I am growing weak. I see it as merely a sign that my days as human are coming to a close.

I have no regrets and you may think that this is from having lived a full and virtuous life. However when I look back I will admit that there were things I wished I had done differently. My lack of regret is not that I walked through my life having done all that is great and amazing. My lack of regret comes from something much grander.

My days now are quiet and still. They seem long but I fill them with reflection. Within reflection I am allowing myself to see beyond the simple human realms of my life experience, beyond all that I have achieved; not only in this life but those I have lived before.

I have now come to understand and truly connect with a calling that has been with me since I separated from the oneness. I can hear the absolute truth of my being and it sings to me a song so beautiful that my eyes fill with tears.

I will leave this body that I have used this past sixty-seven years quite soon. I will do it knowing that I will return to my wholeness as it was at the dawn of time.

I will do this because I allowed myself to hear the calling from my essence. The voice that called out to me to come home. The voice that offered me the freedom to rise above the chaos of existence and walk the Earth with clarity and strength.

It called to me in the darkest times but I know now it was there even within the most elated of times.

I sit here now and make one last prayer as I look out to my garden. I pray that others will know the beauty of hearing the call. And when they do I will walk with them and we will sing and dance to the music of their oneness.

So once again I will invite you to come along with me to hear your own music. When you are ready, let's go for a walk....

Kuthumi

# CHAPTER ONE

I was born of starlight and laughter.

The day of my birth soon went into the night of my birth. As my mother shrieked with yet another pain the midwife would yell over her cries with a joke, so that as the pain subsided my mother would collapse back upon her pillows laughing.

"A child born amidst laughter knows humour and good will. Let a child be born amongst angst and so thus their life will be one of tragedy and confusion."

This was the midwife's motto and she truly believed it had not failed her yet. It was also what she snapped at my father when he finally beat upon the door in the late afternoon to question her methods.

He sighed as she closed the door and turned to his butler.

"Have you ever known such a birthing method?" he asked the servant.

"No, Sir," the servant answered plainly as he shook his head.

My father paced the corridors of our home for several more hours. Night began to fall and as the servants scurried about him lighting lamps he heard an almighty roar of laughter come from the birthing room. He shook his head and told himself that it was better than just hearing his wife in pain. Then he did hear her cry in pain. Though it was followed by a bawdy joke from the midwife, he did not hear any laughter from his wife and then another cry of pain followed quickly.

He could not bear to hear this much longer and called out to his butler.

"Go get our astronomy equipment," my father ordered.

"Really? Tonight?" the butler questioned.

"Yes, yes, yes," my father replied flustered. "What else do you suggest we do as we wait? I fear I am going to wear a trough in the floor."

My father and his butler walked outside into the garden. It was a beautiful night. The moon was just less than half and hanging in the sky like a cup. This meant only the brightest of stars could shine tonight and my father liked this.

"We will mark the positions of the major constellations so that my child will know just what the sky held on the night of their birth," he smiled as he told the butler.

They set up a small table just a small way from the window of the bedroom where my mother was giving birth. He did this quite knowingly and with good reason. For the moment he heard a cry from his child he planned to run inside and be with my mother.

Just as my father looked up at the sky for the first time, the shutters from the bedroom window flung open banging against the walls of the house. He turned to see the midwife leaning out, her huge bosom resting upon the sill.

"Ah, decided to get some fresh air did you? Well we could use some too!" she said and then disappeared back into the room leaving the shutters open. My father could hear her louder than ever now. "Your husband is out playing with stars while you do some true work in here!" she bellowed to my mother.

My father shook his head and began to call out measurements and names to his butler who recorded them upon a scroll.

Another hour passed and while my mother's cries grew more frequent the midwife grew cruder.

"Ah, that child coming out is much bigger than what your husband put into you," she roared as I began to finally make my way out.

Outside my father's face grew dark. He gritted his teeth and muttered something unintelligible through them. His butler dropped his head in the hope of hiding his smirk, but my father did not miss it. He was about to rebuke the man when the most glorious sound made its way through the open window.

It was the sound of my first cries. My father's plans to run inside were suddenly forgotten. All he could do was stand frozen in place, staring at the window.

"Sir, the child is here," the servant whispered and then he began to pack up their instruments and scrolls.

My father did not hear him. All he could hear was me.

Then the midwife appeared at the window holding me in her arms.

"Well, do you think you might like to meet your son," she said and laughed. "He is a fine specimen of a child. I congratulate you."

From behind her my mother cried out, "He is beautiful!"

My father finally remembered how his feet worked and walked to the window. The midwife held me out for him to see and as he gazed upon me he too finally found reason to laugh.

"He is beautiful," he said softly as he smiled.

"Take him," said the midwife and lowered me into his arms.

So as the midwife and the maids finished attending to my mother, with the loving arms of my father embracing me, I spent the first moments of my new life beneath the stars.

It was no wonder that I always felt so at home when I was with them.

 CHAPTER TWO

I may have been born amid laughter and starlight but I was also born into a grand life.

My father was a magus: a high priest of the Zoroastrians. As was his father before him and his father before him. It was a tradition and way of life that all men of my bloodline had followed for over a thousand years. It was without question that this was the way my life would lead and not once did I ever question or doubt it.

The priesthood was as much a part of me as the blood pushing through my veins or the breath within my lungs. It was a grand calling and I honoured it.

The magi that spread the teachings of Zarathustra saw the beauty in all life as they knew the magic of creation. Ahura Mazda had shown this to Zarathustra upon a mountain as Zarathustra called out for enlightenment.

Zarathustra, our grand prophet and founder, had wandered from his village, frustrated with the suffering and futility that he believed life was. He walked knowing that he needed to be alone and quiet to gain the understanding of why the world was like this. He arrived at the base of a mountain and he knew he would climb it.

When Zarathustra reached the summit he sat and observed the lands. The quiet and stillness revealed far more than he could have imagined. Within the solitude he started to see the nuances of nature and he knew within this was the key to the understanding he ached to know.

The clouds threw shadows upon the land and then moved on. The sun warmed his skin and then a breeze would cool it. Zarathustra became aware of a rhythm and the more he allowed himself to feel it the more he realised the rhythm was within him as much as around him.

Zarathustra became aware of his heartbeat and its pounding reminded him of a drum calling him to march. Then another gentle rhythm made itself known. His breath washed in and out of him like waves of the ocean. Zarathustra closed his eyes and surrendered to its grace.

As he did this a voice called him.

"Are you ready?" it asked.

"Yes," replied Zarathustra.

Thus began Zarathustra's time with the energy he would call Ahura Mazda, the creator of all that is.

Mazda showed to Zarathustra the eternal oneness that was the creator. Then from this, sparks flew out to become their own beings. Zarathustra knew each one was a soul dancing away to know themselves and all there was to experience.

That call to experience created dark and light, warmth and cold, good and evil.

"To know experience you must know all it can offer. You must know its depths and heights. Only then can you know the wonder of all that is," Mazda told him.

Zarathustra felt into this and while his heart sang at the joy and beauty, then too his heart broke to see the despair and horror as well. He lay down amongst the rocks and wept.

"Why would we want to know such darkness? Why would you let us suffer?" he cried out to his creator.

A cool breeze washed over him and Zarathustra looked up. Dark clouds had gathered above him. They rumbled and he felt some drops of rain upon his skin. In the distance he saw a bolt of lightning hit the ground.

Then the clouds folded upon themself becoming thin, a wind came and they were pushed from the sky. Sunlight poured down upon the mountain and the scant rain that had fallen dried instantly.

Zarathustra once more felt the rhythm of life and how it all played in harmony. He understood in that moment that every aspect of life was here for a purpose.

Yet something still pulled within him. He thought of men who chose to rob and murder. He saw battles where soldiers were slaughtered for the whims of a conqueror. He pictured women who would sell their bodies for money.

Mazda felt his question before he could even form the words and told Zarathustra to stand up.

"Look to your left," Mazda said.

To the left of the mountain Zarathustra saw that more grey clouds were gathering. They were so thick they cast heavy shadows upon the land. Beneath them the land was desolate and with nothing there of nourishment.

"Look to your right," Mazda said.

To the other side of the mountain, gentle sunlight played upon a lush land. Its trees were full of ripe fruit and a gentle river flowed through it.

"When you leave this mountain, which place would you go to?" Mazda asked him.

Zarathustra smiled and received his answer.

"Which way I should go would be of my choosing," he replied.

"As such choice is the way of all humanity in life," Mazda answered.

Mazda showed Zarathustra that while there was contrast to explore experience, there was also the choice of what to experience. Zarathustra breathed deep with this and saw all the land around the mountain transform into a fertile and abundant land.

"One day you will not need the contrast. One day so many of you will have chosen the light, the abundance and the joy so that the dark will not be needed. Then you will all live in paradise."

This was Mazda's promise to Zarathustra and us all. He walked for many years retelling all that Mazda had told him. He wrote scroll upon scroll that became the basis of all we lived by.

We were but sparks sent by Mazda to enjoy this life. As priests we guided and encouraged people to make good choices, to live in light and joy. For in doing so, not only were we all rewarded with a virtuous and noble life, then too did we invite the time of paradise on Earth.

It would be the Great Awakening; a time when all the contrast could fall away and generation upon generation of magi had awaited its arrival.

CHAPTER THREE

My childhood was simple but full.

The first male child of a magus carries with him great hopes for the future and not just for his bloodline, but for all of humanity.

As my father looked upon me during our first embrace he smiled and whispered, "Fear not little one. Great things lie ahead for us all."

He repeated this to me many times during my childhood. When talk of war arose or when our family heard of another's tragedy he would say it again, though often changing the words.

"Discourse and chaos are part of life, but faith and trust in the future softens them," he said to me when we heard about a skirmish on the Egyptian border which threatened to head east to our home.

I truly believe that all I needed to know was within these simple variations of his belief: a belief that had been handed to him by all our preceding magi forefathers. It was this simplicity that was the foundation of all I was taught.

The stars which were so much a part of my beginning were also to be a huge part of my experience. A magus learnt many things but few were as wonderful or integral to his role as the study of the stars. When one starts to look upon and review the endless charts and recordings it can be quite overwhelming but, as with anything that at first seems complex, one can soon find a simplicity within it.

The stars were certainly like this and my father knew it. By the age of three I had spent as much time in the night air as I had the day. The great garden behind my home was the grandest classroom I would ever know and my father took me here as soon as he decided I was old enough to pay attention in any way that would be useful.

I am most certain the year leading to my second birthday was most unproductive but my father persevered. He would point to a constellation and then to its diagram on a scroll. By the time he had looked back to the sky I would be distracted or possibly yawning.

"Yes I know this makes no sense, but some day it will," he would say to me while looking at the sky.

It was just after I turned two when it did make sense to me. I had been uttering my first words for weeks now and was beginning to make crude sentences. My father revelled in our new mode of communication and pushed my astronomy classes even more, getting me to recite the names of constellations and never laughing once at my infantile attempts to replicate the words.

My father one night lifted me in his arms, as though being closer to the stars would help me see what he saw in them. He pointed at certain stars, kissing me upon the cheek once as I copied his hands and babbled as though teaching him.

Then the most glorious thing happened. A star shot across the sky. It was quick but it was brilliantly stunning, leaving a silver scar across the dark grey for a few seconds. My eyes grew wide, hardly believing what I had seen. My father whooped and bounced me in his arms adding to the fun and making this even more special.

"You saw it Balthasar! You saw it!" he cheered and then pointed to the place where it had flashed. "That will never happen again in that exact way and we shared it together!" he said so excitedly that I could not help but smile back at him. "I wonder who else saw that tonight?" he said as he lowered me to the ground. "We must record this."

Fifty miles west of us an eight year old boy kicked at the ground as his father scratched upon a scroll.

"Gaspar! I cannot believe you are not excited about that," the man grumbled.

The child shrugged his shoulders. "We have seen such things before and we shall again," Gaspar muttered back.

"Yes, but rarely as bright as that, and certainly not in the same position! Surely you have not lost your enthusiasm to see such things already?" his father asked with concern. "Perhaps I have spoiled you by teaching you so much so young … though my father did the same and I still hold some wonder for such things."

Gaspar was not spoiled though. He was simply impatient for the change that he had been told the stars would foresee. Though all the magi had been patiently waiting for thousands of years for such things, at the age of eight he was already weary and wary that his life may simply pass with no significant event to record.

Gaspar knew the fleeting streaks of light that shooting stars offered could someday add up in some way, but he knew already that they meant nothing of the change Mazda predicted. He knew they were but mere winks from the universe to entertain those who kept their vigils. At the age of eight such a realisation had become more of a burden than a revelation.

He sighed as he looked up at the night sky.

"My life will not be wasted recording trivial changes to the sky and humanity," he silently promised himself and kicked at the ground again.

Thirty miles north of me a six month old boy named Melchior stirred in his sleep as his mother looked down upon him. She looked out into her garden where her husband gasped as he too saw the shooting star and began to record it.

# CHAPTER FOUR

When I say I was the firstborn son of my father I say this with some license. I was not necessarily the firstborn but was indeed the first surviving son. Two other males had left my mother's body before I arrived but sadly neither had taken even one breath. When my mother fell pregnant with trepidation and anxiety for the third time, my father nodded his head in acknowledgment but he did not smile with the delight an expectant father might usually.

"We need to do things differently this time Marianna," he said to my mother with the air of one planning a grand journey. "If we change how we do things then we can change the outcome."

So together my mother and father didn't so much reject the traditions and beliefs surrounding pregnancy and birth of their time; they simply twisted them to suit what they believed they needed to do to change what had been.

First of all was to let go of the idea that a woman needed to be bedridden for much of her pregnancy. This was truly only something noble women did anyway. A common woman would toil until she could not bend or her labour pains finally brought her to her knees.

My father, Malchiek, knew this from his counselling, often visiting families where a heavily pregnant woman would be balancing a small child on one hip while picking fruit or stirring a huge pot of soup. Yet somehow noble women needed to lie down as soon as they knew they were with child. Malchiek knew that sometimes women did indeed endure pregnancy as though it were an illness and needed to rest, but my mother was far from this fragility when she fell pregnant.

So first on their agenda was keeping my mother active. Marianna would walk with the maids to market and she would walk the grounds of our home upon my father's arm.

"Your face looks brighter and healthier this time my dear," my father would say to encourage her and he meant every word.

My mother ate the best of everything. Malchiek sent for foods from as far as the land you call Italy for her. There were truffles from southern Italy, dates from Egypt and persimmons from the northeastern reaches of Persia to name but a few. Our head cook would often stand perplexed at her bench looking down at yet another basket or box that had just arrived, delivered by some foreigner who could not explain the contents to her in any words she could understand.

"What am I supposed to do with this?" she would exclaim as she held up a fruit she had never seen or a bag filled with a spice that made her nose burn.

Malchiek would be so patient with her, explaining each ingredient. "You will be known as one of the great chefs of Babylonia when this pregnancy is done," he said to her as she tentatively began to peel yet another alien vegetable.

The final act in all of this was finding a new midwife. The local midwives of the village cried when Malchiek tried to explain why he would not be calling upon them.

"We failed you. We failed our own magus!" one cried but several scowled behind him knowing that most stillbirths were not to do with their limited skills.

"No, no, no!" cried Malchiek. "We just wish to change how we have done things to create a new outcome."

This made the scowling midwives now roll their eyes. As Malchiek left the meeting they looked at one another shaking their heads.

"That is our grand Magus! One who thinks he can alter his wife's ability to bear children simply by who is there to catch the baby. May Mazda truly help him!"

This was what Malchiek believed. He knew intent was as powerful as actions. He knew that he could find the most amazing food in the world for his wife but if he offered it without the awareness of why he had sought it, and if she ate it without the awareness of why it was offered to her, then it would serve no one and no cause.

He had felt the scowls and cynicism of the village women as he spoke and as he walked away he heard the mumbling. Malchiek knew that dismissing their services was probably the most powerful thing he had done to assure my safe delivery. Now he was left to find someone to replace them.

Malchiek asked his servants first. He trusted his household as much as he did his fellow priests or family. He walked into the kitchen as the evening meal was being prepared and was given his usual warm greeting as though a cherished friend had arrived. There were few formalities in our home, yet this did not compromise the respect held by our servants for my family.

"Good day our Lord," shouted out the cook as she continued to cut into some goose. "Do you come to instruct as to the new seeds that arrived today?"

"No, I come to ask some totally non-food related advice," he replied with a laugh.

Every person in the kitchen stopped what they were doing and looked at my father. The cook put down her huge knife and wiped her hands upon her apron as her face took on a quite serious expression. She gestured for him to take a seat. Everyone else kept their eyes upon my father.

My father did not sit and spoke clearly and calmly as he looked about the room. "I need to know if any of you can tell me of a competent midwife that would be in a neighbouring village. I wish to seek someone new to deliver the child your mistress is expecting. They just need to be able to travel here in a suitable time when Marianna goes into labour."

The servants looked about themselves for a few seconds. Many of them knew of women nearby who could do such things, but to recommend someone who may in fact deliver yet another stillborn child for their master made them hesitate.

From the back of the kitchen though, a timid maid stepped forward. She knew someone and she could not hold back from mentioning her.

"I do Sir," she said almost faltering and barely able to look my father in the eye. "Her ways are somewhat different but she is highly spoken of—and—and—rarely does she—um—ah—have any—difficulties."

The maid had struggled to find the words to deal with the issues she knew Malchiek wanted not to repeat but he had heard nothing past the word "different". That was the one word he had hoped for and he knew immediately this was the woman who would deliver me.

So to endure the midwife's "humour", as hard as it had been, it had also been seen as something of necessity and purpose. When my father finally held me in his arms and saw my chest and belly fill with determined and deliberate breaths he knew I was here to stay.

Malchiek also believed the worst of what I could possibly endure was also over. This may seem odd given what lies ahead for even a simple life, but my father saw my ability to simply be born as something magical and a sign that I could survive anything.

Three sisters followed me and he saw that within them all. And when my sisters in turn successfully gave birth to their own babies, he saw this as confirmation of their blessings as well. Not surprisingly each of my mother's subsequent births followed the procedures carried out within my time in her womb. After all, if you change a pattern to change an outcome then you would repeat a pattern to repeat an outcome.

When my father visited the midwife to book her services the second time, she was both bemused and elated – and did not hesitate to say so.

"Well my Lord, I must say I am surprised to see you—and yet not at all surprised at the same time!" she said with a laugh.

"I don't understand your techniques but what I do understand is that it works. For that I cannot consider another to be with my wife to deliver our children," he said most humbly.

Malchiek used the story of the midwife many times over as my sisters and I grew up. Whenever we seemed perplexed by something that was intangible or that relied upon our faith, her story would be recounted.

"The details and nuances of 'why' do not matter. That just makes sense for up here," he would say and tap at his forehead. Then he would point to his heart. "Faith and trust come from here ... and here is what lets us all enjoy the magic in life without knowing 'how' or 'why'. Here," he would keep tapping at his chest. "Here is the passion and power to make life much more than what we see and hear. If I had not listened to this then I would not have the four of you."

And for that we were all grateful.

CHAPTER FIVE

At the age of five my education and training went into its next phase as I was now old enough to enter temple. Children were not allowed into such places until adolescence and my early entry was only due to my family lineage and the fact that I would one day be a magus myself.

"Here," said the eldest of my sisters as she handed me a twig. "Take this for the great fire so Mazda will hear my prayers."

I looked at the twig and didn't know whether to laugh or not but behind my sister I saw my father looking at us with a most serious face.

"We will offer that to the great fire with honour for you Marit," he said and now looked me in the eye. "Won't we Balthasar?"

"Yes. Yes we will," I answered as I nodded my head.

The great fire was the central part of the public section of a Zoroastrian temple. It was in essence our altar, symbolising our god and therefore being the focus of rituals and prayers. People of the village and surrounds brought bundles of wood to keep it burning constantly and most temples needed a storage space next to the temple for such things.

As each person brought their stacks of wood as an offering they would take one piece into the temple and place it into the circular pit in the centre of the room which held the fire. Then they would drop to their knees and pray. They would pray for Mazda to guide them in life, to help them make good clear choices and they would pray for the awakening that had been promised to arrive.

As they left they would be given a piece of charcoal; the cooled remnants from the excess coals that built up in the altar pit. This served two purposes. Firstly it allowed the priests to clear the inevitable accumulation of embers at the base of the fire, allowing more fresh wood to be placed on for prayers. Secondly it was taken from the temple by worshippers as a reminder of how their offering would be transformed, and also as a symbol for the transformation of themselves through their prayer.

Many would rub the charcoal upon their foreheads to let others know they had been to temple, making a design something akin to an asterisk or star. As others passed them by they would touch their own foreheads to acknowledge the person's visit to temple and to remind themselves to do the same.

The charcoal would sit in the villager's home until it was replaced with a new piece. The old piece would go into the stove fire and invariably the meal cooked from the fire it contributed to would be deemed the tastiest that week! After all the power of Mazda had been within the flame that cooked it.

I climbed the steps of our temple for the first time that day. It was at the base that I would have usually farewelled my father and then returned home. Today though I stepped up onto the first and then second step, then I stopped. Malchiek took a few more paces up the stairs until he realised I had stopped.

"What is it Balthasar?" he asked with a smile but he knew the answer already.

I could not answer and each time I looked up at the colonnade surrounding the temple the feeling within me grew stronger. Malchiek came back down the stairs, stopping on the stair just above me. He bent down, resting his right hand upon his knee and spoke with the softest voice I would ever hear.

"I remember the first time my father took me to temple. I thought I would faint to finally be so close to Mazda. All the stories I had been told would now become real and not just be some words from my father's mouth," he said with a smile and caressed my hair to comfort me. "You will not forget today. Today will make real all you have been told, and remove some things that you had imagined. That can be uncomfortable to have our imagination both confirmed and cancelled, but trust me when I tell you that knowing reality is much more satisfying to your soul."

With that we walked up the stairs once more. This time though I picked up my pace and grabbed at my father's coat. I may be about to have my imagination pulled into reality but I would at least do so close by my father.

There were only twenty stairs to the temple but to my small frame it seemed much more. Each step we took made the temple seem even larger and this made me feel that Mazda was even larger than I had believed him to be. I grabbed at Malchiek's coat even tighter making it pull at his neck. He didn't stop for a second though and I saw him smile.

We reached the top and Malchiek gently reached down and pulled my hand from his coat. Without looking down for more than a second, he then looked ahead and said softly, "You have to walk in of your own accord. No man can be dragged to god, no matter their age."

I did not understand but I also knew not to question. I resisted all temptation to look around me and be distracted by my surrounds and walked in at my father's side.

Our local temple was designed along the basic format of all larger Zoroastrian places of worship. It was set upon a platform to raise it above the ordinary buildings of the town it was located in, with stairs on all four sides leading up to the terrace that surrounded the building.

There were doorways at the front and to each side to dispel the heat of the fire and allow fresh air in. All entered by the doors at the front of the temple. This was the side which faced and looked down upon the town. Temples were always built on the northern or highest edge of a village. It gave the air of a grand master guarding and watching over the people at all times and the trail of smoke that constantly snaked out from the great fire through the openings in its roof, also reminded the people of what resided in here.

When you climbed up to the temple you were reminded of how Zarathustra himself climbed his mountain to connect with Mazda. Each person who made their way here was seen to re-enact his very journey to begin our religion.

As we stepped through the door, that first instance of the light dimming and your eyes beginning to adjust soon falters again as you set sight upon the great fire. It sat within a pit in the centre of the room. Four immense pillars at the edge of the pit pushed the roof above it up several feet, creating a gap which allowed the smoke out, then around these pillars a balustrade of marble circled the fire and the pillars. This railing had gaps in it at four equal places and it was in these spaces that people stepped forward to place some wood upon the fire before stepping back behind the barrier to kneel and pray.

Some brought with them a pillow to soften the floor beneath their knees whilst others knelt upon the marble floor as though it was no matter. Some prayed in silence, while others seemed to emit a low hum as they softly spoke their hopes to Mazda. Priests walked amongst them softly touching their heads or shoulders as though Mazda himself was giving them a gentle acknowledgment.

All the while the great fire churned before them with its own soft pulse, every now and then emitting a snap or a pop as an ember exploded.

The first time I stood before the great fire was amazing. After all I had been told it could have been somewhat disappointing to simply see a great bundle of heat and light in the centre of the temple. I had seen fires before. I watched our cook maintain the fire in our kitchen ovens and I had sat around braziers in winter with my family. But to stand before this immense fire and to know what it symbolised was incredible.

I stood with my mouth open; firstly at its immense size and then at the very fact that I was finally within the temple and before it. My father left a moment for me to take it all in.

"It is beautiful, is it not?" he asked me and all I could do was nod. "Stay and watch it some more," he said and walked off.

I didn't think for a minute that I wanted to follow him. Instead I made my way around the edge of the room, careful not to disturb the prayers or priests. I wanted to see this fire from every way I could. When I made my way back to where I had started I finally remembered the twig from Marit that I still held in my hand. I walked to the nearest space within the balustrade and tentatively threw it upon the fire. It disappeared within the flames and then I too knelt down, closed my eyes and began to pray.

I prayed that I not be a disappointment to my father. I prayed to grow strong and wise and serve Mazda as best I could. I prayed for the health of my family. I prayed for the care of my village. Then when I decided I had covered all that needed to be prayed for I opened my eyes and looked once more at the fire.

Somehow now it seemed different. The whips of flame that jumped up from the embers seemed even more definite, as though each one sprung from the wood independently. Some were deep red; others had streaks of yellow and orange. A knot in one of the pieces of wood exploded and I jumped in my place as sparks shot out from the pit just missing a nearby priest. He brushed at his coat making sure none were embedding in his clothing.

I looked at his face and saw he did not panic as it seemed that this was a perfectly regular thing for him to deal with. Within seconds he was back to walking amongst the people. I watched him for a while longer as he moved about the room, his face staying calm and relaxed. He would stop by a young woman and place his hand upon her head and I noticed that as he did his chest rose with a deep deliberate breath.

Then the priest moved on to an old man who had tears fall down his face as he mouthed his prayers. The priest stopped and then softly dropped onto his knees beside the man, gently placing an arm over his shoulders. Once again I saw the priest's body fill with breath and slowly the old man's tears stopped and his face lightened. The priest stood up and moved on without a word or a change in his expression.

I would have liked to watch more but heard my father's voice above me. "That is enough from this room for now. Let me show you the rest of temple."

The room of the great fire was the only one that the people of the village were allowed into and this is all they needed access to in order to fulfil their responsibilities and spiritual growth. Behind the room of the fire were the libraries – one dedicated to the teachings of Zarathustra, while the other held the astronomy teachings and records. Only priests, acolytes and students were allowed into these rooms.

There was a doorway at the back of the room of the great fire that led to the libraries. This was a huge ornate door much like the double door that

37

formed the main entrance. It swung without a sound and the only way you would know it had moved was the slight breeze it sent to the fire giving the flames a momentary rush.

My father pushed me through the doorway and pulled it closed behind him.

"We never leave this door open any longer than is necessary," he said and then explained. "We cannot risk a spark or stray ember to find their way to the libraries."

I nodded emphatically as I pictured the fire growing as large as the temple itself and devouring everything in its path. Not surprisingly there was little wood in the temple aside from that which fuelled the fire. The doors were of metal while the walls, floor and most of the roofs were of stone. When we walked into the libraries, even the shelving was made of the immaculate marble and granite that was elsewhere.

The scant furniture and panels of the roofing was all that was flammable apart from the precious scrolls. The irony of having a god represented by a force that could destroy the very records of his teachings, and to have them in close proximity to each other was not lost upon the priests. Behind the temple there was another cluster of buildings that completed the temple complex. There was one small stone replica of the temple and in this was housed a duplicate library. It had only taken one fire to sweep through one temple to teach our religion how to preserve and protect what was necessary.

Alongside the second library were storage spaces for the excess wood brought as offerings, and another small building served as a larder for food for the priests. To the side of these small buildings was a long building and in here was a dormitory, including a bathing area and kitchen. This is where students and pilgrims could stay if no accommodation in the village was offered them. Despite the hospitality and generosity of the village the dormitory was regularly full; as much from desire to be close to temple as it was a necessity.

Today I would stay in the libraries with my father. I will never forget his smile as he pulled that first scroll from the shelves and turned to face me.

"You remember all I have taught you about reading?" he asked and I nodded. "Good. Then today I wish you to read me the first book of the Avesta."

With that he sat beside me, uncurled the scroll and pointed to the first characters upon it.

"Begin," he said and I did.

CHAPTER SIX

The next five years were intense and demanding upon me. Being the son of a high magus did not spare me from the requirements of study. We were expected to learn and memorize a book of the Avesta each year so that by the age of twelve we could recite them all by memory.

This pushed us in many ways; it embedded the teachings deep within us by way of the words but even more profound was the impact of reciting the words over and over again upon our spirit. Some days were like torture; your mouth would turn dry and your tongue would seem like it was paralysed. Other days something would touch your heart as you said it so that you could do nothing but cry. Some days you decided you hated Mazda and all he shared with Zarathustra and other days made you humbled to be part of such a tradition.

The repetition over and over tested our commitment. It also made us go deeper and deeper into the teachings. There were parts which at first seemed small and yet to say them a thousand times made them as big as any other part of the teachings. It made you realise how every single word was necessary, how every page was necessary and that no book of the Avesta was more important than another.

I sat upon the top step of the temple one day looking out upon our village and pondered this. As I did I looked at the village in a new way. I saw that no building was more important than another – our temple would have no value if it did not have a village to look upon, the bakery fed so many and the simple village home housed a family that was cherished. It all worked together and if one part was missing then it all changed.

Yes, everything, no matter how small, was important.

The method of repetitive learning not only helped us see outside of ourselves with greater depth but it also opened up parts within us. There were days when the repetition became like a chant; even dissolving into a hum which would seem like a meditative mantra. The words would just seem like sounds with no meaning after a while and the movement of your tongue and lips would fall into a rhythm.

Suddenly, even though you were still reciting perfectly, the sounds would seem to separate from the thoughts behind the words. Syllables, phrases and sentences were no longer anything tangible to the one who was speaking them. A wave of surrender and stillness would come over you. It was within this space that you would really feel the truth of what was written.

The first time it happened I was so confused that I ran to find my father who was in the astronomy library. I was breathing quickly and my face was red. As my father looked at me he felt my panic and reacted accordingly.

"Oh no! Has the great fire gone out?" he said and began to make way to the door behind me.

"No, no, no," I said shaking my head.

"Well then, what else has you in such a state?" he asked as he walked back and stood before me.

I explained as best I could while he kept a calm and composed expression. When I finished he put one hand upon my shoulder and smiled.

"Son, I do believe you are ready for a mountain retreat," he said calmly and smiled.

The next day we made way for one of the mountains on the outskirts of our village. In Babylonia no village was too far from such mountains. They provided shelter for the townships as well as places to forage. For a magus it was the place where you were able to relive Zarathustra's time of revelation and hopefully gain your own personal insights.

I was ten when my father walked me out of the village. Each of us carried only a small canteen of water. I knew little of what we were setting out for and despite a constant stream of questions from me there was still little discussion on what was about to happen. My father's answers were clipped but far from terse.

"Balthasar, this is not the time for such a barrage of questions," my father finally gasped.

"Well it might have been nice to have informed me of such before we started," I muttered back. It was the first time I had challenged my father in any way and he stopped in his tracks, looking at me with an air of frustration which was also a first for us both.

"Yes I suppose it might have but that is not the way of this stage of your learning. This is about opening up even more that which you felt at the temple." With that he walked on and despite this cryptic answer tempting me to ask a hundred more questions I kept my mouth shut tight.

My feet kept slipping as we walked the narrow trail up the mountain giving me all the reasons I needed at my age to be even more frustrated and defiant. Malchiek, though he too faltered every now and then, remained composed and regal as ever.

"I do believe that Zarathustra turned himself into a goat to accomplish this part of his journey," I called out jokingly as I gathered myself from yet another fall.

Malchiek did not respond or react. I straightened my clothes and continued on.

When we reached near the summit my father stopped and pointed. I looked and saw that he was motioning to a small cave within the rocks on the side of the mountain. A modest tree stood to the left and its branches curved over most of the opening.

Malchiek stepped forward and pulled some of the branches aside and I could now see the opening and space beyond was much bigger than I had first thought. He stepped inside and I would later find out it was to check that the space was clear of the remains of any previous inhabitants be they human or animal. When he could see it was truly empty he walked back out to me.

"Go inside and begin your recitations. When you reach that feeling that you spoke to me of, delve into it even more. Allow it to open up," he

43

said hardly making eye contact with me. "I will go now. You can return when you feel complete but that should not be before at least two nights." With that he began to walk back down the mountain.

I began to scramble after him. "But I only have enough water for today and no food!" I cried out.

"You will have Mazda with you. That is all you need," he said without looking back and quickened his pace.

I stopped and looked around me. It was no use to simply run after my father as I am sure he would have just dragged me back to the cave. I slumped down on the ground, drew my knees up to my chest and hugged them as I watched the small cloud of dust that followed my father back down the mountain.

I stretched my neck up and looked at the sky. There was not a cloud in sight and though there was a slight breeze the heat of the sun became uncomfortable. I stood, looked one last time at my father making his way back to the village and entered into the cave.

Once inside I soon forgot the heat from outside and actually shivered from how cool it was in the dark with the tree blocking any sunlight that tried to shine into the cave.

No food, no water and no blanket either I realised. I dumped myself unceremoniously down on the hard floor of the cave and sighed as I looked around. There may have been no bodies but as my eyes adjusted I saw a few discarded canteens. Picking them up and shaking them I was not surprised to find they were long empty. They would have been no use to me full anyway as I would have had no idea how long the water had been stagnating within them.

To the back of the space though I found something that would be useful. Heaped in a pile that at first I thought was a rock was indeed a blanket. It was musty, dusty and had several bugs making it their home but it would serve me well. I took it outside and shook it as best I could. Unfortunately most of the dust blew back upon me making me admire and respect our servants with a new perspective.

I watched as the insects that the blanket had housed fell to the ground and scurried away. I wished I was leaving too. Instead I went back into the dank cavern and sat down cross-legged. Pulling the blanket over my shoulders I began the recitations as Malchiek had instructed me.

I continued on for hours, stopping only to sip at my water or investigate some foreign sound that had distracted me. Not once did I get even close to the sensation that had been the cause of me being left in this hole in the mountainside. The sun began to fall and it was then that I truly wished I was heading home. My stomach began to growl and this increased as night fell.

With the sun completely set the temperature fell even more within the cave and my eyes grew heavy. I lay down upon the stone floor and every part of me ached for the comfort of my soft bed.

I was now tired, cold, uncomfortable and desperately hungry. The worst though was that I was now also lonely. To think of my home and its physical comforts were one thing; now as I thought of my family the tears began to fall.

I have no shame to tell you that I cried like a small child. As I did I cursed Zarathustra and all that he thought he heard upon his mountain.

At my home my family gathered around the dinner table. My mother feigned a smile as Malchiek described leaving me upon the mountain.

They had discussed it the night before when Malchiek told Marianna that I was ready for such a retreat.

"He is still a boy, Malchiek," Marianna protested softly.

"This will help him become a man," answered Malchiek firmly.

That did little to stop her maternal instincts from worrying for her son spending a night, or possibly nights, exposed to nature despite the "assurance" of the cave.

"Where is Balthasar?" asked Marit when she realised what they were discussing.

"Your brother is experiencing his first mountain retreat. He will pray and recite the Avesta upon the mountain to expand his connection with Mazda," Malchiek answered matter-of-factly.

"When will he come back?" asked Suzana, my second sister.

"When he is ready," said Malchiek in the same manner as before.

"When will that be?" Suzana pushed.

"It may be some days," answered Malchiek and filled his mouth with food in the hope the girls would see this as a sign to stop their questions.

"Is he going to sleep there?" asked Marit with her eyes wide.

"Yes!" snapped Malchiek.

"What if a jackal eats him!" shrieked Marit and burst into tears inspiring Suzana as well as our youngest sister, Aluna, to join in crying at this thought.

Seeing all three of her daughters cry was the final straw for Marianna and she too now let her tears flow upon hearing Marit say the words that she had been thinking and fearing. The girls seeing their mother cry saw this as license to now upgrade their sobs to wails, which in turn made Marianna's tears pour with even more ease.

Malchiek looked about the women surrounding him, shook his head and then did something he rarely ever did—he raised his voice.

"Stop this! Stop this now!" he said loudly and though it was far from shouting, to my mother and sisters it was as powerful. They began to gather themselves as Malchiek continued. "Balthasar will not be eaten. I spent nights in that cave and was not eaten by a jackal… as did my father… and—and his father… and his father before him. Not one of them was eaten by a jackal. No one in this family has been eaten by a jackal. No one will be eaten by a jackal. You forget that he does this in service to Mazda! Mazda will not allow such things to happen to one who serves him with such honour. Now, please, let us eat and tonight in your prayers you can pay respect to your brother and all he does for our family and humanity."

With that the family all went back to eating but no one was so hungry after that discussion. Meals were picked at between sniffs and the occasional catch of breath as the girls pushed their tears back to escape another lecture.

In the meantime my own tears had subsided also. I watched how the moonlight dappled through the tree branches onto the floor in the cave and was thankful that the moon would be like a lamp for me, saving me from complete darkness. Then I realised that the night animals would also be taking advantage of this light to hunt.

I thought of the jackals making their way amongst the animal hutches and stables around the village and wondered if they might smell me out up here. I was not so big yet; they might mistake me for a lamb or calf! As I thought this I heard one of the animals howl out into the night and I shivered but not from the cold. I pulled my legs and arms in close, making the blanket as tight as I could around me and decided to stay awake. That way I would be ready if one did make their way to me.

I did fall asleep though. It happened just as the dawn began to break. Seeing the pink in the sky made me relax and this brought on sleep quicker than ever before. It had been almost twenty-four hours without sleep so that was not so surprising. Even the hard floor and my hunger could not hold me back and I slept well into the day.

When I woke it was past midday and as I stepped outside to stretch and relieve myself I realised this and was somewhat grateful.

"Well I have managed to survive some more time here in a most efficient way," I thought to myself and had a little chuckle but then my smile dropped.

It was in that moment I realised that my father or no one else had been to check on me. Surely they would have woken me to berate me for sleeping into the day if they had been here.

"I could have been eaten and they would not know," I realised and then horrified myself by contemplating that they did not care either.

I imagined life in my home continuing on as though I had never been there. My father would have to choose another male to succeed him at temple and I pictured him travelling about Babylonia to find a candidate.

At home though the opposite was true. My father walked to temple that morning trying to not think about me but as he looked up at the mountain he felt something pull inside him. My mother kept finding ways to be alone so she could shed some tears without upsetting my sisters or the servants. Marit began to pack a small bag with food to bring to me and hopefully have me return home with her.

"What if you get eaten by a jackal?" suggested Suzana and Marit dropped the bag, abandoning her plan in an instant.

I spent the afternoon sitting outside in the sun, having had enough of the damp and dark of the cave. I tried my recitations but could not concentrate as thoughts of my family abandoning me here with no care for my life kept surfacing.

I created delusions that my father would teach a string of successors but all would fail and he would rue the day he had left me here. My sisters would never marry because of how our parents had treated their only male child. Who would allow their own son to marry into such a family!

Standing up to go back inside I looked down and saw one of the bugs that I had shaken from the blanket the day before.

"Why are you still here?" I asked. "You could go anywhere yet you stay in this stupid place."

I kicked at it and it ran away under some rocks. Then it struck me—why did I stay here? I could leave. Father had not said I could not leave. He just said that it should take about two nights not that I had to stay two nights. I had suffered one already and even to think about the second made my blood run cold.

Would it matter that I had not explored my connection with Mazda as he had directed? I wondered what he would do if I was honest—and then pondered the possibility of just lying—but I knew that would never work.

Malchiek would know in an instant if I tried to deceive him. Beside I had no idea as to what I could conjure up to impress him anyway. All I knew was that I was to recite the Avesta until I had that same sensation and, with this fear of being left out here to die, that was never going to happen.

I decided to head home and even the dread of appearing a failure to my father was no deterrent. The sun was getting close to the horizon and I knew I would not make it home before dark. I did not care. It would at least seem as though I had spent a full day doing my recitations and perhaps then I could claim part of the night as well, though I knew this was fanciful.

I folded the blanket, apologising to the bugs for using their home for one night. "Trust me, I will never use it again!" I declared before placing it to the back of the cave and heading down the mountain.

When I reached home it was just as the evening meal was being finished. Tonight there were no dramatics. There was barely any conversation as all kept their eyes down upon their food lest they catch sight of my empty seat. Malchiek was just about to dismiss the girls to their evening prayers when he heard a commotion at the front door.

"See what is happening," he said to a servant standing close by.

Before he had a chance to leave though the household's main butler came into the room, his face was red and he seemed flustered.

"Master Balthasar has returned home," he said as calmly as he could but his voice was filled with excitement.

My father's mouth dropped but before he could do or say anything the room filled with shrieks of delight from Marianna and the girls. They jumped from their chairs and all ran to the front vestibule where I was waiting for them.

Malchiek walked slowly and steadily down the corridor to greet me. When he finally arrived at the front of the house he could barely see me as I was buried in my mother's arms with my sisters also clutching upon whatever part of me they could.

"You're alright, you're alright…" my mother said over and over through her sobbing and squeezed me so tight that I thought I might not breathe again. Six other little hands pulled at my clothes and dug into my legs, scratching me and making my clothes cut into me. I did not worry though. All I could think was that they cared. They had missed me and they cared.

Then over the edge of my mother's embrace I saw my father standing at a distance. His hand was on his heart and I saw his eyes were red though he let not one tear fall. He walked to the huddle before him and placed his hand upon my head.

"Welcome home Son," he said softly. "Bathe, eat and sleep. We shall talk in the morning."

With that he walked off to his private study.

I bathed and ate with my mother and sisters surrounding me. They asked endless questions about my short time upon the mountain but thankfully none that broached upon the more esoteric aspects of the experience.

Marit wanted to know if I actually saw a jackal.

"No, but I heard one," I replied and she shook her head at the thought.

Suzana wanted to know if I was scared.

"Only when it got dark and I missed you all," I said and my mother grabbed me again to hug me as she kissed the top of my head.

Aluna sat back from them all and frowned. At the age of five she might not have known the details of what had been done to me but she knew what it might suggest. She slipped away from us all and found my father in his study.

"Aluna, should you not be partaking of your prayers now? Is your brother finally in bed?" he asked as he looked up from his desk to her.

Aluna walked to him slowly with her frown still firm upon her face. Malchiek now saw her expression clearly as she stepped into the lamplight from his desk.

"What is it my love?" he asked and put his hand out to her.

Aluna did not offer her hand though. "Will you be taking Marit to the mountain next?" she asked bluntly.

Malchiek dropped his hand as he shook his head. "No, only males studying to become a magus do such things. Young girls connect with Mazda in other ways."

Aluna sighed and finally smiled. If Marit would not be left upon the mountain then neither would she or Suzana.

"Thank you Father. I will go back to my prayers. Good night," she said and stood upon her toes to kiss him a farewell.

That night as the girls gathered to say their prayers before bed Aluna leant to Suzana and whispered, "We don't have to sleep on the mountain. That is just for boys!"

"Oh of course it is!" snapped Suzana. "You are such a baby that you do not know such things." Suzana then shut her eyes to say her prayers.

Aluna pouted for a moment but then smiled. She might be the baby who knew the least of them all but that was nothing compared to the relief she felt at knowing she would not be left upon the mountain by their father. She too closed her eyes and began her prayers.

Aluna's first prayer was to give thanks to Mazda that she had been born a girl.

CHAPTER SEVEN

I crawled into bed that night sinking into the soft mattress with a sigh, pulling the downy pillows under my head and gathering the silky blankets up to my chin. My stomach was full once again and fears of my family not caring were long gone.

My delight at being back in the luxuries of my home though was soon replaced with thoughts of how my meeting with my father would go in the morning. Thankfully I was still exhausted from the lack of sleep the night before and my trek home that evening. I slipped into sleep within minutes but the comfort of sleep was not to be as my night filled with the most lucid of dreams.

My dream began back upon the mountain.

"No!" I cried out when I realised where I was. It was nighttime again and a full moon glowed in the clear sky lighting everything below it a pale silver blue. I heard jackals howling and then other animal noises that I did not know, yet instinctively felt would do me harm should our paths cross.

I saw the goat trail that led down the mountain and began to run, falling so often that it soon seemed that I was on the ground more than I stood. The further I tried to walk the more the trail was blocked with boulders that I had to climb around or thick trees that grabbed at my clothes pulling me backwards.

All the while it seemed I would never reach the bottom of the mountain. It was as though the trail grew longer the further I walked it.

Then suddenly I was at the base but nowhere looked like the direction home. The jackals howled again and they seemed closer. I grew frantic as I searched around me for some clue in the landscape as to which way to walk home but nothing seemed familiar.

"The stars. I will use the stars," I thought and looked up but the moon was too bright and none of the constellations were clear enough to distinguish.

"Even you fail me now!" I cried out but then something amazing happened.

The few stars that I could see, though they seemed to be of no significance, started to move. I stood transfixed as I watched them slowly dance through the sky, gliding towards a point above me. As they slid close together they merged into one bright dazzling star that almost rivalled the moon for brightness despite being so much smaller.

Merged as one, this super star began to move again, gliding ever so slowly but without a doubt that it was moving. I realised it was showing me the way home and as I began to follow it, the star's movement quickened as well, as though my recognition of its movement now sealed our agreement for it to carry out its purpose.

I walked and the star continued its smooth movement ahead of me. I looked up the whole time not ever needing to know where my feet would step next. My trust in this star was implicit.

Then it stopped. I glanced down for the first time since leaving the mountain base and saw my home just ahead of me. Above me the star broke up into its separate parts once again and they glided back to their proper places in the heavens.

That was all I could recall when I awoke but it was what I decided to tell my father. He sat silently and listened, taking a deep breath when I finished. I decided to speak before he could.

"I honour and respect the ways of my forefathers and our religion but I see no point in sitting in discomfort to gain insight when clearly I was able to do so in the ease of my bed with a full stomach. I know this dream was to show me my connection with the skies and that Mazda will always guide me through them. I will not go to the mountain again."

Though my words were determined my voice was soft and I dared not look my father in the eye as I spoke them. I waited for his rebuke and explanation as to why I was wrong and when my next retreat would be.

Malchiek stood and stepped towards me. He placed his hand upon my head, as he always did in lieu of a hug, and then spoke as softly as I had.

"I have no doubt your dream was confirmation as to how Mazda will use you in this life. There will be no more retreats that are not of your choosing. Instead you will increase your astrological studies—if you so choose?"

I looked up at my father, smiled and nodded.

"I so choose," was my reply.

We made our way to temple and my father gathered any other priests who were attending that day, calling them into the astronomy library for a meeting. There were six of them there that day ranging from decades of experience to a few years. The last to enter the room was the one who I had watched walk amongst the people on my first day.

There were no other students arrived yet. When my father began to speak I realised that I was the only student that would be included and this made me somewhat nervous. This only increased when I realised that my father was speaking about my retreat and the dream that had resulted.

"Balthasar, I want you to tell our brothers about your dream. Do not spare any details as several are proficient dream interpreters and will know what even the slightest symbol represents," Malchiek said and nodded when he finished indicating for me to begin.

Instantly my mouth went dry and my throat tightened. I couldn't remember the general idea of my dream let alone the details or symbols that my father had hoped I would reveal. I looked about me as the six magi gazed at me intently waiting for me to begin. It was deathly silent, so much so that I could hear the hum of the great fire through the doors. Finally, after what felt like an eternity, yet was barely seconds, I began.

I closed my eyes as I began to speak. It helped not to see the serious faces before me. It also helped me call back the images of my dream, and even more so to feel into what it had been like. It was as though I walked the dream again which was peculiar, as I did not truly walk it at all anyway.

55

When I finally finished I opened my eyes, it was as though every man had held the same posture and expression the entire time of my retelling. In fact they had. Each one had been enthralled and it was a moment more before they moved, with several exchanging glances between them.

One though did not take his eyes from me. "How old are you now?" he asked with great seriousness.

"I am ten, Sir," I answered.

He leant forward, pointed a finger at me and waggling his hand as he did, turned to Malchiek. "You do realise that he has dreamt of the prophecy?" he asked my father and around him several other magi nodded as they muttered their agreement.

"Which prophecy?" said Malchiek calmly. There were many prophecies recorded in the Zoroastrian records and though my father knew just which one my dream referred to he wondered to which one his fellow magus thought this dream connected with.

"Zarathustra had a dream of a guiding star!" answered the magus as he smiled. "I know it is only a secondary story in our records but you do recall it, don't you Malchiek?"

Malchiek nodded. "Yes, yes, of course I do but even Zarathustra said it was inconclusive."

"Inconclusive or yet to be truly revealed?" suggested another magus and the entire room erupted in agreement with the latter.

"Zarathustra himself said the lack of meaning he placed upon this meant that its truth would be revealed when the awakening began," said the first magus and then he looked at me. "To have a child barely upon manhood dream such a thing must surely be a sign that this time is now upon us."

"But all I dreamt about was finding my way home," I sputtered. My simple dream which I had thought was my personal sign to never spend another night upon a mountain with only rocks as a mattress, had become much more. I was not so sure that I was willing to have it now be part of the Great Awakening.

The six magi as well as my father all smiled and several laughed.

"Yes my son," said the first magus as he smiled broadly. "That is what we are all wanting to do; find our way to our true home! We are all wanting Mazda to send us some guidance through the skies. That is the truth of your dream and that you actually were guided means that Mazda has chosen you to lead something grand."

The room fell silent and I furrowed my brow. I was barely five years into my studies and the thought that I now had to prepare for something even grander than the responsibility of temple weighed on me. The men noted my reticence and the magus who I watched on that first day, yet had never heard speak now opened his mouth.

"Balthasar, my feeling is that this dream is far more literal than we can imagine. I do not disagree with Arganus as to its symbolism either," Pieter said holding up his hand in peace to Arganus who had turned to challenge him. Arganus sat back in his chair as Pieter continued. "It is no coincidence that this should happen to confirm your natural talent and calling to astronomy. It is also no coincidence that it should happen at your age to give you purpose to your studies. Many young men fall out of their studies at your age. This is your call to commitment. Clearly you are needed to know such things so that you will be ready for them no matter what age its truth will actually present to you. But mark my words; this dream one day will be a real event in your life."

With that Pieter finished as around him the other magi nodded.

"Does anyone else wish to add something?" asked Malchiek.

"Do you think we should message to other temples to see if any other young students have had such a dream?" asked one.

"A wonderful idea," answered Malchiek. "Compose and send it immediately."

CHAPTER EIGHT

Gaspar had just finished his most hated part of temple life: sorting and breaking the pieces of charcoal into the metal buckets. He did this from the huge pile that sat outside upon the temple terrace where they were left to cool. He hated how his hands turned black and there was invariably always one piece that refused to cool completely. He often was lectured on how loudly he cursed when his hand found it. The last thing a worshipper needed to hear was the foul language of a student magus echoing into the room of the great fire as they prayed.

Gaspar shuffled into the library wiping his hands upon his clothes. He was looking for his father to ask permission to go to the bathing room to clean and then take some time for a meal. His father was sitting reading a scroll when Gaspar entered and he looked up with a smile.

"I have received an interesting message from our brothers to the east. The son of the high magus has had a prophetic dream that speaks of the awakening," he said as he looked intently at his son. "They are asking if any other young men have had such dreams that may connect with his."

With that he read the story of my dream and for the first time in what seemed like years to the older man, his son's face showed some interest in what was being shared. The father finished and asked, "Have you had such a dream my son?"

Gaspar said nothing for a moment and then without saying anything he slowly nodded.

Gaspar had many such dreams though none were exactly the same as mine. As his father read the story of my dream to him the young man felt the energy within it and he knew the sensation well. His own dreams had started at ten years of age also. Some days he woke not remembering them at all and within hours they would be completely lost. Now as he grew older they were becoming more solid and he recalled them with ease.

Gaspar sighed, as his father's eye grew wide. "Why have you not told me of this?" his father asked.

"I am not sure," Gaspar replied as he shrugged his shoulders. "I suppose I believed I was too young for them to be significant."

"That is my fault," said his father. "I give you simple tasks such as sorting the embers and reading. Not once have I asked you of your insights or opinions. But we will change all that today." The father stood and walked to his son, taking the young boy's soot covered hands in his own. "Today we expand your lessons..." he paused for a moment and Gaspar thought he saw tears in the man's face. "...and I ask your forgiveness at underestimating your connection to the teachings by this age. I thought you would follow my path as I walked it but that is not to be. I should have paid more attention to your growth and not assumed we were the same."

Gaspar could hardly find his voice after witnessing such humility from his father, the grand magus. "There is no need for forgiveness," he said barely above a whisper. "Your guidance is what leads me and helps me grow."

His father said nothing and pulled Gaspar against him to softly cry into his son's hair.

This scene, of the high magus having this conversation with their sons and young acolytes played out for several weeks across the lands of Babylonia and her surrounds as Malchiek's letter made its way. Then the letters of reply came back to our temple.

Letter after letter that confirmed, supported and shared that young men my age, or just older, were also having such dreams arrived. I sat with my father as he read them. As he read some he would nod, while others would make him shake his head, yet all the while he smiled.

It was at the end of a particularly long day and my father put down the last of a myriad of scrolls which had arrived. He leant forward, resting his forehead upon his hands and let out a sigh.

"I am never sad to leave temple at the end of the day but today I will truly delight in the comforts of returning home," I heard him say through his hands and I laughed.

"You do look tired Father," I joked. "It has been a very full time since you began writing to the other magi."

At this my father looked up and dropped his hands to the table. His eyes looked even wearier than I had first thought.

"You realise that all this is because of you, don't you?" he said with a smile.

I actually blushed when I heard this. My little dream. My message from Mazda, just for me, was now much more.

When the final replies arrived almost four weeks after Malchiek's initial letter he sat down and wrote once more. He now made a compilation of all that had been shared with him: from the dreams that were almost replicas of mine through to the ones that carried the same message but with different symbols. He listed the boys who dreamed, their age and location. He found common elements throughout; stars that joined together, stars that moved through the sky and the theme of being lost. Then there was the one element that finalised them all. Each dream ended with full closure or completion. No matter the setting, each knew the dream was resolved before waking. Each one spoke of knowing that they found what they had been looking for, that they had completed what they set out to do.

Malchiek listed the details with precision and care so that each magus who read it could only nod in agreement when they read the final line of his letter.

'My dear brothers, I believe we are now in the age of the Great Awakening.'

More letters flowed amongst the brotherhood of magi; some were dramatic and filled with a sense of duty. Others wanted to downplay it, not from lack of faith, but fear they would not fulfil their role properly to allow it.

'We must use some caution until we have more solid signs lest we set about creating false history which will impede the true awakening' one wrote back making Malchiek shake his head and frown.

'It is that caution that will impede it!' he replied.

Soon the doubts and reservations faded away. All the magi throughout Babylonia now looked to the skies with renewed zeal as to what the heavens would show them. Much was made of the slightest finding with scrolls being sent about even the least falling star.

The fervour that had been built up so quickly and dramatically soon calmed down though and thankfully. Many of the magi including my father would chuckle when they thought of how they changed within the few years following my dream. They even spoke of this time as the "Great Excitement". Not once though did they feel that their actions or emotions were uncalled for. In fact this time of heightened enthusiasm was seen as far from unproductive.

"We may not have achieved much within these years but we planted seeds which will germinate in time," Malchiek said to the priests of his temple eight years later.

He was right. Those seeds included creating a new link between the magi across Babylonia that was much needed for our religion and culture. Magi in isolated areas now felt once more that they were part of a brotherhood and not just some adjunct to a community. The villages too felt a new bond grow between them and the temple as their priests communicated.

This also went much further than to just make our people feel joined due to the increase in communication. The priests themselves felt their passion renewed for their religion. To know that the awakening may be possible in their time, or at least to a generation that would know their name, was incredible.

Many who had abandoned their astrology began again. Many who had lost their connection to the teachings and performed rites out of obligation and habit were now walking about their temples with fresh eyes and hearts. The people saw this and responded likewise. In these villages the offerings grew again and their faith in their magi in turn inspired them to put even more energy into their service.

My prophecy of the Great Awakening may still have had some years in which to become reality but another awakening had begun. Our religion and our culture were reawakened with hope and passion.

I do believe that this in itself helped the dawn of the new consciousness that was about to birth. Now you might ask how does a country, a culture or a community help birth a new way by uniting and I will answer thusly: unite together in thought and you create a wave of energy that moves through you all. Unite together in feeling, with passion and with purpose, and that energy radiates out beyond the limits of your human expression.

When Babylonia united together with renewed love for our religion and therefore our culture, we sent a message out to the lands around us. They saw a land in love with itself. They felt a land that was ready for all the delights that any god would bestow upon it.

Now this in turn can inspire others to go one of two ways: they can endeavour to follow and share a life of joy and flow or they can scoff and fall deeper into their lost ways.

To the west of Babylonia the Romans had marched and captured many lands and people. Former empires were ruled by men who were now puppets of Augustus. Roman soldiers walked the streets as reminders to the people that their home was not what it once was. These people too prayed for change but they did not look to the skies for when it would happen. They looked to the men who now pandered to Augustus and they lost all hope that they would ever again be free.

When these people were told of the renewed faith of the Zoroastrians in Babylonia they would scoff and laugh. Indeed it would take something grand such as a new emperor to change the way things were, but even they wondered how any man would rid them of the blight that was Rome. They all knew in their hearts that no ordinary man could end this.

Back in Babylonia and free from the threats of Rome, for now anyway, we continued on with our observations of the stars. We saw constellations move with the accuracy and predictability that they always did.

"Will you ever lose faith in the Great Awakening?" my father asked me one night as we stood outside.

I was twenty years of age when he asked. It had been ten years since my dream.

"Never!" I said without hesitation. "I will never lose faith in change or that humanity deserves to live in joy and harmony."

My father chuckled and grabbed at my shoulder. "Good!" he said.

✳ CHAPTER NINE

Gaspar was now well into manhood. His beard was grown to touch his chest and he loved to stroke at it as it reminded him that he was far from being the young boy who had to sort the charcoal. He walked out onto the terrace where the newest of the acolytes was doing just this.

"I am almost done, Sir," the young boy said with the respect and humility that was expected of him.

"I can see that," Gaspar said and reached to his beard. "Take a bucket full inside for the incense first and then place the rest at the doorway for the worshippers."

The boy nodded and grabbed at the nearest bucket into which he had sorted just the sort of pieces he knew Gaspar liked to burn the incense upon. Gaspar grabbed at his arm as he passed to stop him and looked into the bucket.

"Mmph," Gaspar said. "They are just the right ones for the incense. You are doing well Izrael. How is your reading coming along?"

"Ah … good my Lord. I practice at every opportunity," he replied.

"And do you feel the words?" Gaspar asked.

Izrael felt that Gaspar was pushing for something from him and he didn't know what. He looked down and hesitated, trying to think what he could say to placate his teacher and not appear foolish. The boy decided to just nod.

Gaspar, still holding the boy's arm, leant towards him and whispered. "There is no wrong or right answer. What you feel, you feel, and you feel it when you are ready. Never be afraid that you will tell me the wrong thing. Unless it is that you decide that Zarathustra was told by Mazda to live a life less virtuous."

The boy looked up and saw that Gaspar had a half smile upon his face but he still did not feel comfortable with this interaction. He nodded, hoping it would help the scene end which thankfully it did. Gaspar released his arm and the boy continued on into the temple with the bucket.

Gaspar straightened and sighed. He so wanted to inspire his students and the young men who came to join the temple but he always seemed to intimidate them instead. Gaspar stroked his beard as he looked out at the village below and sighed again.

"Perhaps it is good that I am not so soft with them. Perhaps it is good to have this distance. An air of mystery may be what will inspire them to get to my level of the priesthood," he thought to himself.

But it didn't. Gaspar watched as the students would go to the other priests for counselling when they had issues. Even when they had attended one of his classes they would go to other priests to ask for clarity on what he had shared rather than return to him.

There was an upside though. It meant that Gaspar had spare time that few other priests of the temple did. It gave him more time to read and, even more delightfully, to write.

Gaspar wrote incessantly. He wrote every detail of his insights and what he saw in the night skies. The scrolls were stashed in a room of his home and he knew they may never be read, though in his heart he hoped someday they would.

The vow that he made that night when he had stood with his father twenty years ago under the night sky was still strong within Gaspar. Though parts of his heart ached that he was not living that life out as he imagined, his commitment to the promise with himself did not waver.

'I may not be the great inspiration to my students that a visionary should be but I will do the work I promised to Mazda regardless,' he wrote in one scroll.

But this was far from the truth. His students and acolytes had more respect for him than he could imagine. In fact they were all in awe of him. One even said that when Gaspar spoke it was as though Zarathustra himself was before them. Who in their right mind would go to a man like that

66

to ask for clarity upon something he had just spoken to you, they thought. Who would dare to waste his time?

They knew he wrote incessantly and they knew he had been one of the young men who had the prophecy dreams during the Great Excitement. Gaspar would view the stars from the grounds behind the temple each night. It was a lovely clearing high above the village and he walked here to watch the stars and to teach along with the other senior priests.

The students would often hang in the shadows when the class ended to watch Gaspar in turn watch the heavens. They made note of his posture and how much he wrote.

Gaspar heard them once as they hid, when one spoke out loud, and he assumed they were doing so to mock him. He decided to not validate their rudeness by pretending he was unaware of them. The young men just saw this as a reflection of how immersed he was in his observations and several took this as a cue to look at how easily they were distracted.

"What do you suppose he writes?" one of them asked of the others as they lay in the dormitory and should have been falling asleep. "Why does he not share what he writes with us?"

"It must be too advanced for us," another proposed.

"I asked Markus. He said he does not even share with him or the other elders," another said.

"Pah! As if he would tell you otherwise!" an older boy said above a whisper drawing a round of shhh-es and hushes from the ones trying to sleep. He ignored them and continued on. "The high priests are sworn to protect certain knowledge. As if he would tell you if they did share amongst themselves!"

With that this older boy suggested the unthinkable. "I say we go to his home and we find his private library and read these scrolls!"

"You're an idiot and a fool," replied Izrael from his corner. "What would that achieve?"

"We can know just what we are heading towards. We can know why these men act like they are better than us," he replied.

"They are better than us! That's why they are high priests and we are students. You think you will push time forward by reading some private scrolls? Well then you might also think that your beard will grow faster if you simply decide the rest of the year has been lived out."

With that Izrael turned his back on the conversation and tried to sleep. Behind him though he heard the boys plotting to visit Gaspar's scrolls.

The next morning Gaspar taught a class about the Avesta as he always did on that day. The boys were their typical respectful and obedient selves, though it seemed that they were even more reluctant to make eye contact than was usual. It also seemed as though they left the room quicker than normal when he dismissed them.

Izrael though lingered behind. He sat in his chair picking at his finger-nails.

"You can go Izrael. All the others are long gone," Gaspar said quite bemused to actually have a student stay a second longer than they needed.

Izrael looked up and said plainly, "I need to tell you something."

With that he told of the other boys plans to sneak into his home and read the scrolls that they knew their teacher wrote.

"And why would they do this? Are they planning to destroy them?" asked Gaspar with as much concern as he did with curiosity.

Izrael shook his head. "No. It is because they feel it will help them know the wisdom you have."

Gaspar shook his head.

"This makes no sense. I share all my wisdom with them in my teach-ings," he said but he knew this was a lie and Izrael looked him square in the eye as though he too knew it was an untruth.

Gaspar took in a deep breath. "You must tell them that they are not ready for anything within these scrolls. They will learn all that we teachers and priests know in time. They would not understand half of what I write about."

"I cannot stop them. Five are making their way to your home this evening before the sun sets but while you are still at temple. They will pretend to be doing a run to the markets for the kitchen," Izrael replied.

Gaspar nodded. "Thank you Izrael. Go now."

That afternoon, just as they planned, the group of boys made their way to Gaspar's home on the outskirts of the village. They clambered over the garden wall at the back of the home knowing that the servants would all be in the kitchen or living areas getting ready for their master's return in a few hours.

As with most homes of the region they knew Gaspar's study would lead onto the garden area and so carefully one snuck to the wall of the home and began to pull the shutters gently forward to peer inside and see which room held the scrolls.

At the second window he saw what they were looking for. In the stripe of light that the shutter allowed in, he saw the shelves of writing. Without taking his eyes off them he waved for the others to join him. As they scurried across the garden, looking out for any servants who may see them, the scout opened up the shutter and began to climb through the window.

He walked to the shelves as the others climbed in quietly. It was only when the last one was fully within the room that a voice came from a dark corner.

"Welcome boys!" it said.

They all turned and saw Gaspar leaning against the wall, his arms folded across his chest.

They should have run, but their fear of him made their feet freeze. Besides, he had seen each and every one of them. To run would only put off the inevitable. Instead all they could do was drop their heads and look at the ground. One began to whimper.

"Oh hush!" Gaspar snapped at him. "You are brave enough to enter an elder's home without invitation and yet you cry when you are caught. Shame on you! If you choose such indiscretion at least have some conviction about it!"

With that he let out a slight laugh but no student saw the humour in his words. It just made their blood run even colder with fear.

"Look up! NOW!" Gaspar shouted this last word and they could do nothing but obey.

Looking up at him Gaspar could see the shame in each one's eyes and yet he saw something else also—a hunger that he knew too well. A hunger to know everything now. He sighed and stroked his beard.

"I know what has driven this behaviour. I know it too well. It separated me from my father early in my life and I was blessed that he knew how to heal it," Gaspar began. "Sit!" he demanded.

The boys looked about the room. There was only one chair and they knew that would be for Gaspar. Finally one spoke up.

"There are no chairs, my Lord."

"Well then, the floor will have to suffice," answered Gaspar as he walked to a shelf and gathered a bundle of scrolls.

When the boys were settled upon the floor with their legs crossed and their backs straight their elder walked to them and handed each a scroll.

"Here. Read!" he said thrusting them at the boys.

They looked about at each other and finally one was brave enough to uncurl his, leading the way for the others. There was nothing but silence in the room for the next half an hour until Gaspar spoke again.

"Has this satisfied your curiosity?" he asked while sitting in the single chair, leaning to one side upon the armrest.

None of the boys dared look up at him as they refurled the scrolls.

"Well? I imagine this is about the time you would have had to read before you lost your nerve or a servant heard you in here."

Still no one dared to even look up.

"Do any of you have any questions after reading?"

Still there was no response.

"Well I must say this was very disappointing," Gaspar said with a laugh but not even one half smile was returned to him. "You can all go now. But please - do so through the doorway and my front gate. My gardeners have enough work to do without fixing what has been trampled by errant guests."

He walked to the door of the study, opening it and standing aside. Slowly each of the delinquents stood and made way to the door. They handed their scroll back to Gaspar but still none would lift their faces to make eye contact.

Gaspar smiled at each one as they made way into his corridor. He then realised they would have no idea how to leave the home and called out to a servant to show them to the front door. As they followed the servant Gaspar watched them and sighed, then turned back to his study to return the scrolls to their place.

As he did he looked about and pondered on just why the boys had felt the need to do so but he knew. He had seen it in their eyes in that brief moment he had been allowed to look into them.

Gaspar sat down hard into his chair and sighed yet again, then reached up to his beard but his hand stopped before it touched the hairs. It fell to his lap instead and he let out another slow breath as he looked at his scrolls.

"What good do these do sitting here waiting? And waiting for what?" he thought to himself and shook his head.

Gaspar knew the frustration of waiting too well. It had been the spark that had fired his commitment to make his life something of meaning.

It was sometime longer that he sat staring at his shelves full of their curled parchment when a servant appeared to announce that his evening meal was ready. Gaspar nodded to acknowledge the man's message but did not take his eyes from his records. He knew now what needed to be done with his writing.

Each morning Gaspar would finish his breakfast and then make way to temple. The morning after the five students had sat upon his study floor Gaspar instead rose from his dining table and strode to his study. He called for a servant to bring him a satchel and in it he placed a dozen of his scrolls. They were an assortment of astrological observations, his personal reflections as well as his memories from the Great Excitement. When he was satisfied with his choices he slung the satchel on his shoulder and left for the temple.

This morning was not a morning of the usual class format where a priest would stand in front of the students and speak while they listened. Instead on this day the students would study on their own.

So Gaspar walked amongst them in the library, the dormitory and wherever they chose to work. He did this still carrying his satchel. He went to each of the five boys in turn, tapping them on the shoulder and then when they looked up at him with wide-eyes, he would simply say, "Make way to the classroom."

He saw how their faces turned red while one even went white and he knew they were expecting this to lead to their punishment. So when he went to a sixth boy and that boy walked into the classroom last of all, each of the rogues were suspicious and one spoke out loud.

"Izrael! Well I suppose the informer should be included in this. How else would Gaspar have known what was going to happen yesterday," said the boy.

Gaspar though was right behind Izrael and stepped into the room only a pace behind him. Before Izrael could deny or defend his actions Gaspar spoke.

"I knew because a servant saw you heading to my home despite your claims to be going to market," he said loudly and once again all the boys dropped their eyes. "Oh wonderful! You can plot to break into a home and compromise my privacy, yet once more when I stand before you, then you all act like girls. Look up or this will turn from my intended class to the punishment you deserve."

The boys all looked up though many still had red faces. Their eyes now were not filled with shame but with curiosity as to what Gaspar meant by a class. There was also a palpable sense of relief as well.

"Thank you," sighed Gaspar as he put his hand into the satchel and drew out the scrolls he had packed. He placed them on his desk at the front of the room then stood leaning against it and looked at each boy in turn. "I chose each of you for this class not so much because of the actions you have made in the last few days but for what I can see in your eyes … when you show them to me, that is!"

He stopped and gave a slight chuckle though no one joined in. Gaspar gathered himself and picked up the scrolls and handed two to each boy. As he walked the room he spoke again.

"I know the fire that is the desire to know everything. I know the push inside that is the passion to be someone who will make a difference, to be someone who is not just another priest. I am hoping that is what made you want to sneak into my study. Was it Jishti?" he leaned down close to the eldest boy so that their noses almost touched and the boy had nowhere to look but into his eyes.

The boy nodded nervously. "Yes it was my Lord. We just wanted to know more of you—to know more of what you store in your personal wisdom."

Gaspar straightened and raised an eyebrow, then nodded. "And I am flattered," he replied. "And this is the rare moment when the student gives the teacher a lesson. You have made me realise my writings need to be shared, but I am not so sure any others are ready for them. I choose you six to be the test for this. We will meet once a week and if I feel it is of benefit then we will make more time. If you show some promise then we invite more students. I just need to know that you are willing and committed."

The boys all nodded but this was not enough for Gaspar.

73

"A nod is not a vow. I need your word upon this. Izrael you begin," he said quite solemnly and pointed to Izrael.

Izrael looked about him but the other boys would not support him with any gestures of encouragement. Their teacher may have covered for him but they were not convinced of his innocence or how deserved of friendship he was. They were nowhere near to giving him any backing just yet.

Izrael knew he embarked on this on his own. He sat up in his chair, squared his shoulders and remembered all he had been taught of speaking clearly when reciting the Avesta. He nodded to Gaspar and began.

"I give you my commitment to honour your sharing and to live its wisdom. I promise that I will always serve Mazda and humanity the best way I can with all that I am about to learn. This is my vow to you … and to myself."

He finished with another nod and though he sat back in his chair his posture did not slump or diminish.

The other boys looked at Izrael with wide-eyes and slack jaws. Not one of them could have conjured such words to express exactly what Gaspar had asked of them. Part of them was in awe of him while another part of them burned with jealousy.

"Thank Mazda he spoke first," one said to another later. "Else he would have made us all look like fools."

In turn each of the boys repeated the vow almost exactly the same, stumbling over parts as they tried to replicate it. Gaspar smiled at each one, knowing that though the words were a struggle for some, the intention was clear.

As the last one spoke and finished he let out a laugh and clapped his hands together, "Let us begin…"

The class was nowhere near a fulfilling experience that first day for either the teacher or the students. The young men were too anxious to ask questions and even if the nerves had abated they were so overwhelmed by what they were reading to even form a question. Gaspar too was at odds as to how he should even structure the class.

So the boys read and Gaspar watched them. He waited for the pause he knew was them stopping for a moment and this was when he would approach and ask them about what they had read. The student would stammer an answer and Gaspar knew that they had not understood a word of what they had read. He would then just nod and say "continue" before walking back to his desk.

That night in the dormitory, far from the ears of any of the priests, the five boys gathered. Izrael was not invited though he could hear them well enough from his bed nearby.

"His astronomy records are like nothing we have been taught so far," gasped one.

"If you think that's hard - wait until you have to read his dream records!" responded another.

They all shook their heads wondering what they had gotten themselves into.

On his bed Izrael could not help but laugh and the others turned and scoffed at him.

"I don't know why you laugh. If you had kept your mouth shut then no one, including you, would be in this situation!" Jishti hissed at him.

Izrael sat up in his bed still laughing at them. "You wanted to know more. Your impatience led you to an act of disrespect that has given you an immense opportunity and still you are not happy. One of the greatest magi of our province has opened his very soul to us and you sit here like washerwomen despising the rain for your misfortune. I suppose one day you will hate the Great Fire for warming you." Izrael burst out laughing once again.

Jishti stood and walked over to Izrael so that he looked down upon him. "You started this with your mouth and I suggest you finish it thus. Go tell your beloved magus that this class is a failure and that we do not wish to attend anymore."

Izrael's smile widened even more. "That sounds like there is a threat behind it!"

"There is!"

"Well then. I must indeed speak with our teacher tomorrow," said Izrael biting his lip to not laugh once more. Then he lay down and turned his back upon the boys.

Behind him though he heard Jishti mutter as he walked away, "Call me a washer-woman…"

Izrael may not have made a sound but the boys saw his body shake from laughter.

The next day Izrael did go to talk to Gaspar but he made sure to do so when none of the other boys were around to see.

Gaspar smiled when he saw him approach and Izrael smiled warmly back making the teacher feel he had finally made a connection with his students.

"Good day, my son," said Gaspar. "Have you a question about our class yesterday?"

"Good day, my Lord. Indeed I do," replied Izrael. "I wish to ask about the astronomy record I was reading about …"

With that Izrael began a genuine discussion about what he had read. For even though he too had been overwhelmed by what had been laid before him, he was wise enough to know it was an honour to read the personal records of a high magus and was not going to waste the opportunity to discuss them further. Gaspar's delight at Izrael's interest combined with his student's enthusiasm allowed them to have a most productive discussion. Izrael nodded with contentment as they finished.

"No other student has come to me with questions," Gaspar said with a leading expression and hoped this would encourage Izrael to share anything the others may have said.

Izrael had only been waiting to complete their more genuine discussion to let Gaspar know exactly what his fellow students had been saying.

"Well, my Lord – it seems they found the first class quite daunting and question whether it should continue," the young man said.

Izrael didn't drop his eyes once and Gaspar even thought that he had a slight smile as he spoke. Regardless, Gaspar was not sure whether to be angry or amused.

"How ridiculous!" cried out Gaspar and his voice echoed out from the room in which they were talking. "After what they did! That is like—like…"

"Washer-women complaining about the rain?" suggested Izrael.

"What?" said Gaspar and looked at him puzzled.

"Well, the rain would make a washer-woman's role difficult but it would fill the rivers and her tubs for washing the next day," Izrael explained.

Gaspar burst out laughing. "A convoluted if somewhat perfect analogy," he said through his laughter. "The class will continue. If anything it will teach these boys some perseverance." Gaspar shook his head. "Imagine if we all gave up the minute we did not understand something or that it was too hard."

That night in the dormitory Jishti stood next to Izrael's bed as he turned down the blankets.

"Well, did you speak with our Lord?" Jishti asked.

Izrael plumped his pillow and dropped it down on the bed. "Yes," he replied simply.

"Well? And?" asked Jishti.

"He said he will see us all at the same time next week." Izrael turned his head away to hide his smile which he knew would make the boy angry.

Jishti grabbed his arm and pulled Izrael to turn his face towards him. "You bastard! You encouraged him didn't you?"

Izrael's smile dropped off his face and he stepped forward making Jishti lean back. "How the hell do you influence a man of wisdom? And how does avoiding wisdom make you such a man? Perhaps you should ask these questions in our next class?"

With that Izrael shrugged the boy's hand off his shoulder.

"Get some sleep," Izrael snapped at him. "Perhaps in your dreams you could ask Mazda to show what would suit you better than being a magus. Perhaps he might show you some clothes that need washing!"

Izrael heard some sniggers from the beds around him and Jishti recoiled as he heard them also. He glared one more time at Izrael and walked away.

When the exclusive class resumed the following week, Gaspar assumed that some of the boys would express their discomfort by simply not attending but as he waited at the desk all six boys walked in. He looked at each one in turn and nodded, offering them a smile which they sheepishly offered back.

"Before we begin I wish to clarify something," Gaspar began. "The vow you made to me last week is only binding while you desire to be a student of this class. If you so choose to end these particular studies with me, then you are released from our agreement. Just as you are always free to leave temple school, then so too are you free to leave this class."

He looked about the students who were casting glances at each other. This was their way out and they knew it. Izrael though kept his head down to hide his smile.

"So, having had a taste of what this class holds for you, is there any-one of you that would like to end their time with these studies?" Gaspar asked and looked amongst them.

He saw several swallow hard as they tried to catch each other's eyes and he also saw how some kept their breath high in their chest. Not one of them stood though. Not even Jishti.

"Really? No one?" asked Gaspar with a smile and he walked to stand in front of Jishti. "No one thinks this is too hard? No one thinks they will do better without this class?" He looked down at the boy. "No one thinks it is too scary?"

There was still no response from any of them.

"Good. Then we will continue on," he said and began to hand out some scrolls.

Izrael could not help himself and he walked to Jishti to tease him as they left class but something stopped him. He watched the boy walk from the classroom with a posture that struck something inside him. Suddenly he knew to taunt him would only be using the boy's discomfort to make himself feel clever and that was not the spirit of a magus.

That night in the dormitory Izrael walked to Jishti's bed.

Jishti looked up at him, with eyes resigned to being mocked. "What?" he said dejectedly.

"I am glad you will stay in the class. I look forward to us studying more together," Izrael said simply and then walked back to his bed.

There was never another threat or taunt made between the two and the term "washer-woman" was never used again. Well, not as a serious insult anyway.

# CHAPTER TEN

My own studies had taken on a very individual flavour since my dream when I was ten. Like Gaspar I had at that time made my own very personal commitment to my connection to the magi and as a magus. It was like the lineage that was coded into my blood was woken fully. I not only studied to respect my father and my heritage but I also did it as though there was nothing else to consider.

Yes I had that sense from birth and affirmed at age ten, but as I entered manhood it expanded. The more I dived into my studies and the more I connected with the Avesta, then even more the joy of being a magus swept through me.

The teen years of an aspiring magus are the most challenging while being the most fun as well. You are nurtured and amused by the elders whilst also having your concepts and habits tested. In return, you amuse and challenge your elders. I had the opportunity to do this with my father as one of my guides and while it should have strained our relationship it was often far from the tension it could have been.

That was with all facets of my studies except for the astronomy.

I will be the first to admit that I had developed a slight arrogance after my dream as to my connection to the stars. It became something of a quest for my father to knock that back into the reverence and humility that it was considered to warrant.

You see there was an aspect of our astronomy that few know about us. Yes we mapped and recorded the constellations and events that you could trace back from now. We understood the waxing and waning of the moon and how everything shifted because of the rotation of the Earth upon its axis and its own movement around the Sun. There was no great mystery to any of that. It had been studied and recorded for tens of thousands of years before us.

The facet that we added was watching for change. It was in how we looked to the skies at night. In an instant any magi worth his salt could look up and name stars and their position. Any magi with the barest of studies could know the season from the sky. It was when we looked beyond that simple initial layer of the night sky that we connected to the energy of communicating with Mazda. That my dear friend takes time, trust and commitment to connect with and some never achieved it.

Though my father knew I had in my dream state connected with it, he now feared that the adulation heaped upon me after my dream would kill off the connection I had opened. He knew the discipline he had shown in taking me to the mountain had begun this and, even though that had not turned out the way he had thought it would, he knew now he must restore that discipline for me to continue on.

So each night after we had looked upon the stars and confirmed they were all in their place, after we had noted any falling or shooting stars, we would then go into the deeper connection with the sky. It was then we would stop talking. It was then we would find our own space, rest our hands behind our back and look up.

Each one of us would find an area to focus on: whether it was a constellation of the zodiac or somewhere in-between, it did not matter. You just found a place to focus. You stayed still and quiet. You slowed your thoughts and all that you were present to was the twinkling lights above you. It was then something amazing would happen.

As you can imagine, in the ancient world there were no large cities with huge amounts of electrical light at night. So every star that could be seen was seen. There was no interference with how you saw them apart from the glow of the moon or if there were clouds.

But on a clear night when the moon was small, the vista of stars was spectacular. There is no word that explains how it looked. To even write this for you now I feel my heart swell at how magnificent it was - as though there was barely any blank sky between them.

So we would be still and silent and stare. Then when you were truly quiet and calm in every facet of your being, the sky would open. The stars would expand and the sky looked even bigger. The gaps between the stars would grow so that you were looking beyond them.

Then you would become aware that there was much more in the universe than these simple orbs. You would feel how much there was to know and how small you were.

In that instant you allowed yourself to connect with this power. This power we called Azura Mazda and for some we heard his voice. And we listened.

To come back from this was both disappointing but affirming. We mourned the loss of the connection but we grew from those moments of communication. Sometimes we would bring back words, other times it was an image or a sensation. This is what we recorded in our personal journals. This was our personal connection with Mazda.

Though we all knew our intimate connections in that communication state were unique, we also knew that many of us heard and sensed similar things. It was in the similarities that we hoped to connect and confirm the coming of the Great Awakening.

It was a general consensus that the ability to enter this state as we watched the skies took time and no one had ever shown an immediate affinity to it. Yes, there had been some who could do it quicker than others but it was believed that one could not do this in less than ten years.

So you began when you completed your initial studies of the Avesta at twelve years of age and you were supposedly competent at this more in-depth study of the night sky by twenty-two. It was also agreed that this talent was never complete, so in using the word competent you may also have used the word 'worthy' to describe your status amongst the order of magi.

As we all know the word worthy does not always equate to the word competent.

There I was at age ten having lucid dreams of the night sky communicating to me which then led to me having my astronomy studies fast-forwarded. So that when I was twelve I was already two years ahead of my peers. This story was all I needed to think I was above the lessons that we were all given to explore and expand this important part of our service to Mazda.

I was caught openly yawning several times; something that was seen as a huge disrespect to your teachers. I questioned methods and asked questions with impertinence, both of which disrupted the class and annoyed my fellow students.

Being the son of the high magus meant many of the reprimands I was due to have spoken to me were withheld. When I did it to my own father though, as he instructed a class, he knew I needed some correction.

I was around sixteen at the time. So yes, my petulance had been indulged and ignored for some time. I was actually at our family home being instructed by my father within our own garden, in much the same spot that he stood as I was birthed. There was only the two of us that night, as well as his faithful butler nearby as always.

The time came for us to be still and meditate upon the stars. My father took up his posture and nearby so did I. Within a minute though the distractions that plagued me when I did this set in. At first it would be an itch that would make me move and then it would be the thoughts that would come into my head. I would think of our meal that night or what classes were set for tomorrow.

My father sensed all this but pretended to keep his own focus. Tonight, he had decided, would be the last time I would make light of this. He saw me itch and ignored it. He felt my focus wane and though his blood warmed, he still remained in his place. It was when I started to squirm; moving my head and rolling my shoulders that he spoke.

"Stay still," he said firmly.

"I am uncomfortable. It is unnatural to stay in such a posture for so long," I moaned and kept tilting my head from side to side to stretch my neck.

"It is what is necessary and it is getting beyond that discomfort that allows the connection," Malchiek continued without moving a muscle.

"But I have such connections within the comfort of my bed," I protested, my defiance justified by the dreams I continued to have at that time.

"You need to be with the stars in your awake, conscious state," Malchiek went on, still remaining calm, or so I thought.

"Fine, then I shall lie down and not strain my neck to do so," I pouted and made myself comfortable upon the rough grasses of the garden. It was truly uncomfortable and I regretted it the moment I lay down but my father's next words made me resolve to deal with the new taste of discomfort.

"That is not how it is done. Get up!" he said firmly.

"Well perhaps it is time for a new way to be had!" I replied just as determined.

I smoothed my robes around me and then gazed up at the sky once more. The few bumps on the ground along with the tufts of grass and the odd rock were worth the relief to my neck and the sense of achievement in breaking the rules.

My father fell silent because, as he knew would happen, I was soon sound asleep. As he heard my breaths take on the rhythm of sleep he finally turned to look at me with an expression which was torn between amusement and disappointment. He gestured to the butler and together they gathered up the scrolls and equipment.

"Shall I wake the young master?" his butler asked as they headed indoors.

Malchiek shook his head. "No, my son shall remain and complete the lesson in his own way as he has chosen."

With that they returned indoors. When they were inside my father gave one last instruction.

"Lock all the doors and shutters. And do not respond to any calls from my son to be allowed inside," and with that he made his way to his bedroom.

I woke several hours later when the bitter cold of the night air set in. It took me a moment to realise where I was and why. My initial reaction was that my father must have just returned inside but I could tell from the position of the moon that many hours had passed since I lay down.

I jumped up wrapping my arms around me to try to warm up and rushed to the nearest door to get inside. It was locked. I shook it a few times hoping that in my half asleep state I was mistaken—but I was not. I banged on the door and called out to the servants who I knew slept not far from this door but there was no response. Even in the dead of night they would have been there in an instant and this made me anxious.

I tried several more doors and then the shutters all with the same outcome. I leaned against the last door and realised what I feared was true. My father had locked me out to pay for my petulance. This alone should have taught me the lesson he had aimed at but it didn't. It just made me angry.

Walking back out to the garden I looked about for where I would now sleep. I saw the stone benches and knew that apart from the hard surface I could not sleep out in the open. My throat would be on fire tomorrow from the cold air and if I was really unlucky that would make way to my chest.

Then I realised my only choice - the stables. I sighed and groaned as my feet carried me there. I thought about my comfortable bed with its linens and pillows and this made it only worse when I opened the door and walked in.

To the left were the goats and our cow; to the right were the camels. The sheep just fit in where they could. I considered my options - the camels I could lean upon and gain warmth from but they were fickle animals that could decide to dislike you in an instant. The goats on the other hand were timid but had a smell that no soap could remove from you.

I chose the goats. I had already been spat upon this evening in one sense, no need to make that a reality with the camels. I found a place between them and pushed the hay that lined the floor to make a rough mattress. Pulling my robes tight around me I lay down for the night, wishing I had some stars to look at instead of these animals.

It was neither a restful or comfortable sleep and I was relieved when the servants who tended the animals came at dawn to begin milking and letting them out for the day.

"Good day Sir," they all said to me as though opening the barn and finding me there was a normal part of their day.

It seemed the butler had been quite thorough in letting everyone know of my father's little exercise for me.

I sat up, resting back against my hands and looked about me. The animals began their routines, answering the call of the servants and moving about like a well-choreographed dance. They too acted like I had always been here, stepping around me as though I was a bale of hay. It made me feel invisible, as though I may well not have been there at all.

Standing up I brushed off as much hay as I could but I knew there would be much upon my back that my hands did not reach. I daren't ask on the animal servants; they had far too much to do and besides this was something a house servant should look after. So I simply walked back to the house with bits and pieces of straw poking out of my hair and clothes.

I saw the kitchen door was open and walked through it even though this too was not customary for anyone other than a servant. As I figured, I had broken enough of the order of how things were played out so why not keep going. When I entered the kitchen the servants here also acted as though my appearance from outside at this time of day, with my clothes crumpled and my hair looking like the beginnings of a bird nest, to be as normal as the sunrise. They barely looked at me as they offered their greetings and continued on with getting ready to serve breakfast.

"Breakfast will be served shortly," called the head cook as I began to walk out into the hallway. Just as quickly a servant brushed past me carrying the first tray to set at the table for our family. The smell drove me insane and I picked up my pace to follow the tray in hopes I might pull something from it before it reached the table.

I was just about to do this when my father stepped before me. He would not look me in the eye and used the excuse that he was adjusting his clothes to keep from doing so.

"Make your way to the dining table," he said coldly and then turned to lead the way.

My mother and sisters were already there, looking down at the table and seemed grateful that the first tray was being placed so they could focus on the food. I could do nothing but smile as I realised they too were in on playing out whatever my father had told the servants. We all muttered our greetings and I sat down.

Aluna though could not help herself and glanced sideways at me. The moment she saw the straw embedded in my hair and the rumpled state of my clothes she gave way to laughter, catching herself but not quick enough for my father not to notice.

"Aluna!" snapped my father but within the space of time he was able to utter this one name, Suzana and Marit also stole a glimpse and they too had to catch their laughter.

My father in turn called out their names but it was no use. It was the infectious type of laughter that could not be contained and the three girls collapsed into fits and I now joined them.

Malchiek finally looked fully at me as did my mother. When they both saw the extent of my appearance they too joined in.

"We need to check his hair for eggs," squealed Marit sending us all into fresh bursts of laughter.

The servants continued to bring in our food and they too walked out with broad smiles only to break into giggles when they were a safe distance in the hallway.

"Did you see him?" cried out one as he went back into the kitchen.

"We all did!" answered the cook dabbing tears from her eyes, weeping with laughter as each servant returned with their take on my appearance.

Back in the dining room, our family mirth subsided and we began to eat.

"What is it with you and having such experiences with sleeping out of your bed?" Marit asked.

"Perhaps you should ask Father as both times have been his doing?" I said and though I smiled we all knew that this was not completely in jest.

"Yes it has been only twice and some years apart. Both times I wished to teach you something. The first time you taught me, but this time I gather that is not the case. What say you of your experience this time Balthasar?" he questioned, looking at me with his chin tilted upward waiting for my response.

"I suppose I have been shown the merit of being more willing to follow the methods that are being offered to me," I replied.

"And what else?" he asked, raising his eyebrows.

"That I should not take the comfort and respect of my home for granted, Sir." Tears came to my eyes as I said this. "I know I am blessed and I thought I appreciated all that you offer me. But I see now I have fallen into disrespect—not only for my studies which is bad enough but to do so to my home and family is truly having lost my way."

My father looked at each and every one of us in turn as he now spoke and there was not a smile to be seen or a giggle to be heard.

"Never ever take your life for granted. Not one part of it. Whether it is the roof above your head or your health. Give thanks every day and Mazda will send you more blessings to fill your life. Each day I give thanks for all I have and all that you are," he waved his hand at each one of us. "Stop being thankful and you stop being worthy of the gift of life." Malchiek looked at me now. "Step from this one more time and what occurred last night will truly be a comedy compared to the life I will send you off to endure."

He wiped his mouth, signifying his meal was ended and stood up.

"I will now go about my day. May you all enjoy the day you create," he said and left the room.

Those were the same words my father spoke to us every day as he finished breakfast. I always felt so much love within them but today I felt something else. It was also a warning.

CHAPTER ELEVEN

My approach to my studies now took a whole new depth as my irreverence gave way to the honour and attentiveness they required. I no longer saw myself as "gifted" or above the traditional ways of my teachings. I saw now that by truly immersing myself into what was offered to me that then I was free to express myself with them as my foundation.

For that is what education is—it is the bones on which to build your personal wisdom. There must always be that phase, no matter your experience or your insights, that requires you to be just a student: to listen and to take in. That builds your foundations and then you are free to construct upon this whatever glorious expression of a building you see fit.

So I truly, truly listened when my teachers spoke and as I did this I heard far more than their words. Just as I had when reciting the Avesta, I now felt beneath and in-between the words. I sensed more of the man who was guiding me and this in itself was an amazing lesson. I saw in them much more than a person who had simply learnt these ways before me. I could now sense their commitment to spirit, their love of teaching the ways of Mazda and their passion for what Zarathustra had brought forth for us all.

I could suddenly see beyond what to some was simply religion or a culture. I could feel into how what we said and did effected far more than someone's perspective or beliefs. As a priesthood we were expanding the wisdom handed down to us for generations. It was not passing on information; it was nurturing a consciousness that we were all connected to.

Now that I had surrendered my ego and allowed myself to see this I could see into the very soul of the men who taught me. I sensed that it was not just this human incarnation of themselves that was devoted to it; it had with them the essence from the very source of all that is. I too now realised that the circumstance of being born the son of a magus was not coincidence. My role as a magus, to expand the teachings and to prepare for the Great Awakening, was not a mere synchronicity of events that had been arranged by Mazda. It was a part of me, present from my first moments separated from all that is. It was a part of me that would call out to me if I ever strayed from my role.

Something that intimate, that ingrained into the very essence of you is never truly lost or missing. It is just that you stop listening and feeling it.

Or you can create great ways for it to come back closer. For me sleeping one night in the barn with our animals was all that it took. Hearing my father's warning was just the final embellishment it needed.

Now when I stood outside beneath the stars I would take in a deep breath and truly feel the majesty they offered to me. My neck never got sore, no matter how long I stood and looked up. I never got bored and I never was tempted to lie down again.

As I began this new relationship with the night sky I saw more than I had ever seen before.

But even more amazingly, I heard them. I could hear tones and symphonies within them. Some nights it was like a lullaby, some nights I could hear drums beating.

Then one night I heard a voice.

"I will call you and you will come."

That was all that it said. I smiled and nodded.

"Yes I will," I replied.

I was eighteen years old when I first heard the voice. At first I believed it was Mazda talking to me and really who else would have need to talk to me in this way? As the years passed though the voice changed and some nights I heard more than one. I knew this was no longer just Mazda talking to me.

When I went to my father and told him of the voice I first heard, his response was simple and expected.

"Of course it is Mazda talking to you," he said emphatically and that was the end of the conversation.

When I went back a few years later and explained the voice had changed and there were others Malchiek did not respond so quickly or confidently.

"What are they saying?" he said quietly.

"Much the same as Mazda; that they will be calling upon me and that to keep aware of when that will be," I said hesitantly.

"They have said more have they not?" Malchiek pushed and he was right.

I had held back because many times what they said was not so clear or made no sense. Well not in words anyway. I tried to explain this and as I did Malchiek's eyes grew wide.

I was not the first to be a "hearer" as well as a "seer". Seers amongst the magi were common; in fact all magi were seers, whether it was through meditating with the stars or the great fire. Yes many heard Mazda but the hearers who heard other voices were much more rare and there were reasons for this that made Malchiek so nervous for me.

Many hearers ended up having breakdowns or leaving the priesthood. One such man had studied alongside Malchiek. Side by side they entered the priesthood and indeed this man would have been a high priest along with Malchiek if not for the voices he heard that eventually drove him crazy.

Samuel heard his first voice while praying by the great fire at the age of fifteen. He confided in his teachers and they all said the same thing; that it was the voice of Mazda choosing him to hear instead of just seeing and feeling. Samuel knew this was rare and his pride swelled.

Soon he became obsessed with hearing this voice. He would sit by the fire whenever he could to call upon it. Then when he felt comfortable with this he pushed it to speak to him at night while he lay in bed. As had the voice I heard, Samuel soon heard the voice change. It took on another quality and the messages it shared turned from gentle encouragement to dark demands.

The voice began to ask Samuel to do things against what he was taught. He soon found himself deserting his studies and teachings to walk outside the village to hide in the wilderness for days at a time. Alone, separated from all his support, the voice could now have Samuel to himself, convincing him that he did not need his brotherhood or family.

Samuel would wander back to temple, his eyes dark and his frame growing so thin. He would challenge the high priests and make scenes amongst the villagers as they worshipped. This would escalate until he just disappeared again.

Malchiek watched the slow descent into madness; thankful he had not been cursed with this talent. He heard the high priests talk about Samuel as they tried to figure out what to do. Prayers were not working and then one of them uttered the words no one else had wanted to.

"It is a demon in him," the high priest said and they all nodded.

There was only one way they knew how to deal with this. The last time such a thing had occurred was in a village nearby over a decade ago. One of the priests there had succumbed to a voice that was not of Mazda. His plight was so bad that he ended up killing a priest as he began to cleanse his temple of what he was told were the blemishes within its walls.

Several of our town's magi travelled to this temple to see what solution they had sought to reconcile the situation.

"There is only one way to end this. You need to cleanse him with the power of Mazda and that is via the great fire," the high priest of that temple said to them.

"Burn him? That is barbaric. We cannot kill our brother no matter his circumstance!" replied one of our magi as they all recoiled in horror.

"No, no, no! Not burn him. Just hold him before the fire. Make him look into it. When he sees the truth of Mazda within the flames he will remember the truth within himself. That is the only way to drive out this demon: by getting him to reconnect with Mazda. It could take hours but it is the only way."

With that he showed the men the temple records of how this was done with their priest. It had taken six men to hold him down. It took four hours before he exhausted himself enough to no longer struggle. In ten hours his eyes cleared and then tears had flowed. He called out to Mazda to forgive him. He cursed the voice that allowed the demon within him.

He never heard another voice.

Back at our temple the magi waited for Samuel to return from his latest disappearance. They prepared themselves physically with ropes and pieces of leather to restrain him. They also prepared themselves emotionally by praying and asking for guidance from Mazda.

Samuel eventually stumbled back to temple after fourteen days out in the wilderness. As usual he stood at the main doorway declaring that he had important news to share with them all that must be listened to straight away.

The few villagers within the temple hurriedly left. Everyone in the village knew of Samuel's condition and also the plans to cleanse him. As they departed the priests in the fire room approached him and encouraged him to speak while another went to call any other priests serving that day.

"How wonderful you are back, Brother Samuel. Come sit by the fire and tell us your message," one of the priests said to him softly, gesturing for him to come to the centre of the room by the fire.

"I have no time to sit!" Samuel snapped back. "That is what I need to tell you. There is no need for us to sit in temple anymore." He pointed at the fire. "We don't need the fire!"

The priests all did their best to not react to this but many took in a sharp breath at his words. As the rest of the priests arrived in the room, several which were behind Samuel nodded to the one talking to him.

Then they all moved in on him.

There were ten who grabbed him initially and it took all their strength to restrain him. Two of them tied his hands while another two tied his feet.

Samuel fought as hard as he could.

"They told me you would do this! But you cannot control me! I know the true power. I am the true power because I know the truth," he shouted, all the while fighting against what was being done to him.

With his feet and hands secure, the priests sat him up facing the fire. He continued to struggle against their hands and the cords around his wrists and ankles.

"This is your truth my brother. Samuel, look into the flames and re-member who you are. Remember why you began this and that you can end this," one of the priests said to him.

For a moment Samuel looked deep into the fire. Then he closed his eyes and began to howl. It was a deep guttural animalistic sound and within it was the word 'no'. He continued to do this for two hours, with the voices of the priests taking turns to repeat the words "remember who you are" to him over and over again.

The screams and howls of Samuel would subside. He would open his eyes but as soon as he saw the fire he would close his eyes and the ago-nised screaming would begin once more. It echoed out to the village and to the younger priests, including Malchiek, who had been told to stay in the library.

Samuel's body exhausted first and he slumped in the arms of the priests holding him. This took six hours. His voice cried out for another two hours.

Outside the sun began to set. The priests who had taken turns holding him were also drained but knew their work was not over. They lowered Samuel so that he could lie upon the floor but kept his hands and feet tied up.

"We will hold vigil with him overnight," said the eldest. "By dawn he will be returned to the brother that we know and love."

The students were sent home or to the dormitory. The priests sat around Samuel and continued their prayers as he slept. Eventually they too sought sleep on the hard temple floor. Several stayed awake though, watch-ing Samuel for any change.

Just before dawn they saw his face soften and woke the others. Then they all sat waiting for Samuel to wake when he was ready.

He never did. Within those moments before dawn Samuel's spirit slipped away. Resigned to the struggle that had set in within Samuel it was the easiest way to end the battle he was living with.

"We did the only thing we knew to do," the eldest said to them. "This is the solution from Mazda. He needed to take him back deep into his embrace to heal him. Samuel was far more damaged than we knew."

The priests all nodded. It was the only explanation that made any sense and it was the one offered to the students when they arrived for their lessons.

Malchiek nodded as he was told. He had not slept so well that night. The howls and screams of Samuel had echoed in his head until he was deep in sleep: then he dreamt of demons carrying priests away.

Now as I confided in him, Malchiek could hear Samuel's screams again and they sent a chill up his spine.

We were at home at the time. Malchiek grabbed me by the arm and took me into his private study.

"Sit," he said and paced the room as he decided how to deal with this. "Have you told anyone else?" he continued.

"No," I said and almost laughed. "I don't see what you seem so concerned about."

"No, you wouldn't. You cannot see when you are within that space," my father said and once more I was resigned to the cryptic manner in which he often shared something.

Malchiek stopped pacing and pulled a chair to sit beside me. He grabbed my right hand within both of his and raised it to his mouth to kiss it. Then he lowered his head and began to pray to Mazda out loud.

"Oh grand creator! Protect my son from any others who choose to speak to him. Guide him to listen to only your divine and almighty wisdom..." and so he went on.

I was glad that his eyes were closed so that he could not see me smile. I am sure he would have decided that it was a demon that had made me think this was amusing. As he went on though I felt the genuine concern and how it was from his love for me that he was truly speaking. I stopped smiling so that when he finished his prayer and opened his eyes he saw my face softened and my eyes wet with tears.

"Tell me what you fear and I will assure you that I will never allow that within me," I said.

With that I heard the story of Samuel from my father as he continued to hold my hand and tears fell down both our faces. I felt the depth of his fear and I also heard the truth in the story.

When Malchiek finished I looked him in the eye and repeated the words, "I will never allow that within me."

It was much the same promise that Gaspar had made at age eight. It was the commitment to be a clear channel for whatever Mazda was calling upon me to complete in my life.

Within that declaration I made it known to any entity or spirit who was not seeking and supporting the awakening of humanity that they were not welcome to be part of my experience. In that moment I made it known to myself that the ability to hear was not a game to play. It was not something to manipulate or push to be anything other than what it presented itself as.

For now this was simply to hear that my connection to Mazda was real. I did not need to hear the words or call upon him for more messages. He would come to me when he was ready and when I was ready to hear.

With this pledge to myself to remain pure in what I heard, the voice once again changed. I heard now a voice not so dissimilar to mine and it would never change again.

The next time I heard it was a week later. I was out looking at the stars, gazing upon my favourite constellation of Virgo, the house I was born under. As I looked within the spaces between the sparkling lights I heard two simple words.

"Thank you..."

CHAPTER TWELVE

While Gaspar and I were involved in defining who we were as magi, Melchior was doing the same within his home and temple. He had chosen to be born in a much simpler place within such exciting times.

Melchior's family temple was one of the smallest in all of Babylonia in all respects. There were barely ten stairs raising it from the ground and the greatest number of priests serving it at any time was ten. It rarely housed any pilgrims or visiting magi. There were no secondary buildings or even a spare library.

The small village it served had a population of fewer than two hundred and this included the farms that lay on the outskirts in the foothills and those that lived in the cliff walls above them. These people were referred to by the main villagers as the "ones on the edges" and most times it was like they were a separate race. The only thing that brought them all together as a community was worship at the temple.

Each day some of the ones from the edges would make their way through the village centre to come and worship, carrying the scant bundles of wood they might find on the way. The main villagers would smile and nod, not from any social politeness but because they knew it dishonoured Mazda to do otherwise.

When Melchior was ten he stood at the top stair of the temple and watched a family from the cliffs make their way towards him. He saw how people moved out of their way, or turned their heads so they could avoid even the basic courtesy that they felt obliged to offer.

He saw the young son of the family stop to talk to another young boy of the village, only for that boy's mother to pull him roughly away before they could interact. Nobody saw that except Melchior and his eyes grew dark.

"I do not understand it, Father," he said that night at the dinner table. "We are all created by Mazda. We all come to temple and yet we feel we can do this to one another."

"It is because they choose to live differently," his father said casually and slurped upon his soup.

"Is that reason to not be warm to another? It is not like they are bandits or worship the old gods that do not give us hope," Melchior reasoned.

"No, but it is the way of man," sighed his father and ripped at some bread to throw in his soup. "And it will change when the awakening is real."

"But if we change how we treat one another then does that not make the awakening a reality now," Melchior said with his brow furrowed in frustration.

His father sighed again and sipped his wine.

"Melchior, you think too much," was all he said and drank some more.

It was true, Melchior thought a lot. He thought constantly. There was barely a moment when his mind was not processing something he had been told or read or that he had felt during a meditation. His energy was in a constant state of acquiring information, then dissecting it and looking to expand upon it.

Melchior was one of those children who was never satisfied with any response he was given or any explanation offered. He would ask a question and even when given an answer would have to explore its truth. Thus by ten years of age he acquired a hefty amount of injuries as he found out for himself the limits and rules of the physical world. These were only matched by the amount of lectures from his father as he tested the boundaries of his parents' authority as well.

"You can never just believe something can you?" his father yelled at him one day.

To Melchior this was not the insult or criticism his father had intended it to be. To Melchior to just accept something as stated meant to him that he was not being a true magus. For Melchior felt that to be a true leader, a solid teacher and a man who could inspire faith in others, then he himself should understand every detail of life with as much knowledge as possible.

Melchior needed to feel the heat of a fire, the itch from a stinging weed and the sourness from a whole mouthful of lemon: the latter of which had amused his family to no end. He also needed to know exactly how the astronomy instruments calculated the movement of stars so far away. Melchior insisted on seeing the full writings of the Avesta and not just what was shown to him as a student.

"You are not ready for this yet!" one of the elders snapped at him when at eight he snuck into the library to read ahead of his lessons.

"Well if I am not then why was I able to do so," Melchior reasoned.

Well he thought it to be reason. To his teachers it was insolence and one of the most common injuries he would suffer was the pulling of his ear by an exasperated teacher as he was led to his father.

"Why can't you just listen?" his father groaned one day.

Melchior shrugged. He truly did not know why he needed to test everything and everyone so much—well not at his young age anyway. That understanding would come when he was eighteen.

It was a beautiful clear night. The sort where every star shone as bright as it could thanks to the new moon. Melchior loved these nights as his measurements were made so easily. When he was finished with his beloved instruments he would then placate his father by doing the meditation that we all carried out with the stars.

Melchior though never did this in the way we all did. He did not go into that space where the sky became much more than the simple sparkling dots. Melchior would double-check his measurements and his records from his memory. He would scan the stars, reciting their names, much like a test. Every so often he would stop to mark his progress by reading over his scrolls or even remeasuring to affirm what his eyes had reassessed.

Then one night in the daze of reciting the names he heard something.

Melchior looked about him thinking one of the nearby students had spoken but they all continued their gaze upwards in the reverie they always did. Melchior looked back up at the sky and continued on naming the stars then he heard the whisper again.

"It's me," it called to him.

"Who?" said Melchior aloud and the other magi there hushed him.

"It's me. I'll be back soon and you will help me," the voice replied and then there was silence.

Melchior looked about him. He knew no one else had heard it. Melchior also instinctively knew they would not know what had happened; well not in any way that would satisfy his mind.

He went to bed that night without mentioning it to anyone, not even his father. Melchior knew that he had to find out what this was on his own.

✳ CHAPTER THIRTEEN

Time in temple life passes much differently to a common life. I know that sounds rather egotistical or out of touch in some way but it is true. Years, weeks, days and even minutes are different. Common life is filled with routine which makes time different. The mundane routines of life exhausts time but a life spent with committed activity fills time.

The pretention of saying such a thing would make it seem that I saw a regular villager's life as drudgery and full of chores and deeds to simply survive. Now for the most part this is true; which is why religion has always been so important. It gives some meaning and purpose to all of the toil.

Life as a priest is the opposite; our lives are based on the meaning with the basics of survival there to support our work with spirit. This alone changes the whole dynamics of life.

When you wake each day with the knowing that day is simply another to explore the connection to Mazda and to inspire others to know their connection then it somehow alters the basic physics you live within. Time seems more fluid, food gives you nutrition in a whole new way, and your mind allows itself to see much more.

Now on the surface this seems like I have painted temple life as something magical and almost supernatural. In some parts this is true because it does become so different to a common life. Connect to spirit and you allow so much more into your life.

The flipside of this is that you can forget what a common life can entail and for a priest who must counsel and inspire the residents of his town that cannot be. The true wise man, the one who his villagers run to for support and insight was the priest who was so connected with spirit, yet understood the trials outside of temple. It was all about awareness and balance; and this was the greatest thing I learnt from my elders.

I saw them tested (for want of a better word) each day as they listened to the villagers who came to us dismayed or disillusioned. I heard them say pretty much the same words no matter the circumstance or the event that brought the person to them. As I watched over the years though I realised it was not the words spoken that gave comfort. It was in the way they listened.

The priest would often invite the villager to kneel with them before the great fire, or they may sit together in the library. I would see the priest take a deep breath and something would change in their face. I called it their "listening face". It was more than a certain look though, something seemed to open in their eyes.

The villager would speak, and the priest would lean towards them, though never touch them, just to be close enough to truly hear the words spoken. Sometimes they would nod, but that was the strongest reaction they would show. The story would be ended and the priest would say some simple words in return, sometimes their own but always something from the writings. I would then watch the villager stand and walk away, almost as though they floated.

I ended my student phase when I turned twenty. At this age now I was what you would call an acolyte; not yet a priest but certainly not a student. It was the age where I may be invited or suggested to serve at another temple; usually one more remote that needed priests or be welcomed to remain where I was. Being the son of a resident high priest there was no question I would remain.

This phase also was when we would begin to counsel. Before we were allowed to do so we sat with an elder as he counselled, then when we began to receive people they in turn would sit with us.

I was assigned to an elder called Rassan. He was somewhat of an enigma to me mostly in part due to his elusive nature. Having not been one of my main teachers I had rarely heard him speak and then it was just in prayers when we gathered. On the morning that Malchiek announced that we would be paired, Rassan simply nodded and motioned with his hand for me to follow him.

We walked together into the room of the great fire and Rassan went to stand so that he could look into it.

"I am looking forward—" I began but was stopped by a simple raised hand.

I then too looked into the fire and made a quick prayer that I do well with this phase of my priesthood. Within minutes we heard footsteps behind us. I turned to see a small man, most likely a farmer, standing at the doorway. He pulled his hat from his head and crumpled it in his hands. Rassan called him into the temple with no words, just the same hand gesture that he had beckoned me to follow him with.

The farmer walked in slowly, eyeing me and then looking at Rassan. Rassan nodded and the farmer nodded back. Then with another simple hand gesture Rassan motioned for the man to kneel before the fire. When he did so, Rassan kneeled to his right and I to his left. The farmer looked up at Rassan, who nodded gently and then finally some words were spoken as the man began his sharing.

I kept my eyes down as he began, after all I was just here as an observer and to look at either my elder or the man seemed to intrude upon their process together. As the man spoke though I could not help but look up. What he shared was a combination of bizarre and affronting. I had never heard such things in my life. The farmer spoke of his desires for women including the sister of his wife, of cheating on his measurements with his produce to make more money in order to buy gifts to seduce women and how he was now caught in a web of lies to maintain his games.

My eyes grew wider at each revelation and I looked over to Rassan to see his reaction. It never changed. Rassan's face remained soft and gentle. He nodded tenderly every so often but that was his only response. When the farmer finished, Rassan spoke simply and directly. He reminded the man to pray when his desires distracted him and to come to temple when he felt that was not enough. Rassan also reminded him that the choice to heal his ways would create a solution to undo his lies. Then he led the farmer in prayer before sending him home.

We stood and watched the farmer walk out of the temple. When we could no longer hear his footsteps on the temple stairs I turned to Rassan and opened my mouth to speak. I had barely inhaled in preparation to begin when he looked at me with eyes glaring. I snapped my mouth shut. Then he lifted his hand and pointed to the door which led to our study rooms. I knew to walk there immediately.

Rassan followed me. I could hear his breath and it was not calm. We entered the study room and once more a gesture let me know to sit. Rassan sat opposite and looked at me, his face was red and I could tell he was doing all he could to slow his breath and compose himself.

Then finally he spoke.

"We are not here to be entertained by our congregation. We are here to serve them," he began.

"I know that Rassan, but what he was saying—" I leant forward as I spoke but Rassan's hand flew up, stopping me and making me sit back. He took a deep breath, closed his eyes and spoke once more.

"You talk too much and I fear I am going to have to use many words to make you understand what you need to know about counselling," he said as gently as he could but I could feel he was frustrated. Rassan opened his eyes and went on.

"We listen without judgement. In fact we don't really listen at all. We sit and remember they are a pure soul here experiencing the contrasts that life presents. As we remember that, then so we invite them to remember as well," he said and I saw the softness return to his face. "Do you understand?"

I nodded, not because I understood but because I was too scared to upset my teacher anymore.

"These people are not the stories they tell. They are souls helping to birth the new consciousness. They too want the Great Awakening. When they come to us that is what they are truly asking for. The details are just a story."

I nodded because with this I now understood.

That was the most Rassan ever spoke to me on one day because it was the most he ever needed to explain to me.

Within two years I was receiving villagers on my own as was expected. No longer an acolyte but now as a fully-fledged priest. It was wonderful! No longer a child or a student. I was, what I thought, complete.

Life was as grand as ever. My home with my family was my haven away from the sanctuary of temple. My two eldest sisters were married and in their own homes with the youngest betrothed. I had routines to follow that supported my temple service and was abundant in all things I humanly needed. I didn't want anything to change.

But choosing for things not to change is not supportive of life. Change is inevitable. It is how we choose for change to happen and how we deal with it when it does that shapes our experience.

So one day I arrived at temple, the way I always did. I woke just before sunrise for my private prayers in my bedroom. My butler would come at the usual time to wash, dress and groom me. I would breakfast with my family then walk with my father to temple. At temple we would hear how the night shift had gone and we would see that the fire was stable. Then each priest would attend to his individual duties.

On this day I was to receive people for counselling. When Malchiek told me this, one of the younger priests who had been on the night shift rolled his eyes. I looked at him with an expression to quiz his reaction.

"There has been a young woman here since before dawn. We found her on the side terrace during the night and made her come inside to the warmth of the fire and to get her to eat. She fell asleep soon after," he explained. "She is not a villager and she has a rough dialect that seems northern. We didn't ask too much of her. It seemed she had been travelling without food and shelter for some time and she needed her rest more than anything else last night."

I nodded and made my way back into the main room of the temple. The woman was curled up against a pillar to the side of the room, grasping a blanket she had been given around her. She looked so tiny; it would have been easy to miss her amongst the shadows of the temple.

As I approached her she seemed to curl up tighter so I did not go too close. Besides I was now an imposing six feet tall so standing over anyone was a bit daunting. I squatted down and softly said, "Will you not join me by the fire?"

I saw her eyes measure me for a second and then she nodded. I walked back to the fire, sat cross-legged and felt her settle beside me.

"So my dear, what brings you here?" I said with a smile. I knew instinctively, as had the night priests that this story would be far from mild. No young woman seeks refuge in a temple for trivial reasons.

As I readied myself, remembering all I knew about feeling the beauty of the soul beside me, the young woman dropped her head to her chest and began to cry.

Elana was only just sixteen when she arrived in my village but she had lived so much more than years could measure.

She was the only child to be born of her parents. Her mother had long been thought barren and had indeed almost passed the age of what was considered childbearing for even the most fertile woman.

"The gods must have sent her to us knowing we were only now ready," said her father when Elana was born. "Though sending me a son to help me on the farm would have been more a blessing," he thought to himself.

Despite this she was dubbed his 'little miracle' and everything she did delighted and enchanted her parents as well you could imagine. Elana was not the most beautiful child but the limitless love and adoration offered her gave her a radiance that made people see otherwise. They were drawn to her, especially when she went to town with her mother. Elana loved the attention and never shied away from anyone. Why would she when it meant compliments and treats might be offered to her?

So to Elana it did not seem odd that her cousin, Tomas who helped her father on the farm, would want to chat with her or have her sit on his lap as he ate his lunch. Then as she grew older, for Tomas to be happy for her to play nearby as he ploughed or picked crops.

But when she was six this started to feel wrong. Elana could not explain it but something in Tomas' eyes changed when he looked at her. She caught him staring sometimes and it gave her gooseflesh. The innocence of a child cannot measure or know where this feeling was going. So that first day when he beckoned for her to come with him into the barn she walked with him despite her feelings.

Now she knew what that darkness in his eyes was and he had passed it onto her. Elana walked back to the house trembling that day. She wanted to tell her parents. She wanted to throw herself into her mother's arms and weep but Tomas was too clever to let that bond spoil his needs. When he was finished he grabbed Elana by her upper arm and squeezed it just enough to hurt but not bruise.

"If you tell anyone I will hurt you, then hurt your parents," he whispered.

It was a simple but powerful threat. Along with his act it was more than enough to dim a beautiful glow in a blessed child.

The deception continued on for years. Tomas never took Elana's virginity. He was smart enough to know that was something that could be proven, especially once she started to bleed and might bear a child. Given he was the only man Elana was ever alone with upon the farm it would have meant instant accusations that he was sure the child would confirm. So instead he settled for groping her or pushing her hands and mouth upon his body.

Having her virginity was the one thing Elana felt she could claim as a victory over this continual torture. As she grew older she also was able to be more ingenious as to avoid providing opportunity for Tomas to abuse her. In fact when she reached thirteen she became so adept, thanks to her chores and housekeeping that the acts ended.

Tomas would still look at her with a longing but he too knew the game was over.

Then one night over dinner, just when Elana felt she had reclaimed herself, her father gave her the news she never expected and her world crashed down once again.

"My darling, you are of age to be married. Tomas has asked for your hand and I have said yes. He is family and knows the land here. It will be good for all of us," he said and yet curiously never looked up from his plate once.

"No!" screamed Elana and she brought her fists down upon the table. "I won't be his wife. I won't. I will die before you can make me do this!" Tears streamed down her face as her parents looked on stunned. It was the first outburst they had ever witnessed from their daughter.

"Darling, it will be alright. You know we wouldn't do this if it was not for the best," her mother said reaching out for her hand. Elana threw her mother's hand back at her.

"Stop this now!" yelled her father. "This is how it will be! No one else has come asking. All I have to offer as dowry is this farm and animals. Tomas is the best you will get. Be grateful and stop acting like you deserve more!"

This speech from her father was far worse than anything Tomas had ever done to her. The one thing that had helped her survive all those years was the voice inside that told her she was better than this, that there would be an end to the abuse and that she could have joy once more in her life.

Elana ran from the house crying, desperate to get away from her father's words and her mother's tears. Yet outside all she saw were reminders of the monster she was now promised to; the barn where he first led her, the trees he would push her against and the rocks he would hide her behind.

The voice inside rose up.

"No!" it said. "No more!"

Elana nodded. "He will not have the one last piece of me that he has been saving. Never!" She thought as she took a deep breath. "I will change this."

"Yes!" answered the voice inside.

Elana calmed herself and went back into the house. Her parents were still at the table and looked at her.

"I accept your choice and ask you to forgive my behaviour," Elana said plainly.

Her father nodded. "Thank you, daughter. In time you will see this is for the best."

"Yes I know," Elana responded before bidding them goodnight and heading to bed.

The next time she saw Tomas he was grinning from ear to ear.

"Imagine, all these years of preparing you. Now you will be mine forever," he said.

Elana did not respond though she fought every instinct to spit in his face. Tomas could believe whatever he wanted, for Elana knew how this would play out.

The wedding was set for fall, when the crops slowed. So Elana had eight months to work her plan. She played her part perfectly for three more months, listening politely as her mother told her the duties of a wife or watching bemusedly as her father and Tomas made plans for future crops.

Then one night after an ordinary day, she waited for her father and mother's snores to drift through the house. Elana gathered the satchel she had made, filled it with some bread, cheese, biscuits and fruit, and walked from her home for the last time ever.

She turned when she got to the road and took one final look at the house. Her heart sank to know she would not see her parents' faces again, but the alternative was more than she could bear.

"No more..." she said softly.

No more abuser, no more being less than what she deserved. No matter the cost.

Elana should have been scared, heading off into the world alone and with only a satchel of food and the clothes on her back. Yet she had never felt so free. She knew with all her heart that Mazda would protect her and guide her on.

And so she walked ... and walked ... and walked....

Sometimes she hid as travellers passed her by; other times she was not afraid to beg for some wine or to crawl into a barn for shelter at night.

Eventually she arrived within a large city. Here she could walk and people assumed she was a servant on business.

"Whose house are you from?" asked a fruit merchant in the markets as he caught her eyeing his stock.

"None," she answered.

"You are not from around here are you?" he said and folded his arms.

Elana shook her head. The merchant unfolded his arms and threw her an apple which she began to devour.

"Heavens child! When did you last eat?" he asked.

"Two days ago," Elana replied, her mouth still full of apple.

The merchant leaned in, his eyes glistening. "You know I could give you a much better meal if you would do me a favour," he leered.

Elana threw the remainder of the apple on the ground, spat out what was in her mouth and walked away.

"You won't survive long with that attitude!" he yelled after her.

"Yes I will!" said Elana through gritted teeth.

She kept walking through the town and decided to try something new. Elana found her way to the back lanes that allowed servants to take goods home and enter the houses without being seen by the nobility. She walked until she could see a door open and hear some people inside. These doors all opened into the kitchens where there was always someone preparing food or doing some chore.

At the first open door she walked up but before she could say anything a broom was waved at her.

"No beggars!" yelled a voice from behind the broom and Elana continued on the laneway.

More doors were open but they did not feel right. Then one did. She could hear loud talk from inside and the voices seemed warm. Elana walked to the threshold and as heads turned to look at her she began with these words.

"I am not a beggar but if you could spare me some food and perhaps somewhere to sleep I would gladly do some chores or errands for you," she said.

There was a woman and a man inside the kitchen. The woman was standing at the table while the man sat.

"Be gone!" spat the man as he threw his hand in the air.

"Oh hush Mattias! She is a child. Come in, come in," said the woman as she wiped her hands on her apron and waved Elana to a chair. "Look at you! When was the last time you bathed, you are covered in dust. Where is your family?"

Elana began to speak but she did not tell her story. She told a new story. One that would dissolve her past and let her start over.

She was now an orphan, with no other family, making her way and hoping to find a home. It was simple but believable and one that did not lead to too many questions.

"What do you know to do?" asked the woman.

"I can cook and clean," Elana offered.

The man and woman laughed. "Well I should hope so for your age," teased Mattias.

"Can you pluck a chicken? Do you know a bad piece of meat? Do you know how to thrash a carpet?" asked the woman.

Elana nodded even though she knew nothing of carpets.

"Well, let us keep you here for a few days. When we see your worth then we will ask mistress about having you stay on," said the woman smiling. "Now take this," she handed Elana a jug. "Go back down the lane to the well and fill it. When you get back you can have some bread."

When Elana walked out Mattias turned to the woman. "Eva, what do you think you are doing?"

"Ahhh. We need another pair of hands. All she wants is room and food. Mistress will be grateful," she explained.

Elana's few days of trial turned to weeks and then months. Life became settled and routine and she loved it, even when Mattias teased her, as he loved to do. Then one day that inevitable change came upon her.

Elana was walking through the markets, avoiding the sleazy fruit merchant, when she felt something. It was dark and heavy, so familiar and yet something that was out of place. She looked up and saw Tomas in the distance, peering at some goods.

She froze in place, trying to convince herself that her eyes were deceiving her but the more she watched the more she knew it was him. Then just as she gathered herself to run Tomas glanced up and their eyes met. It was barely a second but Elana knew he could tell it was her.

Running back into the kitchen and the safety of her new home, Elana gathered herself.

"Maybe he didn't see me. Even if he did, how would he know where to find me?" these questions plus more ran through her thoughts. Then the worst thought came to her.

What would he do if he did find her?

There was not one possibility that made her feel comfortable.

Why was he there anyway? Farmers didn't travel. The only explanation was that he was there searching for her. This made the implications of being found even worse. Tomas was here to claim what he believed was his.

She needed to leave the town immediately but to do so in daylight was too risky. Elana once more acted out her duties within her home as expected, praying each moment that there would be no knock upon their door. Then for the second time, she gathered some supplies and made her way.

Elana knew she had not travelled far enough when she had stopped at that first town. So she ventured as far south as her feet could take her. She walked for over a year, foraging, begging and working for food and shelter. Though tempted to stay in some places she knew that she was not far enough from Tomas yet. Anytime a place seemed safe or welcoming, that voice inside her would say, "not far enough" and she would keep walking.

When she arrived at our temple she was exhausted in every way possible. Her body ached from walking. Her mind was spent from the constant wondering of where her next meal would come from or where she would sleep that night. Mostly though, her spirit was worn out from being in constant flight from her abuser.

Elana had sought refuge in several of our temples as she had travelled so she thought nothing special of mine. Sometimes that is the best way to invite a miracle into your life.

She usually told the same story; that she was an orphan travelling south to find some family. Today though as she sat with me, the voice inside said, "tell this one the truth." And so she spoke the truth.

I sat and listened as I always did, keeping my balance even when I felt my heart shatter into a thousand shards as she spoke of what Tomas had done. When I looked at her feet, that were now calloused and caked with dust, my resolve could not remain. Tears fell down my face also.

"You will come to my home and bathe and eat," I said as plainly as I could, not looking up so that she could not see my tears.

I stood up and offered my hand to Elana to rise also. As she stood she continued to speak.

"I can ... do chores for your home ... to repay you..." she offered as she spoke through the last of her tears.

"There is no need for that. I am a priest and this is what we do for the needy," I said in what I believed was my most stoic voice.

Elana though saw the tears in my eyes and inside her something softened. She had not felt that for someone else since—well actually she could never remember feeling that for anyone. It felt weird and yet wonderful.

"Now you know why you could tell him," was all the voice would say.

I walked Elana to my home after letting the other priests know I would be gone. Rassan saw my red eyes and just shook his head. I didn't care for his reaction and ignored it. It was more what my parents would say that worried me.

Malchiek was visiting homes so only my mother was there to greet us. As always she played the most gracious hostess, filling her words with "of course" and "my dear" and supported with a gentle smile even as she watched one of the servants walk Elana away to bathe her.

Then my mother turned to me, her brow dropped, pushing her smile right off her face.

"Balthasar, what are you doing? She could have been cared for at temple," she said with her eyes searching into mine.

"I don't know..." was all I could say softly back.

"Oh yes you do!" snapped my mother and walked off.

I knew I wanted to offer Elana the comfort of a home. I wanted her to feel that she could stop running, that she was safe and no one would hurt her. I had never wanted to protect someone so much in my life—not even my sisters.

I didn't know why.

I didn't care why.

I went to follow my mother. We needed to discuss adding a new maid to our house.

Elana joined our household. I told her story to my mother and it was enough to make her at least feel partly as I did about providing a new home for her.

"You are lucky she is not useless," my mother said to me six months later when it was evident Elana was far from this.

Elana cooked, cleaned and helped in any way asked of her and she did so without question or heavy heart.

One night as I was out stargazing with Malchiek, we heard someone approaching. It was Elana carrying a small dish.

"Sirs, I don't mean to disturb you but I have brought you some sweets. I thought you might like something as you work," she said as she placed the dish upon the small table amongst our scrolls and instruments. "It's something my mother taught me to make."

It was the first time Elana had spoken of her family in any way since at the temple with me at our first meeting. I heard her voice break a little as she did and noticed she looked down for a moment. Then with a deep breath she looked back up.

"I hope you enjoy them. I used that honey brought to us by your friend," she smiled and then walked back into the house.

In the dish were some small cakes; about two bites each in size. They looked plain but you could smell the Persian honey that they had been soaked in. I grabbed one and took half into my mouth. The sweetness was consuming. I had intended to keep stargazing as I chewed but I couldn't.

"That's why we don't eat as we do our star studies," laughed Malchiek. "It's just a distraction."

This was more than the distraction of the food. I picked up another. With every mouthful a rush of thoughts and emotions came to me. I remembered the first time I saw Elana sitting curled up against the pillar in temple. Then I heard her sobs as she told her story. I saw how she looked after she had her first bath and was dressed in fresh clothes.

Mostly I felt in my chest that sensation I always felt when I saw or even thought of Elana. Now I knew what that feeling was.

"Father, I want to marry Elana," I said while looking up at the stars.

Malchiek kept his eyes upwards also and plainly replied. "You want to marry a servant?"

"She is not a servant."

"So you want to marry a refugee?"

"She is not a refugee."

I heard Malchiek sigh and then he looked to me and I to him.

"You know, I saw this coming. We all did. The other priests warned me," Malchiek began. "I had a whole speech prepared. I had other women to suggest to you. I had your standing as a priest to throw at you." With that Malchiek shook his head slowly and smiled. "But I know any words would be useless. If I deny you this woman, you will live with such a wound in your heart that you will be no use as a priest—or a son for that matter. Marry her but promise me you will remain here as a priest."

I nodded my agreement as Malchiek walked to the table and picked up a cake. He took a huge bite and then shook his head as he laughed.

"Holy blessings, this is delicious. I would be marrying her too if I could!" he exclaimed as he shoved the last piece of the cake into his mouth.

CHAPTER FOURTEEN

It seems I have not said so much about the Great Awakening whilst I have shared how my life progressed. Please be assured that as all I have written about occurred, so too the magi, including those at my temple, were constantly talking about this.

Letters continued to be written. Dreams continued to be recorded. Debates raged and the stars gave up their secrets from time to time.

At Gaspar's temple, I will admit that more was being done than any-where else. He had assembled his acolytes and together they were in the depths of analysing every record that was held. This they combined with their daily fire meditations or those as they looked to the heavens at night.

Within his small group they had seers and even those who heard words, though thankfully none were showing any signs of delusion or imbalance with this. Gaspar though always led the way. He was the one who could interpret the dreams, make sense of the visions and who could explain the words. Mostly though he was the one who knew how to guide what they needed to do to bring forth the right message at the right time in the right way.

"Tonight we will breathe beneath the stars," Gaspar would say. "Do not force anything. I will know it. Let the energy come to whichever of you is ready to receive."

Other days it would be at the fire, or perhaps they would just read. Each one of the young men trusted his leadership implicitly.

It was Gaspar's dreams that were his greatest connection to the new consciousness that was coming in and there was one that he would have over and over. It was so simple but the symbolism was immense. He kept seeing an egg begin to crack and split open. Never though, would he see what was emerging and that drove him crazy. It also provided him with fire to keep exploring what the dream was telling him and he believed the answer would reveal itself in his studies and correspondence some day.

Gaspar knew the dream was both literal and symbolic.

121

'I know it is about a new birth because that is what we are doing. We are birthing a new era. Why cannot I see what is next? What will emerge?' Gaspar wrote to us all.

I remember sitting back in my chair as I read this. I will admit that I had a bit of a chuckle too. Gaspar amused me greatly with his letters. They were so full of his experiences and wisdom, yet there too was such naivety and longing. I put all that aside and closed my eyes whilst still holding his letter.

I imagined the egg, whole and intact. I felt into the energy put into creating the egg, the fertilisation and then the incubation. I imagined that moment when the chick inside knew they were ready to emerge and the strength it needed to push through the shell to begin its new life. Suddenly I knew what was in the shell. I leant forward in my chair and picked up my quill.

'My dear brother Gaspar,

What if you cannot see what is inside because it is not created yet? Yes this time of ours is a birth but what if, unlike a usual birth where the form of the offspring is known, instead the offspring is being formed as we create the birth. The Great Awakening may not be so much about setting free what is already here. It may not even be about simply allowing what is asleep or dormant to awake. The awakening may be what we in fact are creating in this moment.

In love and honour

Balthasar'

Gaspar smiled when he read this. He even laughed a little.

"I will have to meet this brother one day," he thought to himself.

That night Gaspar had his egg dream again. The egg shook and cracked as always. Finally the fracture along its surface went the circumference of the shell and it fell open. Gaspar could look inside. It was empty.

Melchior in his much simpler temple with only his elders as company immersed himself in astronomy. Now we all studied astronomy in a basic sense in that we all knew the constellations and their movements through the seasons. As well we all knew the meditation in which to be still and feel beyond the pattern of lights.

Few though truly studied with detail the art of measuring them. To be quite frank, that element of the study could be quite boring to one without a mathematical mind, such as myself. To those like Melchior, the precision of using instruments to gauge and check positions was infinitely satisfying. I believe men such as Melchior kept us "in place" and grounded, which I realise is somewhat of a pun given the subject.

Melchior and those like him would be the ones to confirm or deny when we believed we had seen an irregularity. In my library was a collection of letters from these men along the lines of;

'Dear Brother,

Thank you for your beautiful sharing of what you observed. However my measurements of that night showed no such anomaly....'

Our astronomers kept our emotions in check and thankfully so, lest we all acted upon them without good reason.

My father once said to me, after a particularly bad fight with one of my sisters that had ended in some very hurtful words:

"You cannot let your emotions drive your actions. They make you irrational."

At the time I thought he was talking to me alone but he was speaking of emotions in general. If every magi reacted to an emotion our religion would have been a mess. The beauty of our brotherhood was in keeping ourselves balanced with the support we offered, with the array of talents we held and with our faith in something much greater than anything we could imagine.

We had astronomers to keep our visions clear, our seers to keep our faith flowing and we had wise elders as our foundation. Together we had knowing; that knowing that we were all part of something so much grander.

Melchior visited our temple with his father when he was eighteen. I was told to watch him as he measured the stars in the hope that I may too be inspired to do more of this. I had barely shrugged off the petulance of my teens at the time and I could not help but act bemused as I observed him.

Melchior was as slow as a snail. He lifted his instruments and stood like a statue. You could barely see him move the parts of the instrument. Then he would just as slowly lower his arms and look at the instrument for what seemed an eternity before softly placing it upon the table. Then he would lift his quill to record what he had measured.

Melchior did this over and over. It even felt like he got slower each time. It was tedious and almost painful to watch.

"Do you not tire of your measuring?" I finally asked when our fathers had moved away.

Melchior just shook his head. He was used to such comments and in fact mine was one of the kinder he had heard from someone close to his age.

"Really?" I pushed. "Your father is not within ear distance. You can tell me. I won't repeat your words."

Melchior sighed and looked up at me. "I do not tire of my work because my work does not tire of me."

"What?" I said screwing up my face.

"I did not think you would understand," Melchior said looking back to his writing.

I wanted to make a retort but our fathers were walking back to us. Instead I looked back up to the stars.

"Is it not inspiring to watch your brother Melchior do these measurements with such passion?" my father asked me.

"It is on the verge of hypnotic such is his commitment," I said as straight-faced as I could.

The following night I sat out with Melchior again. I knew he was not comfortable with me thanks to my attitude the night before and to be honest I felt somewhat embarrassed. As he began his work I carried a chair from the house and sat beside him.

"Is that so you won't have as far to fall when I bore you to sleep?" Melchior said without looking at me.

"No, it is so I can watch you in comfort. I apologise for my words last night," I said. "I lay in bed last night thinking about your words; of your work never tiring of you. We all have our own ways of connecting with spirit and you made me realise that this is your connection."

I sought out Melchior's eyes when I finished and he finally turned to me.

"Thank you," was all he said.

So I watched as Melchior made his measurements and records. I even allowed myself to be intrigued by some of what he shared as he did so. Then when he seemed to be done I stood up.

"Now perhaps you would like to share with me my way of connecting?" I asked.

Melchior nodded and came and stood beside me. I said nothing but looked up and he followed my lead. We both stared for some time.

"Can you hear them?" I asked.

"No," was said softly beside me.

We stood in silence for a while longer. I stared into the heavens, feeling them expand before me. A shooting star flared across the sky and I felt Melchior move beside me, desperate to record the area of sky it had been seen in. I turned to watch him scratching his observation. He looked unsettled as he did so. When he finished he looked up and with the little lamplight we had I could see a blush across his cheeks.

"I heard that one," was all he said and then he walked quickly into the house.

That night Gaspar had a new dream that was set to repeat itself. He was standing out under the night sky when three camels appeared before him. Each one was saddled and loaded ready for a journey.

Gaspar walked closer to see what was packed upon them. One was loaded with scrolls of all kinds: some new, some ancient - but all were filled with teachings. The second was filled with star charts and instruments to measure the skies, while the third was laden with foods.

"Where are you going? Where are your riders?" Gaspar would ask them each time this dream came to him.

That was where the dream would end.

CHAPTER FIFTEEN

My connection was becoming my bliss. Not that I was not happy with the other parts of my life, but nothing satisfied me as it did to stand beneath the stars and hear what the universe had to share with me.

Temple was my duty to our order, counselling was my service to others. To stand beneath the night sky was my love affair with spirit.

One night as I finished my dinner and wiped my mouth I caught Elana smiling, holding back some laughter.

I smiled back. "And what of my manners do you find so amusing, my love?" I asked her.

"I love how you become a child when you know it is time to be with the stars," she answered. "I can see on your face how your thoughts of the day evaporate. You start to smile and eat faster so you can begin."

I laughed out loud. "True, true! Nothing else matters when I am beneath the night sky, except for you my love!" I kissed the top of her head as I walked past her to make my way outside.

I did have a ritual each night that I played out before my stargazing but it was not one of what you would call physical acts. At dinner with Elana and the rest of my family, as I ate I would feel myself slowly change into someone different. The way my mind would be replaying all that I had read or heard during the day would slowly dissolve. My thoughts as to what needed to be done the next day would also fade away. All that would be inside me would suddenly shift so that all that I could consider was walking outside.

My family knew it well. Elana could see it in my eyes when I had made the shift. My conversation would taper off and she knew to not initiate any more talk with me. I was there in front of her but not in any way to hold discussion with. In fact she learnt quite quickly that even if I were to respond, I would have no memory of what was spoken, even minutes later.

I would end my meal, kiss my wife a farewell and walk to the garden behind our home. It was a wonderful open area, on a slight rise that fell away to a field below before the land rose up again into nearby hills. I would face north as I stood to begin, close my eyes, take a deep breath then slowly open them as I looked up.

Beside me on a small table, my butler would have readied some parchment, a quill and some ink. Beside that would be a clay incense burner, a lump of charcoal smouldering inside with the resin of some frankincense smoking on top of it. The scent of that resin helping to pull me into the beautiful space I loved so much.

My eyes would search into the sky, and at first I would feel the very human part of me see the intense beauty of the stars. It filled me with wonder every night: how this magnificence had been gifted to us by Mazda. Then I would close my eyes and take another deep breath. This time before I would open them I would make a quick prayer to Mazda.

"Dearest Lord, maker of all things, that of which I am born, let me see with your eyes, hear with your ears and feel with your soul."

It was my own prayer and when I said the words they were spoken with every fibre of my being. I knew that when I opened my eyes this time that I would not be seeing the stars with the simple human eyes I was born with. I would now see them with divine sight. What I loved even more was to listen with divine hearing.

When I opened my eyes it was as though the very Earth had fallen away. There was just me and the stars. The space around me became infinite. I would take another deep breath and the distance between the stars would open up. The sky would show me even more stars and planets than anyone could see at first. I liked to call these the "immeasurable" because they were not of the dimension of ordinary space and time. Indeed if you held an instrument to them, the first layer of stars would close in as though to protect them.

It was when I allowed myself to dive into this space, not just of the stars but of my surrounds also, that my listening would then open. Some nights I would hear music, other nights it was a voice, clear and sharp. Some nights I would just feel sensations within my body. I knew no matter what I heard or felt that it was all perfect and appropriate.

It took me some time to accept this though. When I first started to hear the voice, my father monitored me closely for fear of my losing sanity with it. Many nights he would watch me from afar as I looked at the stars. At least once a week he would make sure we had a full conversation about what I was hearing. One time I sought him after a frustrating time.

"Some nights I hear no voice!" I declared in exasperation as a wave of relief swept through my father.

"That is fine," he tried to comfort me, while inside he was relieved that my ability to hear the voice may be dissipating and end up merely being a phase. "Hearing such things can pass. Then you can concentrate on other ways of your studies."

"No Father, I still hear. Some nights instead of a voice I hear musical tones, or a low vibration," I explained. "Why does it change? Why is it doing this?"

My father sighed and shrugged his shoulders. We were now well into unknown territory with this.

That night Malchiek lay in bed wide-awake wondering what to do with me. My mother could feel him stirring beside her.

"What is it Malchiek? Why can't you sleep?" she asked.

"One son. I was given one son, talented and committed to the priesthood. Why was that not enough? Why does he have to always take the more complicated way to be what he is?" he sighed and rubbed his forehead.

My mother sat up in bed and turned to my father. "Because though you have one son you hold as much for him as a hundred. Because we birthed him in a time of great changes and you know as well as I do that these changes cannot be brought about by ordinary men." She opened her mouth to say more but thought better of it and lay down again, now as wide-awake as my father.

"You would have made a wonderful priest," was all my father could say.

A good night's sleep followed my mother's wisdom - eventually. The next day my father took me to visit the oldest priest of our village. Barenma was long retired, having left temple way before I even first climbed the steps. His longevity was often seen as gift from Mazda for his immaculate service to spirit.

"It is said that he never lost his temper even as a child. At that young age he knew instinctively to stay with what was good and holy. As he grew he refused to let the ways of man distract him from this peace he had chosen," Malchiek told me once.

"But surely that is a myth created to make us want to emulate him," I sputtered before even considering my words.

"Balthasar! Your ability to question what is presented you and your disrespect for what is presented you have a fine line between them that is rapidly getting thinner."

"But Father, let us be realistic! No man surely can suppress such an emotion over an entire lifetime. And to not have the ability to anger as a child ... well ... does that not suggest some—er—mental deficiency?" I posed and laughed as I did so.

The questioning did not upset Malchiek but the laughter did.

"Firstly Balthasar, what part of you believes that all men are designed of the same form and spirit? If we are all of the same template then consciousness would never change for how could change ever begin if we were locked into the same design?" Malchiek began, being wary of allowing his own anger to bubble up.

"Secondly," he continued. "It is easy to judge others as "deficient" because of their differences. If we dismissed people for their differences then we would also miss any gifts they also had. Would you like to be judged deficient and dismissed by the priesthood for your ability to hear the voice you do when you stargaze?"

I didn't need to answer.

Barenma's home was not so far from ours and as we walked there Malchiek reminded me of my response when I was first told of this elder many years before.

"I trust you will keep your respect in measure today in his presence?" he asked in what was a blend of threat and plea.

I stopped walking and threw my hands in the air.

"I—you—why do you have to assume that I have not changed as I have aged?" I cried out to him.

Malchiek just laughed and kept walking.

When we arrived at Barenma's house we received the customary greeting by his servants. Our feet and hands were washed clear of dust with rose water and a cup of honeyed tea soothed our mouth and throat. We were then ushered into the salon and seated with no Barenma in sight. The servant nodded and left.

It was a typical salon that was within any wealthy Babylonian's home. A room designed for greeting and entertaining guests. It was filled with lounges and chairs, with small tables between them for any refreshments offered. The walls would be draped with embroideries of landscapes or paintings, often of the family. This salon was somewhat different though.

Instead of the usual pleasant scenes or colours adorning the walls, the embroideries were of the night skies. I jumped from my seat and walked to look closer as soon as the servant left the room. Some I wanted to touch, others I took a step back from so I could just take in all their details.

Most were accurate representations that I assumed had been used for teaching, even though we used nothing like this at temple. Then one made me miss a breath. It was one that as I walked before it I instinctively took a step back from. It was the largest in all the room and upon it the stars had been woven into the deep indigo background with gold thread. The tapestry ran the height of the room and most of the width.

I took three steps back to take it all in but bumped into one of the chairs.

"Be careful Balthasar!" hissed my father but I barely heard him.

All I could do was look into the tapestry and suddenly something magical happened. It was as though it came alive. The gold thread started twinkling and the indigo between grew even darker spreading out beyond the borders of the fabric. The room fell away behind me and it was exactly how it felt to be outside at night.

I heard that voice say "See it is not just at night and outside..." which I did not understand. Then I heard tones of music which fell away to be replaced by a dense vibration below my feet.

"Tell me what you feel?"

It was a new voice and I heard it from behind me.

"I can hear Mazda, I can hear the stars and I can hear the Earth beneath me. I do not know what it means though?" I replied with a tremor in my voice.

"There is no meaning. It is a connection. Tell me what you feel?" the voice asked again.

I took a deep breath and my eyes searched into the tapestry, looking between the gold threads.

"I see the eternity of Mazda. I hear the dance of the new awakening. I feel how ready this Earth is," I answered.

"And that is all you need," replied the voice once more from behind me. "Now if you would care to take a seat I would like to serve you some afternoon tea."

In one breath I was back in the room. The gold thread shone as normal and I could see the limits of the embroidery. I heard my father take in a deep breath as I turned around. Malchiek's eyes met mine and he forced a smile, then he nodded to the doorway.

There standing was the most fragile man I had ever seen. He stood on his own but grasped a walking stick as though his life depended on it.

"Hello Brother Barenma. It is so good to finally meet you," I said and made my way to sit down.

We ate, we drank and we made small talk. No more was needed to be said about what I heard when I connected to the stars. It was what I felt - no more, no less. It needed no analysis or dissection. It was my bridge to spirit and that relationship was all I needed to bring to me what was needed to guide the awakening.

This moment with Barenma was what inspired my reply to Gaspar about his egg dream; it was about trusting that we were creating this as we moved along. There was no set plan for the awakening because man would create it when they were ready. There was no divine plan from Mazda as to when or how it would happen. His love for us set humanity free to live as we chose. It was allowing our connection to spirit that let Mazda know we were ready and the more of us that chose this, well then the more ready humanity was to allow consciousness to shift.

So as each one of us allowed the connection, then the awakening progressed and came closer into our reality. This was the birthing; this was the egg starting to crack. There was no point in trying to figure how it would look or feel because as each man or woman connected to spirit it would shift. It would speed up, because when anyone allows themselves this divine, immaculate connection, then "all that is" has to respond. The greater the call, the faster and deeper the response.

So when I allowed myself to feel this beneath the stars, it was not just about what I was going to see or hear from the grand creator. It was also about what I was sending out from me to all that is.

That was what Barenma taught me. When I truly grasped this years later as I watched Melchior take his measurements I understood why Barenma was never angered by others or by circumstance.

When you have your connection with spirit, it is so pure and eternal that it satisfies every part of your being. You feel how complete you are and how trivial your human concerns are.

More so than this - when you feel into how perfectly Mazda has placed all of creation to allow for our beautiful expansion into the birth of heaven on Earth, you then slip into something amazing; acceptance.

The acceptance of all that is. That we, with Mazda designed this experience for our learning and to know our worthiness of life with joy. To know each person plays with this design in their own way. To know that as a priest I could guide them to their connection and their acceptance of all that is.

To live life with this knowing leaves no room for anger.

I also certainly made sure that my children would know of Barenma and what he taught me.

So each night now I stood out under the night sky and I did not push my senses to hear anything. I simply stood in the wonder of being part of this Great Awakening. I breathed in deep to feel myself connect with Mazda and let him know that I was willing and ready to be part of this new birth of consciousness.

With this something amazing began to happen. I felt into parts of me that I didn't know existed. From within me someone else began to emerge.

I had always looked ahead of me to my father and the other high priests and seen their wisdom as a product of their studies and experience. Now I felt a wisdom emerging from within me that was immediate and eternal. It was not the wisdom from books or stories or learnt in anyway. It was like a seed that had been planted in me by Mazda that I had to water.

Each night as I breathed with the universe I fed that seed and let it sprout. It was not a wisdom that I could share with words, but it was one that could be felt by others in my presence. I had felt it with Barenma, Rassan and of course my father. It was a presence that could not be taught in any way, thus not all priests carried it with them. Yes, many could spout the words to inspire but few could encourage or comfort you just with their presence.

This wonderful sense of being so much more than a simple man; that I was so connected to Mazda and the changes of the world, carried with me from the night. It walked with me to temple, it smiled at my wife and it was within the money I paid in the markets for goods. Each night I breathed with the stars, the connection expanded and became more of my life.

One night Elana came out to bring me some tea and honey cakes as I stargazed. She stood back and watched me, waiting for me to take pause.

"It is a warm night, you need some refreshment," she said and turned to walk back inside.

"Stay," I beckoned with my hand and pointed to a seat at the table that held my scrolls and now my supper. I too sat for some rest.

I looked back up as I sipped my tea.

"Do you hear much tonight?" Elana asked.

"Tonight I have been hearing drums but I fear that is a wedding across the plain," I said and we both laughed. "No my dear, tonight I am just happy to be with Mazda and enjoy the beauty of the sky."

Elana nodded and I could feel there was something more.

"What is it, my love? Tell me," I asked.

Elana opened her mouth then closed it and looked down. I knew she would speak in her own time so I took another sip of tea instead of pushing her. Then I gently reached out my hand and took hers into it.

She smiled and looked up. "You have always known just how to be with me," she said softly and I saw a tear fall down her cheek. Then she began.

"You know that I have told you my story in truth and with nothing to hide. However there is one more part of my story that I would like to share. I am not sure why I know to tell you now but as always I trust my sharing is right with you."

I smiled and nodded, giving her hand a gentle squeeze of assurance.

"You see, my love," Elana continued. "I too hear a voice."

Elana looked into my eyes measuring my reaction and to be honest, at first I did not know what to make of this. I was about to ask Elana to share more with me when she spoke again.

This time she told about when she first heard it, as Tomas pushed his hands under her dress. Then she told of how the voice spoke to her as she lay in bed each night as her mind replayed all that Tomas had done. It told her over and over that she was alright and that this would end.

Elana told me how the voice told her to leave her family, to keep walking and how it even told her to trust me.

"I know it cannot be of any evil, for each time I listen and hear her words, my life has led to more joy. It has saved me and brought me to you. I do not hear her so often but when I do I listen," she finished.

"I know that voice too. I hear one within me that seems to share the same things." I stopped as I had a quick chuckle and then just as quickly I stopped myself. "I do not mean to make small of what it guided you through. My voice has not had such things to deal with. Instead it has had to weather my impetuousness and self-righteousness!"

I shook my head as I contemplated some of my past behaviour while Elana now smiled at me. Taking a deep breath, I squeezed her hand within mine.

"And to think you did not need discipline or the stars to open your hearing. Just the desire for something better."

I looked back up to the stars and sighed deeply.

"Perhaps—perhaps it takes something so big—so—so—I cannot think of the words..." Elana said softly and she dropped her head.

I knew what she was trying to say. Was it her trauma that brought the

136

voice forward? Was it my commitment that brought out what I heard? I looked to the stars and asked Mazda for an answer and felt it like a breeze inside me. Then I heard a thousand whispers all around me.

It was the voice that was within a thousand and more people. They were all waiting to be heard. Then I saw them, like shadows, walking around. They were not lost, but pacing as though waiting for something or someone. In an instant I understood.

Each spirit I saw was the embodiment of this voice that Elana and I knew so well. They came to this life with us, a piece of "all that is" that is gifted to us by Mazda. These days you would call it your soul, then we called it bah-ra'an. It was the pure essence of us all, the divine spark that linked us back to Mazda.

That was what I heard and what Elana heard. We had found our way to allow it to be part of our life. Yet before me I saw thousands of souls waiting to be heard, waiting to become part of someone's life.

"But how can they be heard? Why can only some hear them?" I asked of Mazda.

"Who is willing? Who has faith? Who is ready to be all that they can be?" was the answer.

I looked over at Elana who was looking at me quizzically.

"I can tell you were in deep conversation with Mazda," she said. "Can I know what was shared?"

So I told her everything I had seen, heard and felt—then finally what I now understood. Tears fell down her face as she listened.

"That is what I had felt too. Who else would want to save me in my darkest hours but my bah-ra'an? Mazda gifted it to us so we would remember from where we came. It is surely our anchor to keep us with him."

I nodded my head. No words could have put it more perfectly.

CHAPTER SIXTEEN

I find the word maturity so interesting. Most cultures across the ages would say that maturity is the letting go of your childish ways as you step into the role of the adult. I find this definition somewhat sad.

There are many qualities of being a child that I believe we should never relinquish, such as being inquisitive or finding humour in the simplest of things. You see, so many people buy into the idea that to be grown up and wise means that this has to be at the expense of joy and seeing the wonder of life. That to be an adult means a life of responsibility, duty and measured behaviour. To me this seemed to be at the detriment of why we were even upon the Earth.

Now this does not mean that I condone a life of recklessness and disrespect. That I even need to voice this shows how we tie ourselves into such shared beliefs. To me it is much simpler than that.

When my father told me about the midwife who delivered me and of her mantra I understood it completely. Life is how you wish it to be and that can be shared with others in ways that can be inspiring and uplifting. The midwife did it in her own way, taking something that could have been stressful and making it a joyful journey. I often wondered how many ill-fated births were altered to ones of elation because of her attitude.

I once raised this in discussion with my fellow priests at temple.

"If life is given its meaning by how we view it then we can alter life simply by how we choose to view it," I put forward.

I saw several of the older priests take in deep breaths and some even smirked. My father as always tried not to notice their reaction to me.

"So my brother, you believe that you can alter the existence that Mazda has set out for us?" one responded with a half smile across his lips.

"Yes!" I responded emphatically and leaned forward in my chair. "If we are given the choice of good or evil, then why would we not have the choice of joy or despair?"

"Those things are the result of choosing good or evil," was quickly snapped back at me.

This pushed me back into my chair for a moment and my mind began searching into this. All I could see as a response was the face of my beloved Elana.

"But what of those who have not chosen evil but have it put upon them? Do they then lose the right to joy? How many good men do you know of in our town that still suffer bad crops? And how many men of ill repute do you see who have lives that flourish?" I responded.

"The ones who choose evil will eventually face a greater judgement than any human consequence can deliver, and those who suffer ill fate despite a honourable life will ultimately be rewarded and compensated for their suffering," another priest responded as calmly as he could.

None of us were done though. I had stirred up the very essence of thoughts that made any man or woman question the idea of a greater force designing our lives.

"I do not question the ultimate consequences of good or evil," I continued, wary of not inflaming the situation any more. "It is just I believe that if we truly choose joy, then our life will reflect that."

I imagined Elana walking those hundreds of miles to change her life. I then saw the image of my mother in childbirth with me, laughing even though every other time she had given birth she was left in tears.

"What I am saying is this; when we behold the wonder of Mazda and creation, we are not only shown the glory of a virtuous life but we are also offered the opportunity to live that life in wonder and joy.

"As children we are fascinated with everything, every day. Life is a constant adventure. Then somehow as adults we fall into duties and work, losing that sense of excitement and stimulation.

"What if we could do both? What if we could keep the wonder so that our eyes remained as open as they could be? So that we didn't see life as a test of our servitude and merits. So that we lived knowing we had the supreme love of our creator and that we could love every moment of being here, even when it seemed not so joyful."

I said all of this out loud and the room filled with a mix of perplexed expression and bemusement. No one answered for a moment.

Then one of the elders spoke up.

"There is no doubt that we each choose our own life to experience. The 'how' has always been the difference and is the reason we question and seek answers. The truth is that the 'how' can only be answered by the one living that 'how'. I can only tell you how I live and view life, and I know you could never emulate my life. No one can. No other man would ever have my thoughts, my past, my choices, my aspirations or beliefs in the same balance or combination. It is a unique set of dynamics that creates my life.

"Look around this room - here we all are; the same culture, the same religion, the same training, even the same sex. Yet not one of us is truly and completely alike. It is as inspiring as it is frustrating. Thankfully the frustrations are less than the inspiration I receive from you all.

"So yes, my brother, I agree with you. It is entirely possible for you to choose and create joy from that choice. For who am I to know intimately your thoughts and all else of your emotions," he finished and no one in the room moved.

Their faces were now calm and balanced. Then one by one they all began to nod.

The same elder smiled at me. "Now I will be intrigued to see just how you let this unfold."

So that which I had been born of truly became my way. Sometimes it was a struggle, such as times when I would see one of my children ill or a tragedy would beset one of our town's people. My ideals didn't erase the ills or trials of life but what they offered me was a way to step through them and resolve them with ease and grace.

When one of my children did fall ill, I did not weep and imagine funeral plans. I knew to gather the best support I could find. I would sit with them and speak of stories that reminded them of the joy of their life.

When a death was within the village, I most certainly offered my sympathies but I also found a respectful way to speak well of the deceased. So before I left the home the mourners could find some semblance of a smile within their grief.

A bad crop could always be lessened with reminders of what had been stored and the kindness of others in the village.

I truly believed that no matter what life could design for us, we could meet it with our desire to bring it back to the balance of living in joy.

I had this tested on many occasions. Several times I had to leave the home of a death with sneers behind me.

"You do not know of true suffering with your privileged and sheltered life!" a father snapped at me after his daughter died from fever.

This did not sway me. I felt the depths of his misery and would not dare to alter where his emotions held him.

CHAPTER SEVENTEEN

We have spoken much of my beginnings but I know your true curiosity of me is with regards to my famous journey. So let us now speak more of the way this came about.

The correspondence between magi was as active as it had been since my dream so many years before. Amongst the general run of letters, Gaspar and I had developed our own personal connection, with thanks in great part to our sharing of what we saw within his dreams.

'I do believe you are the only one who sees into my dreams with any true insight or value.' He once wrote to me.

To be honest most other magi were frustrated with Gaspar.

"He keeps trying so hard to find meaning in anything he sees, hears or feels," one of our priests muttered when another letter arrived from him. "It is as though he thinks he will force the awakening or some confirmation of it."

I sat back as other priests mumbled their agreement, but I knew where Gaspar was coming from. The older priests throughout our lands seemed to have accepted that the awakening was always ahead of us. At least a hundred generations had waited, so why too shouldn't they? It was as though they did not think they were even worthy to witness it.

Like Gaspar though, I could feel something shifting around me. I could sense it when I looked to the stars or into the great fire. If we decided we were just here to wait then so it would be. But what if we decided that we were tired of waiting?

That night I wrote a very long personal letter to Gaspar.

'Dear brother Gaspar,

I am writing to you as I believe I feel something within and around me that you do too. I truly feel that my lifetime within this era will see much more change than those around me believe. I watch my elders and though

I hold much love and respect for their work, I also see a resignation that what has been, will be.

But how much longer can we wait for prophecies to be played out? How much longer do we wait for the skies to show us something new?

When an egg breaks open, it is because the chick inside is ready to live. What if we now tell Mazda that we are ready for the awakening of mankind? That we are ready and willing to guide men and women into the new world?

What if we choose to now birth the awakening rather than just wait?

Your brother Balthasar'

When I finished writing I folded the letter and made ready to put on a seal. I lifted the candle and was about to pick up the wax block when instead I picked up the letter. Looking at the letter I contemplated all I had written within and shook my head. What was I thinking to write such things? I should burn it.

But that soul voice inside me said, "do not burn your words."

So instead I put the letter down and lifted the wax, making the seal.

The next morning as I was about to give the letter to my butler to send it, I once more hesitated. I made one last prayer to Mazda.

"Please stop me, or stop the letter should the words be blasphemous or wrong."

I did not hear any words or sensations to stop me and so the letter was sent to Gaspar.

Just over a week later the letter was returned to me. However it was not my wax mark upon it but Gaspar's. I opened it with trepidation and saw below my words, Gaspar's response.

It was the single word, 'yes.'

CHAPTER EIGHTEEN

We continued to watch the skies. Comets came and went with no great event around them to make of them much more than the light show they had been. We recorded them anyway.

Gaspar's letters became more frequent as his dreams became more vivid and lucid.

'Some nights it is as though my dream state is more real than this human life. It both excites and confounds me.'

Gaspar's dream of the three camels grew with time. Until one night when they approached, though laden with goods as always, there also were riders on two of them and one of those riders was me.

'You seemed happy to be there. I have no idea who the other magus was, but he seemed quiet. Well he did when compared to you and he was busy watching the skies.'

I laughed out loud when I read this. "Sounds as though he speaks of Melchior," I thought and then it was out of my mind as quickly as I thought it.

The story of that great star has many stories within it. That it was a rare or unique comet that blazed across the sky, somewhat slow enough for us to arrange a caravan and travel hundreds of miles to where it seemed to be going. Or that four stars moved so close that they appeared to be one gigantic star.

Legends can be exciting and glamorous. Myths bend the truth for the drama of a good story. While we were human and not immune to some good drama from time to time, we were also wise men. We were men of the order of Zoroastrians and our dedication to the study of stars was always done with integrity and respect for the reality they reflected to us.

It is such a shame that our records have not been found. There are some that still exist but they are hidden and misunderstood. If they were to be revealed they would explain so much. Once again, as in the times before my lifetime, humanity is just not ready for such things. It will be soon and my spirit will dance with joy when they are shared with you all.

There have been some from your time that have gone over the astronomy records and, with commonsense; they have deduced what was most likely to have occurred. In truth we helped them to realise such things as there comes times for legends and myths to make way for a truth that will help the energy of the event to expand.

So it was that around two thousand and more years ago something significant finally did occur in the sky that warranted our attention and excitement. What I will share with you now will be part history lesson and part astronomy lesson but it will do much to explain why we journeyed based on the travels of some lights in the sky.

For the sake of having you understand the time frame I will relate the story within your current measurements of time as well.

In what would have been September of the year you refer to as 3 BC, a beautiful dance was begun by the planet Jupiter. We knew the planets intimately. Their movements measured our very own movement through the universe. It explained the waxing and waning of the moon, the changes of the seasons and they gave us a gauge for the passage of time.

Jupiter has been studied by man since we first thought to look at the skies. The largest of all the celestial bodies, apart from the sun, it could be seen without any looking glass. Along with Venus, Mercury, Mars and Saturn, Jupiter showed us the routine of the universe. As you can imagine though they were not just balls of light to us, each one held its own significance and stories.

As the largest, Jupiter was not surprisingly called the King of Planets. It was literal but also gave rise to being used symbolically as well, so when Jupiter showed us a difference in its journey we paid attention as it could well mean something about a current king or one about to reign.

The real beauty of watching the planets is that they move amongst a fixed backdrop of stars. The stars were our constants for measurement, while the planets reminded us of where we were amongst the rotations around the sun. Some events occurred annually as you would imagine, while others were far more rare.

So in that month of the forty-eighth year of my life I looked up to see something I had seen several times before. I had seen it aged twelve as I began my studies, then again at twenty-four and once more at thirty-six. Now as a well-experienced magus I watched it once more and smiled.

The cold at night was beginning to have the crispness of our winter months and I pulled my heavy coat tight around me and smiled as I saw Jupiter begin to make its way to Sharu, the star we called the King of Stars. It was the brightest in all the sky and every twelve years the King of Planets made way to cross over it. Such an event was, and is still, called a conjunction; when two celestial bodies reach the closest place they can be in relation to each other.

Just the month before we watched as Venus had done so with Jupiter: an event much more common, that we viewed up to even three times a year. This most recent conjunction of the King with Venus the Mother had been wonderfully close. So close that they seemed to almost touch.

We watched it with wonder but with not much weight to its occurrence other than what we had always expected. Even Gaspar did not sense much in its happening and yet in the months to come it would become one part of something much grander.

I was twelve when I first watched Jupiter cross over Sharu. My father pointed the path out to me, explaining how long it would take and why it took so long to repeat it. I remember nodding, somewhat in awe of what he was telling me.

"Do you think there is a reason that the largest planet interacts with the largest star this way?" I asked. "Surely Mazda has organised it in such a way for some reason?"

Malchiek looked down at me and smiled in a way that I will never forget. It was the first time I had asked a question with such a sense of depth to it and his heart swelled.

"It is a symbol of the king energy for certain…" he began and then paused. "But for many of us we also see it as the father energy, the original creator."

Malchiek paused again and I saw his chest rise as he took a deep breath.

"Whenever I see the play of Jupiter across Sharu I am reminded of Mazda, the eternal father who placed us here. I see Sharu as me, grand and brilliant but in my fixed place with Jupiter as Mazda visiting me to remind me that though I am brilliant, I am small compared to his magnificence."

As I looked up now and saw that Jupiter was once again to make way to Sharu I remembered his words.

"So grand one, you visit again with your son to remind him of the true ruler!" I said out loud and laughed.

"What is so funny?"

It was Malchiek, coming out into the garden, now with his walking stick.

"You should not be out in this cold air," I half jokingly chided him.

He shook his head. "You rarely heed my word so I will not entertain yours. Besides I hear my favourite event has begun."

I nodded and looked up to the sky once more as he came to stand by my side and look up at the grand king making its way across the sky.

"Of all the events that we know and see, this is what I will miss most," Malchiek said quietly.

"Don't say such things as though it will be so soon," I gulped the words as they stuck in my throat. "You will see this several times more!"

Malchiek did not answer but I heard him sigh.

Over the next few nights Jupiter continued to glide through the sky and each night it was closer and closer to Sharu. This time though it felt different. I now wished I had learnt to use the instruments more thoroughly; though something inside me said that this was not about measurement.

At his home in the north, Melchior though was busy with his instruments. He had felt something different too about this crossing of Jupiter and he set about measuring it so that he could prove it.

Melchior measured, then measured again. Then he measured again. Another magus nearby saw him repeat this over and over.

"Melchior, what is happening? This is not like you. I can see you doubt something about what you are observing," he asked.

"Lucius, this crossing is different. Can you feel it?"

Lucius nodded.

"Well it is measuring different as well!" Melchior spat the words out, almost relieved to be doing so.

"Are you certain?" Lucius asked.

"No, that's why I keep measuring. I need to consult the old scrolls," he said.

So the next morning Melchior and Lucius went into their library. They pulled all the scrolls from each year that Jupiter would have made transit across Sharu. Then they meticulously compared the measurement to what Melchior had recorded the past week.

"Each cycle Jupiter has been lower and lower," Lucius said as Melchior nodded.

"And if my measurements are true, then this will be the closest conjunction we have ever seen," Melchior grinned so widely it looked like his face would break open.

"If I weren't so old I might jump with excitement," smiled Lucius.

"Let's do so anyway!" laughed Melchior.

When they had finished with the celebration Melchior sat down to write. He spoke of what all the other magi had noticed or felt; that this current movement of Jupiter was different and that he predicted this as being the closest conjunction of Jupiter with Sharu not just in our lifetimes but in many centuries. When I read out the letter to Malchiek he smiled.

"So the father is coming in to be close with his son," he said and tears filled his eyes.

As Melchior had been making his measurements and consulting the scrolls with Lucius, in the west Gaspar and his acolytes were seeing the same thing. In fact all the magi across Babylonia were seeing it and the letters were arriving thick and fast at our temple: almost as quick as I was sending them out and in reply.

This conjunction was the most significant occurrence that we had all witnessed in our lifetimes, and there were three generations of magi viewing it.

When Gaspar's letter arrived, I took it from the courier and handed him his coin as was the expected thank you.

"Please go to the kitchen and have some refreshment before you continue," I offered him as well.

He jumped from his horse and nodded a thank you. "That is most kind and unexpected but greatly appreciated."

I nodded to a servant nearby. "Take his horse and see it has some water and hay. Your ride needs as much replenishment as you do," I laughed.

"Indeed he does, if not more," nodded the rider.

I did not have to make such gestures, as riders were paid handsomely and did not want for good lodgings or food. But I also knew that such men would be treasures in the upcoming months as the letters would flow even more rapidly and with greater anticipation. They would become our lifeline in a way for allowing whatever was happening to unfold.

Gaspar had looked up to the movement of Jupiter and fell into a trance. He felt as though he was dreaming but awake at the same time. Suddenly the men around him disappeared and his father, who had died years before, was by his side once again.

His father did not speak but he heard the words "do you remember?" and as he looked up to the night sky he saw the shooting star that had agitated him so much as an eight year old.

Then he remembered once more. He remembered the excitement of his father. He remembered the frustration he had felt and the promise he had made to himself.

Then he felt something more. This was his declaration being played out to him. This was his choice becoming reality. This was not just a conjunction. It was part of the Great Awakening.

Within a breath he was back in the present moment. Around him, other magi, the ones he had taught and some older than he, were all gathered. Some measured the movement and position of Jupiter and Sharu. Some just stood in awe.

"He is right. Melchior is right. The measurements cannot be denied," Izrael called out.

A soft gasp washed amongst the men and they all turned their eyes back to Jupiter—all except for Gaspar. He closed his eyes to hold back the tears and put his hand to his heart.

"The forty-six years I have waited for this has been nothing compared to the eternity that mankind has waited," he thought.

Then he opened his eyes again and looked upwards.

The evening of the actual conjunction was incredible. There was not one magus who was indoors or asleep that night. The great fire was trusted to stay alive and within its bounds. How could it do otherwise on such a mystical night?

Not only did all of the priesthood stand and watch but we were joined by family and many of our villagers who also were in awe of what was happening. We all gathered at dusk, with chairs, blankets and pillows and whatever else was needed to make us comfortable.

My priests and I stayed upon our feet, as we did every night. It was part from respect, but also of habit. Tonight of all nights we would act as we were expected to.

My three daughters came from their homes, their own families around them and I smiled upon them all. I looked to my five grandsons, some of whom were already studying with me and those so young they barely understood why they were here. I gathered the youngest in my arms, just as my father had done with me at that age when we would stargaze. Then I went to stand by Malchiek as the sky grew dark enough for the stars to appear.

The blue and pink turned grey and then black. Then there it was - the conjunction of Sharu and Jupiter. My breath caught and I heard Malchiek take a deep breath beside me.

Malchiek slowly nodded.

"What are you sensing Father?" I asked.

"I can hear it" was all he replied.

I looked back at the two bright bodies as they sat one above the other with so little space between them. I kissed my grandson and placed him

152

upon the ground. Then I called upon my soul to witness this magic. I heard it laugh as though I had made a joke in inviting it. Then it whispered something.

"Just the beginning..."

"What do you mean?" I asked it.

There was no answer.

"What do you hear?" asked Malchiek.

I repeated the words. Malchiek said nothing but looked back to Jupiter and Sharu. Then he slowly nodded.

The words frustrated me though. Actually it was not so much the words as the lack of response when I questioned the words. When I finally went to bed in the early hours of morning, I could not sleep. Elana slept beside me, her breathing deep and sometimes with sounds. I looked upon her and was tempted to wake her. She could help me make sense of this, I was sure. I reached out my hand to shake her but pulled it back.

It wouldn't be fair to rouse her. She needed her sleep. These times had made more work not just for the priesthood but for all those around them. Our homes were busy with visiting priests, couriers and extended family. The dormitories at the temples were overflowing with a rush of new students desperate to be part of the awakening.

So in turn our servants and families were busier preparing meals, doing laundry and cleaning guest rooms. It got to the point that there were no available servants to even hire to help with the extra chores.

"We could buy some slaves from Rome?" suggested my chief butler Daride hesitantly.

The rolling of my eyes was enough of an answer. "They bring their own troubles and that I do not need. Besides that would be like having more animals to tend to and I will not have people treated like that in my home. How any man could live just looking for opportunity to escape is beside me. We will just make do and ask Mazda to send the appropriate help when it is needed."

I have to admit that when I suggested praying for help I was half joking. The implicit trust I had in Mazda to provide us with help and support was being sorely tested every time I saw the dark circles under Elana's eyes and those of the servants.

As I looked at her so deep in sleep now, I knew that I could not burden her with anything more. No matter what I was questioning inside me, on the outside I would remain clear and strong. She needed my support as much as I needed hers.

It was within that respect that I trusted Mazda to respect us in providing his support.

CHAPTER NINETEEN

The next day something happened that confirmed my trust completely. I was finishing my lunch when Daride entered the room, his brow creased and his hands wrapped within one another.

"Master, there is a—um—man here. He says he is seeking employment with you," was all he could say.

I wiped my mouth with a cloth and looked at him as a smile broke upon my face.

"Really? Where has he come from?" I asked.

Daride shook his head. "I—I ... did not think to ask. I was too surprised at his gall to approach me. It seems that he is a Kshatrapa. He has the skin and the voice of one."

I sighed deeply. "This is not like you, Daride, to come to me with such things without finding out all you can first!"

"No Sir, it is not..." Daride looked at me and took a deep breath. "He said—he said that he had a dream in which a very old man told him to come here. That he was needed and would not be turned away." Daride paused and took another deep breath. "And ... just ... after our talk of the slaves and your thoughts to pray ... it—it just seemed like I should not ask any more questions of him."

Daride was right. This man was indeed a Kshatrapa, from a region in the west of what is now India. He did not lie about his dream and it had taken some strength to make his way to my home. In fact he had stood outside my home for many days, watching and working up the courage to even walk to one of the doors.

He imagined all the possible outcomes; from being turned away with insults, to being pulled inside and embraced like lost family.

"Why am I here?" he asked himself over and over.

He considered leaving and going back to his homeland. He missed the food and the women. Nothing seemed quite right when you were this far west. But that voice inside, his own bah-ra'an, kept at him.

"You know you need to do this..."

It was like a chant inside him that was both his strength and a curse.

It was that voice that had called him to travel. It was that voice that had called him to leave places, no matter how safe, happy or settled he had become.

"If I could block you out, my life would be so simple!" he had yelled back one night as it kept him awake yet again with its pull. That night as he slept, he dreamt another of those dreams that were more real than his waking hours.

He was standing outside a grand home. Before the home stood the oldest man he had ever seen. Yet he stood straight and majestic, with the vigour of someone much younger than his grey hair and creased skin suggested.

Now his soul voice whispered inside him, "You are needed here."

The old man beckoned with his hand as though confirming the voice.

"Come, my friend. We have much to do," the old man said.

"To do what?" he asked.

But there was no response. There never was. It was what infuriated him about the voice and the dreams. Yet the anger also pushed him to find the answer.

When he arrived outside my home, he knew immediately it was the one in his dream.

"The windows are a bit different," he thought, looking for an excuse to act against what he was feeling.

It was going to take a bit more than different windows to undo what he could feel inside though. Three days later he knocked upon the kitchen door.

"Bring him in to me," I asked of Daride.

"Here in your dining room?" questioned Daride.

"Yes, yes. If he is Kshatrapa then he has come a long way and would be quite hungry. Besides if Mazda has sent him then we treat him as though it is Mazda who has arrived," I answered.

Elana smiled at me. "It is just like how you treated me when I arrived," she said.

"Don't worry I will not marry him!" I said and kissed her hand.

When the Kshatrapa walked into the room I saw him stop almost as though he was startled when he first looked upon me. It was just a split second of shock but I still saw it, though I acted as though I had not. He was what I would call a small man, but only of his stature. Indeed his skin had that warm brown of the Kshatrapas with the soft hands that made them seem eternally young. His thick brown hair was cut short and free of any cloth bindings such as a turban that would have provided the ultimate confirmation of where he had come from.

I extended my hand, indicating a seat for him to fill. As soon as he was seated, a servant appeared and poured some wine.

The Kshatrapa looked at the glass, wanting to grab it but wondering what custom he might break in doing so before being invited to. I did not miss this either and could not help but laugh a little.

"Please, go ahead. We have only one rule within this home about food and that is; if you can see it, then it is yours to take!" Then I laughed openly and warmed to see the Kshatrapa also smile as he took his first sip. "So my friend, please tell me your name."

He took a deep breath and I could feel his nervousness as he began to

157

say the words he had recited within his mind over and over during the past three days as he watched my home. I sat back in my chair and felt Daride also take a breath as he stood behind me. Beside me Elana gave her customary hostess smile and he began.

"Sire, my name is Laal Mahesh and I have come from the East. My name means 'beloved Shiva'. I was named for the God who rebuilds the world when change is needed. Please call me Mahesh." With that he paused, put his hand to his heart and bowed his head.

I acknowledged this by bowing my own head.

"So Mahesh, tell me what has brought you here and why you might think you are needed," I smiled as I spoke. In just telling me of his name I already knew the answer to both parts of my question, but I wanted to hear more.

Mahesh looked down to the wine glass in his hand and though he smiled, I saw tears fill his eyes.

"I wish I had some words that would make sense to tell you," he said softly.

"Oh, do not let that stop you. I have a colleague who tests this of me frequently with his letters," I chuckled and the atmosphere of the room lifted noticeably.

Mahesh softened his shoulders, took another sip of the wine and looked at me.

"I have this voice within that guides me. It does not always make sense, yet something compels me to trust it completely. It also visits me within dreams, becoming images and stories for me to see. It has been telling me to walk west, and it has shown me, within a dream, of your home. In that dream a very old man told me I was needed here. I questioned this yet still found your home and trusted it was the home in my dream. Though you look nothing like the man in my dream..." Mahesh grinned awkwardly at admitting this and I now understood his expression when he first entered the room.

Elana reached to my hand, gently squeezing it.

Mahesh continued. "I have heard stories that there is much happening with your religion. I can only assume and hope that there is some design of the gods that I can help you."

"Well, we only have one god to design our world, but if he sees fit to work with your gods, then that I cannot question!" I said emphatically.

I knew it was Mazda he had seen in his dream. I knew that the voice Mahesh spoke of was his soul. Here he was, ready to help when we needed all the help we could get. I could not deny or reject him due to his origins nor whom he believed created or shaped our reality. To do that would be to go against what the awakening was ultimately all about; this was now the time where we would step into the era of no separation, no differences, no contrasts and no judgments.

As I looked upon Mahesh I knew Mazda's design implicitly. Not only was he sending me some support as I had asked and trusted of him, but he was also sending me a way into dissolving the differences of man. I imagined my home and temple soon full of people of all races.

Elana pulled me back to the moment. She leaned forward and with her beautiful soft voice she spoke to Mahesh. "You speak our language so clearly. How is this?"

Mahesh bowed his head to Elana.

"Madam, thank you for the compliment. I have travelled much since leaving my home and you learn to allow your tongue to be flexible when you rely upon it to aid you in finding food and shelter," he explained.

There was more to this though than simply the need to survive as motivation for learning a language. Mahesh was a master of linguistics and the voice. It was something that had begun as a small child. It had seemed like mimicry at first when at barely twelve months he repeated entire sentences his parents spoke.

When his mother bragged about this to a relative, the uncle had scoffed and said, "Well you can teach a bird to repeat words but they do not understand the words!"

At this Mahesh looked the uncle in the eye and said simply, "I understand."

The uncle had no words for this.

So as he travelled he would sit by people having conversations and listen in to even the smallest of exchanges. Within days he had picked up enough key words, intonations and patterns to have basic conversation. The wonderful thing about the world of our time was that a language did not shift dramatically as you crossed a border. It is not like in your modern times where you can cross from Germany to France and have a totally different language.

In our age, languages flowed and melded across regions. Yes, Mahesh's mother tongue was different from mine completely. But as he had travelled west, he made way into places that knew and used parts of his language. So he blended the two and then so on as he crossed into yet another region. You could imagine it like having on one outfit of clothing, and changing one item at a time for a new piece until you have a completely new costume on.

Mahesh had been travelling for ten years now. So his transformation from Kshatrapa into a man of all languages and cultures had not been so dramatic or sudden. It had been one of slow transformation and assimilation, yet still with the sense of where he had begun. As he sat before me now, I saw someone who, though they claimed to not understand what was driving them, was in fact much more self-assured than he laid claim to.

I turned to Daride, who had remained behind me. "Take our new friend and give him his bed in the servant's quarters." Then I turned to Mahesh. "Bathe, rest and eat. Tomorrow we will decide just how this design shall look."

Mahesh stood and once more with his hand on his heart, he bowed. Deeply this time, not just of his head, but with his body.

"It will be my honour to serve you," he said and then followed Daride out of the room.

Elana picked at some fruit before her and nodded as she smiled.

"I know what you are thinking?" I said.

160

She looked me in the eye, still with her smile and now shook her head.

"No, my love. I doubt that you could," she answered.

"So do please share with me," I pushed.

"I feel like I have just met my brother. Though I have none of which to speak of, and though he was born so far away of another skin and tongue," she said.

"And so do I," was my response.

The next day I appointed Mahesh as butler of the guests, to the great relief of Daride who could now focus upon our family needs. This was still not enough to truly deal with all that faced us though and Mahesh knew it.

A week later he came to me, now carrying himself with all the self-assurance he had lacked on his arrival.

"Sire, please let me send for others to serve you. I know of good men who will work honestly and not expect more than meals and a home."

Two weeks later ten men arrived upon camels and donkeys. They too were Kshatrapas or from the east. All with that chocolate skin and soft hands of Mahesh's homeland.

"Mahesh, we do not have enough beds for these men," I said when I saw how many he recruited.

"They have no need of beds," replied Mahesh.

Indeed they didn't for they had brought tents that were erected on the edge of our property. It was like another wing of the house has been created. Then with their homes established, Mahesh set about designating duties.

Two men joined the kitchens, planting more garden and creating more food. Two others washed laundry from dawn until dusk. Another two helped tend the animals and another two began cleaning every surface of the home. The final two men shadowed Mahesh in making sure that anything a guest needed was provided before they asked.

My original servants were suddenly happier, and the darkness under Elana's eyes lifted.

"If ever we were to ask of proof that we have support from Mazda for what we are doing then it is certainly in the arrival of Mahesh," I said to Elana.

This was to become even more prophetic than I could have imagined. The timing of getting my home in order was more than synchronistic.

CHAPTER TWENTY

Jupiter left its place above Sharu and moved on into the western sky and, for a few days, all magi across Babylonia reflected upon the beauty of the conjunction—all except for Gaspar.

Gaspar was now like a dog with a bone, determined to pull out any meaning he could find in the event. He sat at his desk staring at the chart he and his colleagues had drawn out. He looked at the dates of the conjunction and anything that had occurred in recent months. Gaspar consulted scrolls from all the years of previous Jupiter-Sharu conjunctions. He scratched his beard, he drummed his fingers upon his desk and he prayed out loud for something to reveal itself.

Gaspar was on the verge of collapse, not so much from physical exhaustion but from the sheer fatigue of his mind. He lay his head down upon the desk, crushing some of the scrolls beneath his cheek. Gaspar did not care. His only concern for now was some respite from this struggle to see what he could not find.

Sleep comes easy to a mind which has been depleted. For this is the place Gaspar had reached. In laying down his head, he had not so much surrendered in despair as he had set free the struggle. In that space his body slowed down too and he was soon dreaming.

This was a new dream. There were no eggs and no camels. Before him stood a young man. By his side was a lion, standing calm and regal. In the man's arms was a lamb, also still and peaceful.

"Who are you?" Gaspar asked.

The young man smiled and said gently, "I am you."

Gaspar looked upon the man. "But you are nothing like me. How can this be?"

The man smiled. "You are more like me than you can imagine, and I will return soon to show all men that they are like me."

Gaspar woke and looked about him. He felt as though he had slept for hours but he could tell by the sun outside it had been a much briefer time. He sat up and straightened the crushed scrolls before him.

Then he saw it. The pattern he had been looking for that made sense of everything. The dream had pulled it together.

There within the sky, within the house of the lion, was where it had all happened.

"The lion..." whispered Gaspar. "It has been the lion all along..."

Gaspar reached for a fresh scroll and began yet another letter to me. He wrote quickly and when he finished he looked down upon his words. Gaspar then groaned. He grabbed the letter, crushing it in his hands. He threw it across the room and decided that the day had been long enough. There would be no stargazing tonight. He was even too tired to eat.

With the sun setting, Gaspar called to his butler and announced he would be retiring for the night.

As he collapsed upon his bed, the images of the lion and lamb kept appearing to him. Gaspar thought about what he had written and rejected. It had seemed so clear when he had awoken in the afternoon and yet this doubt for what he had felt was so strong. The back and forth of his clarity with this uncertainty was now effecting him physically and his head actually ached. Gaspar prayed for sleep to end the battle.

Within his sleep there was respite but not by way of emptiness. Once more the young man of his afternoon dream appeared. The lion was beside him and the lamb within his arms as they had been before.

"You are not afraid of the lion?" Gaspar asked him.

The man smiled. "No. Fear is such a waste of life."

Then together they walked, with the lion between them. They were in a desert, with dry mountains to their right. Together they reached a place that looked over a grand city that Gaspar did not know.

"This is Jerusalem. Here my words will be tested and trialled," said the man.

"So the lion is a symbol for Judea?" Gaspar asked.

"If that is what you want it to be, then yes it is," he answered.

"And what of the lamb?" Gaspar asked.

"This is your dream. What would you like it to be?" he asked.

Gaspar shook his head. "I will think about that later."

And that was where the dream ended.

The next morning Gaspar woke and went to his study. He found the crushed scroll upon the floor, took it to his desk and smoothed it out. Gaspar read over the words and within them he knew that he had written a truth, even if it was somewhat disjointed for now. He grabbed a fresh piece of paper and began to write again but something pulled him to pause.

"There will be more..." he heard something within him say. Then Gaspar understood the flux between his clarity and doubts. There was more to what he had written that was yet to be revealed. It was not so much doubt that was eating at his psyche but the sense of there being that which his mind could not grasp yet.

Gaspar took a deep breath. "Well then," he said to the voice within. "I shall write to my colleague so that he shall be as prepared as me."

With that sense of being in readiness rather than searching, Gaspar's mind and body sighed with relief.

'My dear colleague and friend,

We have experienced an amazing event this past week. One that we have known before but that has visited us anew. As I looked upon the conjunction I sensed more than my eyes took in. As I am sure you did as well. You would not indulge me my communications if you did not feel something of substance within them.

I studied all we have seen and more with relation to this. All has occurred in the house of the lion in the sky. We both know this relates to Judea and the West. I know what we have seen thus far cannot confirm anything of substance but my bah-ra'an tells me that there is more to unfold.

With that voice inside me telling me this, I have experienced a dream so full of symbols that I feel I must share it with you as it seems to indicate what is and what will be.

A young man appeared with a lion and a lamb. He told me he will return soon to show all men that they are like him. I received no more information from him other than he is linked with Jerusalem and Judea.

I write to you, not to aggrandise myself as a prophet, but so that someone else may be readied for what is unfolding. In my heart and my spirit I believe we will see a birth of a new king but he will be no ordinary man. He will be one who allows the awakening to truly enter the consciousness of humanity.

I cannot help but feel I am ranting and you would be within reason to disagree and question my sanity. Please know I share with you that you may be prepared and see what perhaps I am not seeing to complete this story. I do not share with anyone else at this time as I doubt anyone else would truly grasp sense of this.

But I trust you as I trust no one else.

In peace

Gaspar'

When I read the letter I did not so much take in words as I felt Gaspar's emotions as he had written it. The frustration of knowing there is more to what we sensed, but yet unable to formulate it into any organised thought. In fact he had done remarkably well to write as he did.

I leant back in my chair, sighed, closed my eyes and prayed to Mazda.

"Please give us strength to stay collected within whatever is unfolding," I whispered.

It was a simple prayer but one that called out to my fears. I did not want our anticipation and expectations to shape how we allowed all this to unfold. As much as I loved Gaspar and his enthusiasm, it also concerned me that he was driving his observations in a certain direction. To do so, we could miss the truth of what was unfolding. We could even close down what Mazda was opening up.

There is a fine balance between participating with spirit and allowing. When you are too active, then you are driving the energy and shaping what occurs. This is not always a bad thing. However when you do so without the sense of the majesty that is the grand creator, then you limit what can occur.

For me this meant creating a dance between the human side of me and my bah-ra'an. I knew implicitly that Mazda gave me my bah-ra'an as a link back to his grandeur. Mazda in creating me had left his mark, like a slice of himself within me to call me back to his warmth and safety. The human part of me had the choice to listen to this or push on with my human needs with no sense of anything grander.

For a magus, it is sometimes even easier to get distracted by the human side, as we have spent a lifetime training to believe we are not so human. From a young age we are taught we have a special connection to Mazda that it is within our blood to guide and teach others of their connection.

So as you can imagine that can in itself be a grand distraction from the balance that all people are capable of. That bias could come in the way of temple politics or abusing others through the power of your position. It is something you still see today; hiding behind a designated holiness to fulfil your needs.

As I read Gaspar's letter, I felt his passion and focus, but I was also

167

wary of how close he was to allowing himself to fall into this imbalance. I lifted my quill and wrote my reply.

'My dear brother and friend,

We are living in exciting times and the signs we have allowed ourselves to see and feel confirm this.

I too have felt and heard that there is more to come.

My sense now is to trust in Mazda and our teachings that all will be shown in the most perfect of times. If we push, then we may miss what is obvious, or worse still, we could close down what is opening.

Let us take time to relax and give thanks to Mazda, rather than question. Let us trust that we will not miss any signs as long as we stay faithful and true to our teachings.

Most of all, let us remember that when humanity is ready, all will be revealed.

In peace

Balthasar'

In all truth that was the hardest letter I had ever written. It addressed my frustration and impatience as much as it did Gaspar's. As I read over it I realised they were not so much my words to him. It was also a letter from Mazda to myself.

I folded it and placed my wax seal upon it. Then I laughed.

"I wonder: should I just have this delivered back to me!" I thought.

When Gaspar received my letter it at first angered him.

"I thought he would understand," he thought to himself.

Then he took a breath, read it again and something within the words worked upon him. He sat back within his chair and smiled.

"So Mazda, I return to my trust of you. I return to my faith with patience," he thought, almost like a prayer.

Yet another voice within him still rose up.

"I will not waste this life."

And with that Gaspar went to his garden to begin his observations for that evening.

CHAPTER TWENTY-ONE

Jupiter continued its path into the western sky. We measured and recorded it and all other movement of the stars as we always did. Things seemed to calm. Our house guests lessened in number and there were no new recruits for the temple. We were still busier than in years before but the calm I had called to within me now seemed to be manifesting around me as well.

The energy within Gaspar's letters also seemed to settle. In honesty though, his dreams were still inviting him to some turmoil. He was doing a remarkable job in keeping his personal balance.

The young man with the lion and lamb continued to appear to him. Some dreams he appeared older, and in other dreams he appeared as a child, but the lion and lamb were always with him.

When the man appeared as the child Gaspar asked him, "Will you tell me what the lamb means?" The child just squealed and ran off into a wheat field with the lamb bouncing behind him, leaving Gaspar with the lion.

Gaspar would wake from each dream with his belief in the man's arrival renewed along with his impatience. Those were the days he made time for extra prayer and it was his prayer time that was his saving grace in these months.

One day as he sat before the great fire of his temple, saying the words he had learnt as a child, he saw something within the fire. It was the lamb, but it was not like any lamb he had ever seen. Within its eyes he saw the strength of the lion.

That night he slept deeply but not without dreaming. The man appeared to him, this time he sat upon a bench within a walled garden. It was nighttime and the garden was lit with lanterns. The lion slept at his feet to the left, while the lamb slept to his right. He was gazing down at both but looked up as Gaspar approached. His eyes were dark, as though he had not slept in days. He feigned a smile at Gaspar and even that seemed to take all his energy.

"I know what the lamb means," said Gaspar.

Now the man smiled and it seemed to be no effort at all.

"Oh good. Now we can all rest," he answered.

And with that the dream ended and Gaspar truly slept for the first time in months.

Then just as we all seemed to be relaxed with what had unfolded, the sky played out something we had never seen before.

Jupiter in its glory, and by simply following its path around the Sun did something that seemed magical, even to our knowledgeable minds. Jupiter stopped moving.

Now you and I both know that this is not possible but such is the illusion of being upon a planet that itself is moving. As we went along our path, so too did others. We all did so at our own pace and course, and thus created the timings of conjunctions and our relationship with one another.

At this time, Jupiter did not stop but appeared to do so from where we were. And then it did something remarkable.

Jupiter began to move backwards through the sky.

Retrograde movements are interesting phenomenon. Like an inverted card or rune, their meaning can seem to reverse. What energies they may have supported in their "rightful" position, the opposite is now in play. Or so we thought.

For most magi it was a delight to see Jupiter do this. For me though it made my heart sink as too it did for Gaspar.

As I began to watch Jupiter move east, I prayed as hard as I could.

"Please Mazda, do not let this be a sign that we have closed off what was begun," I pleaded.

I received no answer and decided to find comfort within. As you say in your time, "no news is good news." I clung to my faith and hope.

Not surprisingly a letter arrived from Gaspar as soon as it could get to me. It was only one line.

'Do you think we have closed off the energies?'

In an instant I remembered the words I heard during the night of the Jupiter-Sharu conjunction.

Only the beginning....

I wrote back to Gaspar and my reply was as simple as his question.

'No. We certainly have not. We were told there is more to come and this, my brother, is part of that.'

Then I wrote a letter to Melchior.

Melchior had grinned from ear to ear when he saw Jupiter stop in its tracks. He loved the patterns of the stars and how they barely faltered from what you could predict. But to finally see something that was not foretold, that seemed truly supernatural, was the most gratifying thing he had ever seen. Melchior was so excited that he almost forgot to measure it. Almost.

The next day as he filed the scroll in the library the eldest magus of his temple walked in.

"So my young brother, I hear the sky offered you a new delight last night," said Adeen softly as he lowered himself into a chair.

"Have you ever known of such a thing in your life?" asked Melchior.

"Yes, but not of Jupiter. This is something that needs to be spoken of and prayed upon," Adeen stated clearly.

Melchior nodded. It was something to know of the place within the sky of the stars and planets. It was another to know of your place within your religion.

Melchior had long ago accepted his talent was in his accurate measurements. He did not have grand prophetic dreams, nor was he a seer. He had only heard a voice that one time when he was younger. The frustration of not being any of those had long dissipated. Admittedly I had helped move that process along when we met all those years ago.

These past months had made that even stronger within him as letters arrived not just from me but from temples throughout Babylonia, asking his advice or confirmation.

"I know this is the talent you have given me to serve you. And I promise to honour that always."

It was both a vow and a prayer that he said to Mazda each night as he scratched upon his scrolls or when he read a letter asking his counsel.

When my letter arrived, asking him of what he made of the retrograde movement, Melchior hesitated in replying.

"He wants my interpretation," was his first response and this made Melchior uneasy. Such things were not of his makeup or interest. He put the letter aside, deciding to write after another night of observing.

That night as he looked at Jupiter again, he did something he had only done once before as Jupiter began its way to Sharu. He decided to predict the path Jupiter would take. Melchior stood and raising his finger he traced the route he was sure Jupiter would follow. When he realised what was about to happen he dropped his hand and grinned even wider than he had when Jupiter stopped.

The next morning he wrote his response.

'Dear brother Balthasar,

I am not one to draw out meanings. You and many others are the ones with that talent.

But with my abilities, I am most certain that we will see the miracle of a second crossing of Sharu within the following months.

In peace

Melchior.'

As always Melchior was right: Jupiter continued back towards Sharu and we had the second conjunction just six months after the first. As the planet approached the star once more, the excitement and anticipation that we had felt for the first conjunction returned and was doubled.

Our homes filled again and our servants worked long hours. My days were taken with letter writing and speaking in temple, my night with conversing with the sky. I still am not sure just how I managed any sleep, but I found time to do so and often took some respite during the afternoon as well.

My sleep was true rest, for Gaspar his sleep was just another way to connect with his work. The dreams of the young man with the lion and lamb had not returned; instead he now once more dreamt of the three camels. They were always saddled and laden with goods, ready for a journey.

Each dream led to a letter sent to me and each one made me smile.

On the night before the second conjunction reached its closest peak, I found a space for myself in the garden so I could listen as best I could. I stared into the stars, my focus upon Jupiter, until all I could see opened up and I saw beyond.

I felt into not just the galaxy of our planets and sun but into all that was beyond as well. I heard the symphony of every celestial body and their play with each other. Then I called out. I called out to Mazda from my bahra'an; that part of me that was also him. I called out to every piece of his creation.

"Show me. Show me what we need to know so that we do not miss your message."

Usually this took me beyond what I was seeing into another realm again, but this time the stars pulled in close again so that I was seeing those closest to me with absolute focus. Then the constellation of the lion glowed bright, almost like it was pulsing.

"Thank you," I whispered.

The lion in the sky. The house of Judea. It was as Gaspar had said it was. We could now have a focus. Though this was to be with caution. There was no news of any birth or even a pregnancy from the West. Nor was there a sign of any uprising, such that a new king may not be born, but arrive as a conqueror.

Once more I took what I felt and measured it with my human sensibilities, so that when I wrote to Gaspar I did so with restraint. I told him that I had received confirmation that what was unfolding was indeed of the house of Judea. I also spoke that we must hold this information within our brotherhood lest we begin a political conflict that was not necessary.

The land and ruling of Judea was volatile as always. Though it and the surrounding area were under Roman rule, it was full of tribes brimming with resentment of the Romans as well as the desire to reclaim their lands.

If we were to send news of what we were witnessing and what we felt it meant, it could lead to even more suspicion. Worse still it could incite actions inspired by the paranoia.

There may well have been a royal or noble pregnancy that was being held secret for fear of assassination or poisoning of the mother. Perhaps there was even an uprising in the planning but the thought of triggering such things made my heart ache.

"Surely the birth of such a man would be with great celebration and grace," I asked to Mazda one night.

I heard a resounding, "yes!"

It was that "yes" that helped to cancel my doubts and fears. It reminded me that we were witnessing a huge step in the Great Awakening; the event that was our promise of peace, balance and freedom. This could not possibly involve war, death or fear.

In Jerusalem, Herod the appointed king, stood high within a tower, looking out over the city and beyond the city walls. Within the walls he saw a calculated certainty and security, while beyond he saw limitless potentials for his undoing.

Such is the life of a man who gains power and position through violence and manipulated allegiance.

"King by name, brute by blood."

It was a slogan bequeathed him by those born of the lands he now ruled.

His supporters had tried to keep it from him, but he had heard it yelled from a crowd when he appeared to speak to the people. It had burned him more than you could imagine, even more than the heckler could have hoped for because Herod knew it was true.

Herod had muttered the phrase one night when he was drunk. One of his ministers was close by and recoiled when he realised that Herod knew of this slander.

"Sire, it is just commoners trying to feel better of the failings of their blood. You are the son of Antipater. You have nobility in your blood. You are loved by Augustus. You were born to rule in such a position!" he exclaimed in a hope to placate Herod.

Herod sneered at the words.

"My father had no aspiration for me other than I breed to continue his bloodline. I am here through my cunning, gall and servitude to Augustus. You are not born with such things. You learn them and then you exploit them as much as you can. That is the royalty of our day," Herod had drawled back.

And that was what Herod saw as he looked out over Judea. He saw a land governed by cunning, gall and servitude. He knew his rule would end the day someone simply outwitted him on all three counts. Every day was spent planning, analysing and revising how he could keep a grip upon his position. He knew how to placate Rome, he knew how to keep the tribes around him repressed but still there was always that lingering fear that it could be taken from him.

To Herod, we Babylonians were docile and uninteresting.

"They keep busy with their temples and farming. Let them continue," was how he explained us to Augustus.

And indeed we were docile and uninteresting. We had no impressive army to threaten but that was because we had nothing great to protect. We were wealthy and abundant but not in the way that was of relevance to Augustus and his empire.

"Let them make our incense and oils. The scant gold and jewels they keep in return are not of consequence to my fortunes," Augustus had declared. Besides, his resources were stretched enough with the empire as it was.

This was how we remained the friendly, inconsequential neighbours: busy with our religion and produce.

This was also how I wanted us to remain for now and not as some trigger for a ruler's paranoia. The last thing I desired was to give need for the Roman army to travel east and visit us for "more details".

Herod himself was even more of a concern. This was a man who had slaughtered even members of his own family to hold his position firm, including three of his own sons. The name of "brute" had not been given lightly to the man.

So the politics of Judea weighed upon me as much as the "yes" from Mazda had comforted me. I knew that Herod had heirs already born and I prayed prayer upon prayer that what we were seeing would be the succession of one of those heirs that would transform the rule of Judea and its people. That surely would have been the most graceful of scenarios.

CHAPTER TWENTY-TWO

Now I have to admit that Gaspar and I were not the only ones to have read the signs presented to us with the conclusions we had deduced. That would make the rest of our brotherhood seem somehow inattentive or ignorant. Many had also begun to have dreams as well that confirmed and drew together the symbolism of the stars and planets we had observed.

The second crossing of Jupiter had ignited a new level of excitement. The vow Gaspar and I had made in keeping what we had felt hidden until more information presented itself proved useless.

Others were dreaming of the young man with the lion and lamb. Many had seen the link to Judea within the house of the lion. All knew this was to be about the birth of a king or leader. As had Gaspar and myself, none felt the story was full in its entirety. Letters were written asking for confirmation or in hope that others had sensed more to round out what they were aware of.

I was standing within the library looking at a desk filled with letters. There was one from every temple within Babylonia and each one contained at least one of three points; the dreams of the young man, the link to Judea and the fear of revealing this to Herod.

Every magus in my temple was also in attendance.

One sighed. "We cannot keep up with such correspondence. By the time our reply reaches most of the recipients the information is almost redundant."

I nodded in reply.

Malchiek was sitting across the room. "There is no time for letter writing anymore. We need to gather. I will write to the elders of each temple. They will send one magus and no more to gather here. We will go through our histories together. We each provide what our temples have seen, dreamt, heard or felt. When that is all assembled together then we can know truly what is unfolding."

There was no sound through the room as everyone paused and imagined this. We all knew this was the most perfect way to deal with the situation.

"One giant gathering. All temples represented. All voices to be heard so that we can act as one," I heard someone beside me say.

"Yes. Let us just make sure they bring their own servants to care for them though," I replied and began to clear the table.

The grand gathering began a month later and though we limited each temple to sending one magus they all arrived with a small entourage. This was both necessary and appreciated. They came upon their camels, laden with clothing and food. Beside them rode butlers, bodyguards, scribes and even musicians. The result being that each temple sent around five people or more to the event.

Our homes overflowed and our grounds filled with the tents to house the help. Servants from distant locales sized each other up, becoming fast friends or wary acquaintances. Within the homes the same occurred between the magi.

There most certainly was a warmth between us but there was also some reservation as well. Most were my age, with the elderly not deemed fit for travel and the young not experienced enough. So the men who congregated had some vigour balanced with enough wisdom and maturity for what would be considered a sensible discussion.

We assembled together in a makeshift amphitheatre - using the steps to the side of the temple as seating while the ground between the temple and the dormitory served as a stage. We even had a platform built upon which those speaking could stand.

Malchiek stepped upon it at the beginning of the first day and all fell silent instantly. He leant against his walking stick and smiled. I saw his breath catch and made way to him for fear there was something wrong. Malchiek put up his hand, gesturing for me to stop then he lowered it to his heart. He spoke then but his voice broke with emotion.

"My heart is so full to see you all here at our home," he quivered and waved his hand at the temple. Malchiek looked over the group of eighty-two men and smiled. "I do not just see a group of men, nor even a group of magi. I see a family gathered together to share the love of our great father Mazda. I see a family with hope for a new birth for all mankind."

He paused again as his voice caught on his last words. Once more he put his hand upon his heart as he regained his breath. Tears filled my eyes as they did for many who were listening.

"I know with all my love for Mazda, with all my hope for humanity and with all my faith for my brotherhood that this gathering will heal all that has been and prepare for what will be. I ask of you only this: honour all who speak and their words, and remember why you are servants of Mazda. If we do this then we honour the awakening that we know is unfolding before our eyes and souls."

With that Malchiek closed his eyes and lowered his head to lead us in prayer.

"Holy creator, beloved father and breath of our lives, bless all those who gather to honour you. We ask of you to guide our words, to protect our gathering and to reveal that which we can use in serving you and the Great Awakening." He paused and opened his eyes. "Let us make this a gathering that will be remembered for eternity."

Every man present nodded in agreement.

Over the day, each magus was given opportunity to speak. Some had much to say while others did not speak at all. In fact by the time we were half-way through the assembly, many simply said that all they had to share had already been shared.

As men spoke I looked amongst the magi. I saw heads nodding as each one of us presented what we had seen and recorded. As the day unfolded recurrent themes and feelings were revealed. Every speech became yet another confirmation to what we had all been experiencing within our own temples.

It was a joy to finally meet so many of my colleagues, many of whom I had only known of through letters and stories. It is interesting how when you finally meet someone they can defy the image and act you had constructed in your mind. Height, voices and demeanour are never truly carried across in the written word. Thankfully all embraced the love of Mazda that I imagined them to have.

There was one magus who did not surprise me with his appearance and that was Gaspar. He was every part the man that I believed that I had grown to know through his letters over the years. In fact the moment I saw him it was not as though we were finally meeting; it was as though we were brothers being reunited. We embraced as though we had done so a thousand times.

Gaspar then held my shoulders and smiled. "I wish I had the words to say how grand this is to meet you.

It won't come as a surprise to you that I billeted Gaspar and Melchior to my home, along with some others that I felt a resonance to. I did this in the hope that they would all reside in harmony with each other as well. Unfortunately the others being unfamiliar with Gaspar found him intimidating and intense.

"I do not think he has spoken of anything but the awakening?" one said to me after Gaspar had left the room.

You see to some an obsession can seem like a blinkered focus, shutting all else of life off. To others it is a driving force that concentrates energy such that there are no distractions or excuses to deviate from your calling. In the latter was how I chose to see Gaspar and his passion for the grand awakening. It was priests such as him that we needed.

One night I headed into the garden where he was already discussing the movement of Jupiter with two of the younger priests who had travelled with him as assistants. I saw the younger men nodding, and then looking up to where Gaspar pointed towards the stars.

I stood and watched, hoping they would notice me and allow for me to make my way into the conversation. Such was their focus though that they did not even see or sense me. I turned and made my way inside.

When Gaspar spoke on that first day, I saw some magi who knew of his ways, take a deep breath as they prepared for what he might say. By the time he was finished every magus sat up straight with eyes wide open.

Gaspar spoke of the house of Judea and the dreams he had of the young man with the lion and the lamb. Then he did what no other had done.

He asked, "how many have dreamed of this man?"

Over half the men raised a hand, while they all looked around to count for themselves and see who else did so.

Gaspar smiled and nodded calmly, though I admit that I gasped when I first saw how many hands went up.

"This can be no coincidence," Gaspar declared and there were murmurs of agreement throughout the gathering.

The dreams were all similar, and some were so close in their details that it would make the listener shiver at the exact replication.

The young man, even though he appeared at different ages, was always the same. Dressed in simple clothes, his dark hair worn long as was his beard, with eyes a pale green that contrasted with his olive skin.

He was always with the lion and the lamb. He always spoke the same words.

"I am just like you. I will return soon to show all men and women that they are like me also."

He never spoke of anything else. As Gaspar stood before the group and saw so many hands raise to say they had dreamt of the same man, part of his heart burned in the hope that they had received answer to the questions that this man would not answer.

"Has he spoken his name to any of you?"

There was silence and the shaking of heads.

"Has he spoken of where he will be born?"

There was also no response to say that has been answered.

"So all we have for now is the signs from the stars," ended Gaspar. "Let us pray that they, along with our dreams, reveal these pieces."

That night I waited until I could find Gaspar alone.

"Why did you not say more of what you feel is happening or who you believe this man to be?" I asked him.

Gaspar took a deep breath and smiled. "Because I feel that will be revealed soon enough."

What Gaspar felt about the dream man was not so different to what many felt. Like us both though they felt they had nothing to back up the sense of so much more. Here we were, waiting for this grand awakening, for this next phase in humanity, where everything would change. Yet we were tied to our old ways of how to let it in.

We measured the stars, we analysed our dreams. Yet underneath all we knew and understood, something was opening up that our minds weren't letting us truly see. We danced around it, writing letters and travelling to each other's homes. Hoping that some other magus had measured something in the sky we hadn't seen. Praying that we would not miss a sign, no matter how small it would be.

Yet every single one of us felt it. It was something inside us we could not put to words. It was a rush of warmth that washed through us as we prayed to Mazda for insight. It was the excitement that made the idea of gathering together so important.

Then when we were gathered, our sensibilities, pride and caution held it back. We all knew we were gathered to share more than what we saw, heard or dreamt but still we played out the roles of being proper and respectful.

I watched Gaspar hold his tongue as things were said and as I did so I became angry. I looked around to others and wondered what they were holding back. Then something within went even further; if we as such wise men could not speak the truth of our feelings, then how would the common man feel to open up to the awakening.

What if our hesitance to be open with each other held back this awakening? What if it stopped this new birth; not just of this man but of the era we had been waiting for so long? What if every generation before us had withheld this expansion simply because of the fear to speak their truth, for fear of breaking traditions and pushing beliefs? The awakening could well have been with us sooner.

My blood boiled at this. There was anger at myself. There was anger at all who had studied before me. I consoled myself at the idea that humanity had not allowed the awakening because it had not been ready. Then this thought angered me more than any other; that any man would delay a life of paradise.

What for? To suffer more? To endure the duality of good and evil?

That made no sense. Why would any god allow that? It could let you question the existence of Mazda and the story he gave Zarathustra.

It was when I got to the point of questioning my creator that I stopped, because I knew how easy it is for one to get lost on such thoughts and reject their creator.

There was my answer. We delay our paradise, because it allows us to even question the very basis of our existence. When we stay in the questions of life, then we miss out on life. We miss out on our connection to Mazda and we miss out on the joys he has created for us to experience. All for the fun of asking the questions.

So what would happen if instead of a magus standing up and asking more questions, sharing more doubts or looking for confirmation—what if one of us stood up and simply shared what he felt and believed? And to do so without fear of the consequence?

I decided to see just what would happen the next day but not before speaking with Gaspar.

He raised his eyebrows and a slight smirk crossed his lips. Then he nodded.

"It is time. If not for you to find the bravery within your impatience, then I may have done so through anger and frustration. It may be what we need to move things forward from being a polite gathering to being something that will achieve some greatness," he said.

So the next day we gathered in the morning as we had done for the past week. Each priest went to the great fire to make individual prayer. I was the first to arrive at the fire and the last to leave. I barely noticed each man as I was so deep in my own meditation.

Gaspar's words had hung on me somewhat. I did not want to speak out of anger or fear or any other emotion. I wanted simply to speak out of my devotion to Mazda and the awakening. So as I looked upon the fire I called upon that devotion. I checked myself over and over until I was clear and certain that it was my commitment that would be my motivation and no other part of me.

All other priests had gathered upon the stairs. All except Gaspar and myself. He waited until he saw me open my eyes and lift my head. Then he walked to my side, placed a hand upon my shoulder and spoke.

"You may be saying the words but you will not be alone. Let me stand beside you so that you speak for us both," he said.

I nodded. "What should I say?"

"What your bah-ra'an tells you to," Gaspar said.

Malchiek began the gathering as always with a group prayer, then asked who would like to speak first. I raised my hand and my father looked at me quizzically but nodded and gestured for me to make way to the podium.

Gaspar stood and walked beside me, which I am forever grateful for, but which made many magi join Malchiek in his puzzled look. We stepped upon the stage and for a moment all time seemed to stop. I looked out upon the faces of all the men before me and no longer did I see a group of well-studied men.

I saw something beyond their eyes and the faces they sat here with. In some I saw the entire village they represented; I saw their farmers and bakers - every "simple" man who sought them for support and clarity. In another face I would see the magus' father and his father before him; as though each generation of his family was waiting to hear me speak. Another face would show me the magus as a child, full of wonder and joy. Then in an instant I saw him thirty years from now as his life began to slow.

It was probably only seconds but it felt like so much longer. I caught my breath and Gaspar gently touched my shoulder reminding me that he was there for support. Thankfully it also brought me to the present moment.

I took a deep breath and asked Mazda to allow my bah-ra'an to speak. Then I began.

"My brothers. I cannot begin to express the delight in being amongst you. In the joy of our sharing in such an exciting time ... and yet another part of me has been quite sad," I began.

At this I saw glances exchanged and some shifted in their place. I took another deep breath and continued.

"It is hard to find the words for what I will say and truth be told I am sure many of you will already know what it is that I try to speak. I fear, my brothers, that in respecting our past, we are denying our future. I fear that in sharing as we have, we are not honouring the real purpose of this gathering. Mazda has called us here. I know it began with an invitation from our temple but we all know a greater purpose has called us together.

"We have all waited so long for this next era to begin. We have watched the skies, we have written the scrolls, we recited the teachings ... but there is so much more happening. Yes we also have our dreams, and what we hear, but I know many of us are feeling something that is like nothing we have felt before. I know this is what has made the conjunction so exciting and why we are all seeking each other out.

"It is time for us to be as open as we can. To share not just what we have already but to share what we are personally feeling and believing.

"We have all agreed that the latest movement of Jupiter is about a new king for Judea. I have felt there is more but like all of you, I am waiting for something to confirm this. And to be frank with you all, I am tired of waiting to have my senses proved to me."

Beside me Gaspar nodded.

"I have sat here with all of you. I have honoured your words and wisdom as though you were my blood for you are my brotherhood. It is that connection with you that lets me feel that you also have the sense that I do about this; that there is more!

"I also sense your frustration as to wanting to know what that is. I too have heard words that promise more to come—and I waited. Then our brother Gaspar wrote to me and found the words to make sense of it.

"This is not just about the birth of a king. This is a man who will bring to us the key for the awakening. In every dream we have about this young man we are not seeing a king. We are seeing our hopes come alive. We are seeing the promise made to Zarathustra become a reality; that a lion and lamb can be together without fear.

"The symbols and signs we see are just markers to entertain us as we open our spirits to what will manifest. There is much more happening than what we see, and I know each and every one of you feel that too. Is that not why you are the ones who came from your temples?"

Slowly every man nodded, even Melchior. I took another deep breath and put my hand upon my heart.

"My prayer for today was to stand before you and speak with a truth from so deep within me that even I might not know the voice that came out. I stand before you now as though I have had shackles released from my heart.

"I do not ask you to dismiss all that we have learnt or all that we respect. But I do ask that you share beyond the boundaries that have been set before us. If we cannot do this here, with a sense of being safe and respected then we cannot do that anywhere.

"I truly believe that in being open, even if our words make no human sense, it will send a message to Mazda that we are willing and ready. In allowing our hearts and bah-ra'an to speak, alongside our wisdom, then we make an invitation for the new energy of the awakening to come to us and be birthed."

As I finished, Gaspar once more reached out to my shoulder; this time gripping it and giving it a squeeze. I felt his love and solidarity in that grip. Before me though I saw something different.

The magi gathered were still making sense of my words. Some looked at their feet, others were muttering to the ones next to them. I looked to Malchiek in the front row and his eyes were dark, burning into me with disapproval. It was only then that I realised I should have spoken to him first.

I knew though that would not have worked. My father would have questioned me so that any doubts I had would have been flamed enough to convince me not speak. I had been very clever in searching out the one man who would instead bolster my determination.

Keeping my eyes locked upon my father's, I swallowed hard and raised my chin a little, as though to make clear that I stood by my words. Likewise Malchiek kept his gaze steady and piercing. It was a look I had not seen since my youth, and I knew one of Malchiek's lectures, which I also had not experienced since my youth, would follow at the first opportunity.

Then something happened that changed all that. Zavan from the east stood up.

"I too have felt all that you said. I believe the man will be an incarnation of Zarathustra to lead the world into the awakening," he said with conviction.

Then Belthsam from the north stood up.

"I too believe this is the birth of a prophet and not a king. The signs of royalty are just to let us know of his majesty," he said with his voice shaking.

Then another and another stood, all sharing the same belief with their own variation. Soon the gathering turned into chaos with magi crying out over each other, while others talked with their neighbour.

I call it chaos in that there was no order, but the warmth and joy that washed through the noise was wonderful. It was as though the energy of the meeting had been dissolved and reset. I had called out for the release of the old ways and that had been embraced with relief and exuberance. It would take some time to call us back into some semblance of calm but it was worth it.

Beside me I heard Gaspar chuckle as we watched the crowd dissolve into bedlam. Then I saw there was one man who remained quiet and still. In the front row Malchiek sat with his head down and his hands folded softly in his lap.

There was little structured discussion for the rest of the morning. Many simply spoke more about their dreams and what they had read the symbols within them to mean. Others spoke of the messages from their own bah-ra'an telling them that there was more to come. In releasing our protocols and etiquette we had found a new way to express ourselves and it was revealing and inspiring.

Malchiek sat still and quiet the whole time. Gaspar and I intuitively kept some order in how things proceeded but seeing my father like this took the shine off what was such a triumphant moment.

Gaspar eventually called time for lunch and our afternoon rest.

"I feel we need some rest after such revelations and discussion to see what we can allow in for the remainder of our gathering," he said as each man made way to their homes.

Malchiek got up slowly and began to walk up the stairs of the temple. I rushed to be by his side, offering my arm to support him but he pulled his arm away.

"Father..." I began to speak but Malchiek shook his head to stop me. I knew better than to push my luck and I let him go. Watching him walk up the stairs I saw him as so much smaller and older than I ever had before. My heart ached wondering what I could do to speak with him, and though something told me to give him space I followed behind him up the stairs.

Malchiek walked into the room of the great fire. Two young acolytes were tending the fire and the fresh wood upon it made it seem hotter than it usually was. I saw my father slowly lower himself to his knees before it, then drop his head in prayer. I silently made way to kneel beside him.

I heard his prayer being murmured from his lips and I too made my own prayer of thanks for all that had unfolded that morning. Then I turned to look at Malchiek and saw tears falling down his face. I sighed not knowing what to say and then thankfully Malchiek turned to face me.

"I tried so hard to make you fear the voices you heard. I wanted you to close them off, to stay with the ways we knew and trusted. But you couldn't and I am glad," he said barely above a whisper.

"So why are you so forlorn Father?" I asked.

"Because you could not share what you felt with me," he continued. "Why did I hear of this today as part of a crowd? Why could you not have come to me?"

I looked at the fire and closed my eyes. I didn't even know how to answer this. Why was it so easy to write letters with Gaspar and yet not speak of it with my own father and teacher?

"Because at best it felt like I was simply writing a story: that this amazing thing unfolding before me was just a fantasy. How dare I assume my feelings were true? How dare I believe that Mazda would show me such things? It felt that I could keep playing with it safely when it was just letters with someone I had never met—and who was even crazier than me. If I had come to you ... if I had come to you..."

I trailed off because I didn't want to say what would come next. I would have been made to analyse every detail: likewise for Gaspar with his fellow temple men. We would have been made to take every dream, voice or sensation and dissect them with writings from the Avesta. Our feelings and intuition would have been compressed into something understandable and measurable. For many of us this was just impossible to do and I also believe that it would have possibly stopped what we were inviting in.

"If I had to come to you—then all would have changed. I am not so sure how," I lied then added. "But for now we should be grateful that all has unfolded as it has. Today was remarkable. It will be remembered always and I know in my heart of hearts that you were a key to this. Your teachings, your temple, your family all were part of this. If not for you, then today would not have existed. That is all that matters; that today happened."

I finished and looked back to the fire.

CHAPTER TWENTY-THREE

Coincidence is a wonderful phenomenon. It can be the confirmation of our beliefs, the answer to our prayers and the miracles that keep our hope alive. That very night coincidence provided us with all three potentials.

After our lunch and afternoon rest, we gathered for a communal meal at the temple so that we were all together as a group for the stargazing that night. As the sun set we made way to the open area behind the temple and when we were all in place the servants extinguished the lamps around us.

It was a beautiful night; the air was crisp but not too cold and the waning moon let as many stars as possible reveal themselves. We all looked to Jupiter, and I heard someone call out for us all to join together in prayer. So we did, not with heads bowed as usual, nor in unison. We kept our heads up, our eyes opened and upon Jupiter and we found our own words in our own way. Some spoke out loud, some prayed silently. We all prayed the same thing; that Mazda would reveal what we needed to know through the sky.

I heard someone rush to my side.

"It has stopped again!"

It was Melchior. His speech was breathless and though he aimed to speak in a whisper anyone close by heard. Not that it was such a secret as any magi with talent in measuring had noticed also. The fact was spread quickly through the crowd, followed by a flurry of tools being lifted to the sky.

"It has! Jupiter has stopped and is heading west again!" Belthsam called out.

I turned to find and walk to Melchior. He stood with his astrolabe in his hand, hanging by his side. His gaze was fixed upwards, his eyes as wide as they could be and his mouth open in awe. Melchior looked towards me, his eyes still wide in wonder. He smiled slightly.

"There is going to be a third conjunction," he said calmly and then looked back to Jupiter.

All around us magi rushed around, confirming measurements with each other and lighting lamps so they could write upon scrolls. Amongst them all, Melchior and I stood, silent and still, looking up at this point of light that had changed our lives. I lifted my arm and placed my hand upon his shoulder. Melchior did not drop his gaze for a second.

I felt someone come to stand to my other side. I expected it to be Malchiek but it wasn't. It was Gaspar. I turned to acknowledge him and saw he had tears streaking his face.

"We asked for something more, and Mazda has given it to us," he said.

Then we both joined Melchior in watching Jupiter once more.

Far to our west and oblivious to anything that was occurring in the sky, a young man looked upon his new wife. She was within the last months of being pregnant.

"I hate to make you travel while you are like this, but you know we must," he said.

His wife ran her hand over her belly. "It will be alright Joseph," she answered. "Yahweh will watch over us."

Joseph nodded. "If only I had so much faith," he thought to himself.

Joseph's faith had been much tested in the previous months. He knew marriage brought responsibility and trials but he hadn't imagined so many and so soon. His young wife, Mary, announced she was with child before they had married or he had even lain with her. Any other man would have ended their betrothal then and there, but not Joseph. He had stayed and listened to her words.

"This is not the child of a man. I have had a divine seed placed within me. I know ... because an angel ... Gabriel ... he came to me and he told me," she had explained with her eyes wide and pleading to be believed, even though she gave him more excuse to reject her.

Joseph couldn't though. As he looked into her eyes he just saw truth. He nodded and stroked her cheek.

"I know. An angel came to speak with me also," he replied. "If we are insane, then we can be damned together, and if not then we can be blessed together. I will not forsake you."

With those words Joseph made a pledge that no marriage vows could match.

As Joseph and Mary began their historic journey to Bethlehem, back in Babylonia we watched as Jupiter began to return to Sharu to cross over the star once more; a triple conjunction within a year that had never been seen or recorded before.

"It's a coronation. Three times. There is no doubt that the father is crowning his son," said Malchiek and anyone who heard these words nodded and agreed. "Mazda is anointing a new king of the world."

We were now all in agreement that all that we had felt, dreamt and seen had been confirmed.

There was one question that now lingered; what do we do now?

"We should send word for any royal births," came the first suggestion.

Riders were sent to scout for news. We heard of the birth of a princess in Egypt but knew the prophet must be male. Then we heard of the arrival of a son to one of the tribes to the north of Judea and our hearts swelled. A week later we heard of his passing.

"They must be of Judea though," Malchiek reminded us all.

We reluctantly sent a scout to Jerusalem to see if Herod had any new heirs. None were recently born or due to do so.

"Thank Mazda the newborn is not of his blood," one magus proclaimed to grunts of agreement.

"What if this is not a noble birth?" questioned David of the south. "Zarathustra was not of royalty or nobility. He was of common blood. What if this is a common birth? How would we ever know where the child is? Perhaps we now just wait to see how the man reveals his teachings over the years as he matures. Maybe it was just our place to record the birth?"

Melchior listened to this and something didn't feel right. That night he went to the garden behind my home with every instrument he had. I saw him and went to see what he was doing. Before I could even speak he raised one hand to stop me.

"Please my brother, leave me to work in silence. I have a feeling that there is something else to reveal to us. I must be alone and quiet," he said without ever looking at me. I walked away instantly, and told the others to keep their distance.

Melchior measured and recorded with more focus and determination than he ever had before. Then he did what he had done before the second crossing of Jupiter. He traced the path as he knew it would be. Yes, the third conjunction would happen. It would be closer than the second, though not as much as the first. Then Melchior let his finger keep moving in the arc he predicted.

I watched him do this from a distance. His index finger tracing through the air, then he stopped and he drew a line with his finger towards the ground. Melchior turned and looked to me, his face spread in a grin.

"I know where we will find him!" he cried out.

Some people predict through their dreams, others through their feelings or intuition. Melchior did so with numbers, lines and his trust in the infallible movement of the stars.

When I walked back to his side his grin was even wider.

"If sailors can find their way to a distant shore by the stars, then why can't we priests use them to find a child?" he said with a laugh and I joined him.

Melchior had foreseen the second conjunction and tonight his finger had traced the path of the impending third. Then he had kept his hand moving and what he saw would happen next made his heart almost explode.

"Three conjunctions with Sharu ... and then a second with Venus!" he proclaimed to me.

My mouth dropped open in awe and I looked up and across to Venus, the brightest star in our sky.

"Twice ... and so soon..." I muttered.

"Yes so soon. The king began his journey with the mother, crowned the son and returns to the mother," Melchior continued. "It is too perfect."

I now shook my head. "But how does this let you know where the child will be?"

Melchior faltered in his response. "I—I—well I ... it just seemed to make sense that the child will be beneath the conjunction of the mother and father," Melchior finished and looked down. "Now I feel I may have been a bit premature in that deduction."

I took a deep breath. "No Melchior, not at all."

There may have been no solid measurement to substantiate Melchior's theory and that was his hesitation now. I knew though that it had been more than his training that allowed his hand to trace that path and come to that conclusion.

"Let's tell Gaspar," I said.

Gaspar was coming out into the garden as we spoke and he could see the expressions on our face. He hurried to join us, then listened calmly as Melchior explained what would be occurring over the coming months.

"When do you think that Jupiter will reach Venus?" he asked.

Melchior shrugged his shoulders. "I don't know that I could say exactly..."

"I don't care for exactly! Will it be weeks, months? Is there a chance it won't happen?" Gaspar spat with frustration now.

Melchior sighed and looked up to the sky. Once more he traced his finger in an arc, this time stopping every inch or so and counting.

He looked back to us and said, "six weeks."

"Six weeks?" Gaspar checked.

"Yes, six weeks," Melchior repeated.

Gaspar now looked down and counted upon his fingers. He stopped at nine.

"Nine months or thereabouts. Jupiter started at Venus, crowned his son and returned to her. All in nine months. If we needed any confirmation that this was a conception and birth then we now have it," he said.

"That is not all," I said softly. Gaspar looked from me to Melchior.

"I believe that the final conjunction will mark the birthplace. We know it is within Judea. The conjunction will show us where," he said plainly waiting for Gaspar's reaction.

Gaspar stroked his beard as he looked off into the distance. A smile made way across his face. Now he knew what the dream of the camels had shown him.

"So if we were to travel to Judea, you believe you could measure the area that the child should be within?" he said, never looking back at either of us.

"I—I actually believe I could take us to an exact village; not just an area," said Melchior and though he had stuttered a little, he spoke with conviction.

Gaspar nodded slowly. "Then I suggest we make way to greet our new prophet."

"Now, now, now!" I said waving my hands. "Let us just calm down one moment. We are yet to even see the third conjunction, let alone the second with Venus. Why don't we just wait until at least the third with Sharu before we make such plans? Besides…" I took a deep breath. "We need to be wary of Herod. I will not make such travels until we are all agreed on how this would be relayed to him. If we cross into his kingdom we will be questioned, and we all know that one wrong answer would cost our lives and even worse, that of others."

Melchior nodded but I could see he was not happy.

"I do not doubt you Melchior. It is just that there is so much at stake here. If we just follow our feelings ... well—well..." I looked at Gaspar who was glaring and I stopped.

"If we follow our feelings and pursue our intuition we will be helping to birth the greatest era of mankind. We will be guiding the release of all that makes life a trial, including despots who think they have right to constrain the lives of others," Gaspar said clenching his jaw.

I sighed and closed my eyes. I knew he was right. That was exactly what I had stood before the gathering and spoke about.

But could one man such as Herod undo all of this? I just did not think that was something worth risking.

"Please, let us present to the others and use the power of our brotherhood to decide what happens next?" I begged.

CHAPTER TWENTY-FOUR

The next day Melchior with his straightforward way spoke of the most recent measurements, as those with the same talents nodded in agreement. Then he described the second conjunction that he predicted to us the night before. This too was greeted with nods, while others leant forward and gasped.

"We never imagined such a sign from Mazda. This is grander than we could have believed," a magus proclaimed.

Then Melchior delivered the final bombshell of his observations.

"And I believe that I can use that meeting with Venus to show where the child is born. As a sailor uses the stars to find land, so too we can use them to find our new prophet," he finished.

There was a momentary pause and silence. Then Belthsam stood up once again, crying out.

"We must go there now and protect him!" he shouted.

Then once more the meeting collapsed into chaos with men standing and shouting. Somehow amongst this Malchiek found his way to the podium, pushing Melchior aside. Then from somewhere in his elderly frame came a voice I had not heard since I was a child.

"ENOUGH!" he shouted so loudly that I believe it echoed off the temple and down into the village. "I will not let us dissolve into this rabble each time there is a revelation. Gentlemen, remember who you are! You are grand magi of the Zoroastrians. You are the ones who carry the words and teachings of the greatest prophet known to history. I will not stand here as we verge onto all our forefathers prepared for and watch you act like Roman senators at a political meeting!

"Yes we are all emotional, but we cannot let those emotions rule our discussion or actions. Sit down, each one of you. Take a breath and join me in prayer. Pray as you will, but pray for some guidance and balance. We must get back to our clarity," he finished and shook his head. Then he gestured for Melchior to take his seat and pray also.

As Melchior ran to his seat, partly horrified at being the initiator of the scene, Malchiek looked over each and every one of us.

"How did it get to this?" he thought and his eyes stopped upon me.

I caught his look and did not miss one scrap of its intent. I dropped my head and prayed.

Malchiek looked upon me as I did so. He recalled all the moments of my life that I had questioned him or our teachings. He remembered the night I had been made to sleep in the barn. Then he thought of the dream I had the night I returned from my short-lived mountain retreat. All of this; the letters, the connections, the anticipation - it had all begun that night with my dream.

He looked to Gaspar, yet another who had dreamt such things at that time, and across to the other sons who also had such dreams, who now all sat here as men. They had all opened this up; they had all allowed the energies to come in. They had all created the events that had made this meeting necessary.

Here Malchiek stood as he looked upon my generation, who were the bulk of the meeting, and a sudden shame washed over him for having yelled at us so.

Now as I looked up I saw my father's face soften. He smiled at me and though it seemed strained I saw within it a certain surrender.

Malchiek looked over all the men one more time. Then he spoke again, so softly that those on the highest stairs only just heard him.

"I am sorry my brothers. Forgive me my anger. It gets so easy to forget one's grace at times of such importance and yet I am the man here who was supposedly reminding you of yours," he sighed and gave a small smile. "Let us all call back our grace as a priesthood, as a family and as guardians of the awakening. Then let us discuss how we shall go to greet our new prophet."

With that he gestured for Melchior to return to the podium to finish his presentation.

We returned to our meeting with the decorum that Malchiek had hoped for, and even when that did dissolve from time to time, he did not allow it to upset him as it had before. Even when he felt his temper rise up, my father would take a deep breath and remember how this had all began.

There was one part of the discussion though that the eldest of the brotherhood were truly needed. That was in the way that we were to deal with Herod.

"There is no way you can enter Judea without asking his audience. To do so would somehow infer you had something to hide. You must be open and warm," one stated and we all knew this was true.

"But can we be so open about what we believe?" Zavan asked.

That was where we all faltered. How do we walk into a man's kingdom and announce the birth of a great prophet and leader without that seeming some threat to him.

"We could just say that we believe a new incarnation of our prophet has been born?" I offered.

There was silence as we all considered this.

"He has his own astrologers, surely they have seen what is happening?" Melchior said.

This was true. Any court or palace had their astronomers and astrologers. They did everything from plan crop planting, to predicting the best time to launch battles. Herod's astronomers thankfully were not so intuitive with their charts and mapping. Unlike us, they simply saw a two dimensional display of lights. Also, they did not have the history and teachings to make them see anything beyond this design. Yes they were watching the dance of Jupiter within Leo but their story was something quite different.

"Sire, this is surely a sign of your majesty and worthiness," they told Herod. "For the king of planets to dance with Sharu and all within the house of the lion, this is surely Yahweh telling all beneath him that this is a glorious time for this land."

When the astrologers left, Herod's chief minister turned to him. "My Lord this is certainly wonderful and must be shared with the people!"

Herod sneered and rolled his eyes. "Why yes, we must tell *my people*. While you are writing the declaration also include that I have eaten a divine apple which has allowed me to grow ten feet tall and shit gold from my arse! They will believe that as much as anything else you tell them."

Indeed when the declaration, minus the suggested storyline of the apple, was shared around the kingdom many did laugh out loud.

"I suppose he will say the sun rising each day is a sign from Yahweh as well as to his right to rule us," an astronomer in the north said.

This astronomer and his priesthood had been watching as Jupiter had made its two crossings, and though they had not predicted as far forward as Melchior, they knew a third was on its way. The Jewish priests too were waiting for signs of a grand birth for their own reasons. They were waiting for the birth of their own saviour.

Their people had survived escape from Egypt. They had wandered the Middle East and established new homes, only to have Rome come and claim the land for their own. Now they lived within the lands of their birth ruled by someone designated to control them. They were permitted to live their religion and customs and they prayed each day for the protection of Yahweh but this was the only true freedom they had.

Their strength came from their own story; that one day they would be delivered back to a paradise upon Earth. And that paradise would be delivered by someone within the sixty-sixth generation of their people, and that generation was now being birthed. Unlike us though, they did not see the events in the sky as being an indicator of this. They would simply wait for the man to reveal himself through his actions.

We too knew of this prophecy. When one of our scouts returned from Judea during their search for news of a birth they reminded us of this. In fact when he had spoken with the astronomers in the north of Judea, they had smiled at the purpose of his visit.

"It is so rare that our religions should overlap with such news," he told his fellow astronomers afterwards. "Surely this is a sign that our messiah is soon to be with us."

It was a thought that was echoed amongst the Jewish priests whenever our news reached them. It stirred the fire of their hope and conviction that the glory of their people would be restored. Unfortunately for most priests that was as far as their interpretation of this birth would go. They were waiting for a conqueror and a new king, and that belief would shape the life and history of what was to unfold.

For us; we were waiting on a new wisdom and awareness to be born. For us this was about the birth of a teacher.

✳ CHAPTER TWENTY-FIVE

When the dust had settled around Melchior's prediction of the upcoming movement of Jupiter and his hopes for what this would show us, we all settled on what we needed to do.

A caravan would travel to find the new child. We had to see for ourselves that this was what we were being shown. It was more than just finding undeniable proof of a birth though; we had to participate with what we had helped to open. If we had created this through our faith and belief, then we must also support and protect it.

Now by support and protect I do not mean that we would head there to act as bodyguards for the infant, but that in our acknowledgement by way of finding him, we also paid honour to all that we had allowed. This journey would be as much about honouring ourselves and our forefathers as it would be the child and the future he would unfurl.

It was almost unanimous that Gaspar, Melchior and I would lead the caravan. Melchior was considered the most important due to his conviction to find the child using Jupiter as his compass. I was honoured due to my role in the Great Excitement as well as being part of the temple to call the meeting. No one dared to contest my suggestion that Gaspar would also lead the journey.

History recalls the journey as being led by three, and even though I mention our three names as being chosen, there were many others. As you can imagine all our brotherhood that were gathered at the temple wanted to travel with us, and many of them did. As much as we would need servants to be with us, we also needed the support of those who studied and knew our ways.

You see we were men of faith but we were also men of reality. Long journeys in our time were perilous; there was possibility of attacks from tribes as well as simply falling prey to an illness. To have just three of us did not make such great odds for who might complete the journey to the child, or even return home to share what had transpired. So along with our servants, we too chose other priests and acolytes to be with us.

Those that remained within Babylonia were not necessarily deemed not worthy to travel. These brothers were the protectors of the knowledge we had gained. They would hold the energy of the journey, praying for our safe passage and return. They would ask Mazda each day as to our progress and watch the skies to see what else was being revealed.

Each one who stayed and held the space for those who travelled was as important as each one who journeyed. We would feel the protection they were creating for us from our home, and in turn it would remind us of the protection from Mazda in his paradise. We may have ventured far from our lands and houses, but we knew in our hearts we were as safe as if we were still there.

Until this day I still offer my thanks for each and every one of them. They were the foundation of all that our journey achieved.

Preparations for the expedition were a mix of hurried plans as well as days that seemed to drag on in time forever. It seemed we had so much to do to get ready and yet we never seemed to get closer to actually departing.

Once the travelling party had been decided upon the remaining energy holders began to return home. For some it was relief, for others it was with hesitation at leaving direct contact with what was unfolding.

"My heart aches to leave and yet I know I am needed within my temple to continue my work," said one as he grabbed the pommel on his saddle, readying himself to climb upon his camel.

"Your heart will travel with them and your soul will know exactly what will happen. It is just your body and mind that makes you believe otherwise," said my father as soberly as he could.

The departing priest nodded his head. "Yes, yes, my elder. I thank you for reminding me," he said and then climbed up onto his ride. He looked down at me as I stood beside Malchiek. "I pray your safe journey," he said to me and nodded his head.

"As I do yours," I replied bowing my head.

The priest sighed and looked up at the sky. I saw him swallow hard.

"We have put so much faith into what will unfold, and all on the movement of some lights in the sky. Let us also pray that Mazda would show us our follies before it is too late," he added then turned his camel to make his way.

I hated his parting comment so much. I actually wanted to spit in his trail to curse his words. Instead I just clenched my fists.

Malchiek looked down to my hands, curled up by my side.

"I could feel his words burn you and I see by your hands that you have allowed that ember to burn hot," Malchiek smirked but I did not see any humour in his words. He continued, "Be prepared for more doubt, especially from those who will not join you. It is their way to console themselves and justify not being there. For those it will be the means to hold onto a life that is safe and predictable."

I nodded in absolute agreement. It was why I had suggested Gaspar as a leader. He did not doubt what was opening up and he was beyond wishing or hoping for it. Gaspar's life passion was to birth the awakening.

Melchior too had no doubts. His joy was in being able to take in every sign that the sky showed him. "Why wait for these symbols and patterns to only question them?" he had once said to me.

Indeed, why wait for what we prayed for, then to only push it away or double guess it? This is what we and generations before us had waited for. It was time to embrace it with every fibre of our beings.

This did not destroy the doubts around me though. One night at dinner, David from the south who would not travel with us, ate with me before leaving for his home. As we discussed the journey I saw his face grow dark.

"What if we are wrong?" he said bluntly. "What if there is no prophet being born? What if the awakening is still generations away or, worse still, is not to happen at all?"

I took a deep breath and put down the bread I was about to dip into my beans. Heat rose up in my chest, then I remembered the words my father had said as the other priest had left.

"What if we are right? What if we don't travel due to our doubts but we were right? Yes, the awakening may happen anyway, but my friend…" I picked up the bread again and pushed it into the beans. "I would rather travel based upon my heart and my passion, than stay here based upon my doubts." I took a mouthful of bread and beans, making David wait until I swallowed. "I would rather return and say 'I was wrong' than sit and wonder what could have been. That my brother, is why I will journey."

I ate some more as David sipped quietly on some wine, but I was not finished.

"Besides, why do we need to act that this is going to be something considered as a failure or success? Imagine if Zarathustra had said 'maybe I should not climb that mountain for I may fall and it be for naught'. Imagine that!" I laughed and reached for my wine. "Does all we do have to be measured? What if we just journey for the joy of discovering what is to be?"

I had gone a bit further than David's question had invited but I did not care. In doing so I had reached a new place of conviction within me; this journey would be whatever it needed to be to support the awakening whenever it would happen. In that moment of realisation I set free whatever would unfold.

CHAPTER TWENTY-SIX

Jupiter moved closer to Sharu and we moved closer to our departure. On the night Jupiter once more sat above the king star, I stood out in the garden with Elana by my side. The rest of the priests scattered around us.

I reached down and took her hand in mine, lifting it to kiss gently. That was when the tears began to fall down her face.

"The very things I love about you, that drew me to you are now going to take you away from me," she said softly.

"And they will return me to you as well," I assured her.

Elana did not smile. She just looked down, then pulled her hand from mine as she turned to walk inside.

I knew within me that I would return but that certainty was not true for everyone around me.

My father lectured me on diplomacy. "The last thing I want is a scroll telling me you have been tied to a stake for disrespecting a custom!"

My mother, now so small and frail, would simply want us to pray together. "My prayers worked when your father took you to the mountain. They will work again," she said.

Likewise my daughters questioned all my preparations and plans. Each query was met with a reserved and steady answer.

"All is well and all will be well."

It annoyed them the first time they heard it but they soon found some comfort in my conviction when I spoke it. I did begin to envy the distance Melchior and Gaspar had from their families.

"That is why I never married!" Gaspar had said when I shared my family's concern.

I saw Melchior drop his eyes though as he thought about his wife who would only learn of his involvement by a scroll.

As Jupiter continued towards Venus we began final preparations. We ensured our animals were well rested and fed, that they were in the best condition possible. There would be a mix of camels, horses and donkeys; each with their own attributes and talents as well as their own needs. Along with these were the men who would care for them on the way.

We hired swordsmen to protect us. They arrived from the north wearing leather armour covered with marks and scuffs from battle. Some even had the stains of blood from their failed competitors. They shook hands with the other men of the caravan and bowed to us.

"It will be a pleasure to protect you," said their captain Naturnus and then smiled broadly as I handed him the first purse of gold. "And it will be even more of a pleasure to receive our final purse on our safe return," he added as he bounced the purse in his hand, listening to the coins jangle within.

The bulk of the caravan would be our fellow priests and acolytes. They were those from the meeting, such as Belthsam, who had been immediate in resonating with the truth of what was happening. They would support us and be there for counsel, as a source of dreams and offering their expertise in star alignments and their knowledge of the places we would travel.

"The greater our resources, then the better prepared we are for whatever will occur," was a general consensus.

We had priests representing every region of Babylonia, every facet of our lives, as well as a gathered knowledge of our teachings and those of the religions we would encounter. It was a mighty brain trust that was as comprehensive as it was diverse. Imagine your Internet search engines in human form and sitting upon camels!

Younger priests and acolytes arrived from the temples of those joining the caravan. They would be there to assist as well as learn. They would be the ones to act as scribes, writing down all that occurred to create new records for our libraries. These younger men would also be a way to ensure an oral history was begun of the journey. They had much more years ahead of them than my fifty-six, and that was many more years to share firsthand what we would encounter.

Then we had our butlers, servants, cooks, physicians and musicians. It had been a unanimous unsaid agreement that we would not travel without comfort or ease. The inclusion of our butlers would mean clean clothes laid out for us, trim beards and perfectly coiled headdresses. The servants would raise and collapse our tents, gather water from wells and clear our plates after we dined. Cooks would bargain and forage for food, then prepare it over open fires. Our musicians would entertain and soothe us when we stopped for rest, as well as amuse anyone who should offer us hospitality along the way.

In all there were around sixty of us, and each one had a list of duties that they would honour. Though they also did much more. I say this referring to not just actions but in that everyone, from the youngest camel handler to the most experienced cook knew the importance of what we were doing. Their role was always going to be much more than just the worker or priest. It was that knowing that I believe saved us from a lot of trouble.

When you travel with an air of dignity and grace: that is how you are received. Villages saw us arrive as grand priests, surrounded by men who loved and honoured us. How could they react otherwise?

If three of us had arrived, dishevelled and hungry, with an air of anxiety, we would have been turned away many times. Instead word spread ahead of a great party searching for new prophet; that we travelled in peace and honoured all who were within our path.

I imagine we may never have needed our swordsmen.

When time came to decide upon which servants would join me I thought it would be an easy choice. My personal butler Daride knew me like he would know his own child. He knew my likes and dislikes, when I rose and what I looked like when hungry or needed rest. To have him with me would be as natural as could be.

213

In fact I completely assumed that he too would see himself with me, but when I spoke about preparations one day I saw his face was anything but enthused.

"Daride, what is wrong? You seem less than excited about this," I put to him.

Daride looked down and I could see he did not want to speak.

"Daride, you may be in service to me but we are also friends. Please be open with me. At this time I could not bear to have you of all people hold your truth from me," I then pleaded.

He looked up and I saw his face was red, and I do believe his hands had a slight tremor.

"I do not wish to journey with you," he blurted out and tears fell down his face.

I ran to him and pulled him into my arms. He collapsed upon my shoulder and began to sob. I held him gently as he cried not saying a word. Nothing needed to be said in that moment.

When Daride's tears stopped, he pulled back and looked into my eyes. "My health has been failing. I can only just do what is required of me here. Though I would wish to serve you to my dying day, I cannot serve you as you deserve upon this trip. I would fail you, and that would pain me more than any ailment I could suffer."

I nodded and said softly, "Of course, stay and serve my home for my return. There will be another who can travel in your place."

I sat at my desk that afternoon and dropped my head into my hands. "How can I travel without Daride?" I thought. He was to be my symbol of home, my enduring link to all that I knew of certainty and comfort. I heard a yell from outside and looked out the window to see someone chasing a goose from the kitchen garden.

It was Mahesh. He was running after the goose, flapping his arms and shrieking to scare it away from the vegetables. When the goose was gone he stopped running and put his hands upon his hips, smiling with satisfaction. Then he stooped down and picked a bean. He shelled it, then threw the contents into his mouth, finishing by throwing the empty shell over his shoulder.

I jumped up and ran to the garden, coming upon Mahesh as he made his way back to the house. He was still chewing the last of the beans in his mouth which he swallowed quickly.

"Sire," he said and bowed.

"Mahesh, you have been with us some months now, have you not?" I asked him.

"Why ... yes Sire. Yes I have," he answered.

"Do you feel you know the ways of my home thoroughly?"

"Yes Sire, though in honesty I still learn much each day," he replied but I knew the humility was not so true.

"Do you have desire to travel more?"

"Not at this time, Sire. I agreed to stay as long as was needed—unless of course that time has come?" he said and tilted his head waiting for a response.

"You are still needed and you are needed to travel. I require you to come with me as my butler."

Mahesh nodded. "Of course, Sire."

Then I am sure he did his best not to smile.

It was a week after the last conjunction that we were ready to leave. The last of our bags and sacks were packed ready to load our animals in the morning. They were piled at the entrance of my home as well as the doorways of the homes the other priests were staying in. In the barns and stables, the satchels of the servants lay waiting also.

Gaspar and I stood and watched as Mahesh and Gaspar's butler Onom, counted our bags one last time, reciting within their heads what should be in each one.

"Do we have enough food?" I said as I looked at the bags.

"We have as much as can be carried and that will not waste. What is important is that we have enough to trade for more food," Gaspar replied and he nodded to one of my sacks.

Gaspar was right. There was only so much food and water you could carry. There were also really only so many days you could be happy on dried bread and hard cheese once your fresh food had been depleted. We could rely on some hospitality offered but a group our size would need to offer some compensation.

That was why within my luggage would be a sack full of the finest frankincense. I had sourced it from the southeast, where the oldest trees lived and provided the finest incense from their resin. We could use it for prayers and it would prove to be a highly prized gift and method of trade. It was as valuable as gold which we would also carry.

Gold would keep our swordsmen happy and loyal, it would soothe a hostile host and it would buy us anything we needed, including safe passage. It was a symbol of power and might, and though we hoped that we would never need to go to such measures, it would be our insurance of sorts should my incense prove not enough.

Our other commodity would be some myrrh that Melchior had sent for. Such was the value of incense in our time that a second sack of the stuff would be more currency. Myrrh would also be used for prayer but its added benefit is that it was also medicinal, and could help everything from a heart condition to the healing of a wound. To be stranded a distance from any village we would need to care for ourselves in any way. The last thing I would hope for was that we would have to leave anyone by a roadside to perish from lack of supplies.

Just before sunrise the next day, every magus on the tour gathered in the temple for our last prayers before the Great Fire. Then Malchiek asked

Mazda to bless and protect each one of us as he handed us a piece of charcoal.

"Carry this with you. It has been part of the fire that burnt during the grand meeting of the magi. Within it is the energy of all who gathered and all that was allowed to be expressed. Carry it with you. Burn it within your fires as you travel, so that the fire of your homeland, the fire of your god, will be with you, protecting and serving you."

Every man kissed that blackened wood before slipping it into their pockets.

With the prayers finished we returned to our homes and billets to eat one last meal before we departed. In my home, I did not eat with my fellow priests. Instead I gathered my family; my three daughters with their husbands and their children, and now even grandchildren. We sat around our grand dining table and ate solemnly as I looked upon them.

I took a deep breath and I remembered why I was doing this. My whole life had been dedicated to my faith and to guiding the new era we had waited so long for. As I looked upon my family, I thought of how paradise on Earth would transform their lives. No more pain in childbirth. No more temptations of someone other than their spouse. No more illness. No more toil to provide an income.

My family did not want for material things, but I knew each and every one of them would have times when they questioned themselves, when they would wish to shrug off their responsibilities or to test their morals. I would journey now to greet the prophet who would show us how to live a life of absolute joy without the trials of life as we knew it.

I looked upon my family and I imagined a thousand families like ours, especially those without the blessings that mine had, and I saw them delivered into paradise. Any trace of fear I had about travelling that was still within me disappeared.

It was at the moment that my eldest son-in-law stood up from his chair and cleared his throat to get our attention. When all fell silent, he raised his glass.

"To our beloved father Balthasar, and to our blessed son Erasmus," he pushed his glass towards one of my grandsons and acolytes who was leaving with me. "Let us pray to Mazda for your safe journey. May you find this babe quickly so we can have you back with us!"

There was a quick round of laughter for which I was grateful. Then he continued with one hand on his heart.

"We may not understand the depths of what you are doing, but we love you for doing it. You are not just our father, you are our saviour and teacher. Each day you are away will make our hearts ache. Each night we will look at the stars knowing you are also and we will know you are not so far."

He choked on the last words and sat down before his emotions engulfed him. I heard Elana beside me sniffle as she held back her tears. I took her hand in mine as I looked down the table to everyone.

"Dear family, let us pray..."

We all bowed our heads and I led them in a simple prayer that part of me wanted to never end. I raised my head and nodded.

"And now I must be on my way..."

Outside, lined along the main street of our town, our men gathered upon camels, horses and donkeys. It was our grand company, ready to make way.

Daride stood beside my camel that was lowered ready for me to climb upon. I could see his eyes were red but his face was as stoic as always. Beside him stood Mahesh, instinctively knowing to let me have my faithful butler have his last moment of service with me. Mahesh climbed upon his own camel behind me and raised it to standing, smiling regally as he did so.

I went to Daride and put my hand upon his shoulder.

"Daride, I can think of no one better to watch over my home as I travel. I know you will do as you should," I said and then quickly climbed upon my saddle before either of us could be too emotional.

Daride handed me the reins. "May Mazda protect and return you to us," was all he could say before walking to stand behind my family.

I leant back and my camel lurched into standing. I gave one last look at the ribbon of men and animals behind me as Gaspar and Melchior steered their camels beside me. I nodded to them and smiled to my family who stood to the side of the road.

"This feels so familiar," I thought and could not imagine when I would ever have experienced such a scene before. The feeling evaporated as Gaspar spoke.

"Let us be on our way. We can make the next town for rest before the true heat of the sun is upon us," he said plainly.

I glanced over to Melchior, as he looked upon my family. His face was heavy and I imagined him picturing his own family and the farewell he had not received from them.

"Yes, my brothers, let us begin," I choked the words as I flipped the reins, waved one last time to my family and moved forward.

✹ CHAPTER TWENTY-SEVEN

We travelled in silence for the first hour. The very fact that we were finally on our way was hard to comprehend. It was all planned so meticulously that no discussion at this point was needed and none of us were particularly fond of small talk.

There was also the fun of adjusting our bodies to such a long camel ride. No one was in a hurry to discuss what they were going through as each hour transpired. Yes, we were accustomed to riding and yes, many of the men had travelled a distance to come to my temple; but this ride would be the longest any of us had travelled and with such a large group.

Even negotiating your space within the caravan was something new, such that a few fights broke out within the first morning. They were just a few terse words here and there but it was not something that could be ignored.

"We must address this immediately or the words will develop into physical reactions," I said to Gaspar and Melchior.

So at the first rest stop, as we gathered under some trees near a well, I spoke to the priests.

"You must be the ones to speak to those within your personal entourage, and this is what you must encourage and enforce amongst them..."

With that we laid out some basic rules. Well actually they were more considerations and behaviours for us all to live by.

Firstly, acknowledge each other's space. Do not ride so close to another that it may hinder their gait, safety and privacy.

Respect that some people may not want to speak or may need some quiet. It is not so hard to tell when someone needed time to himself.

Stop and think. Do not speak in anger at the moment. If someone is doing you wrong, speak to an elder to act as a mediator and gain resolution rather than inflame anything.

Do not speak ill of another for the gain of confidence. Malicious talk would be the greatest challenge to our morale and ambience.

Above all; remember why you were here. That in itself would dissolve much of the human issues we would deal with.

I have to say for the most part, we all stayed true to these agreements.

The first week of our journey was simple and straightforward. We would ride soon after sunrise to make the most ground before it got too hot. Most days we would get to a village or township as the sun reached its peak. If not; we would find somewhere with shade or erect tents and canvasses to rest under.

Wells could be found upon the roadside to fill our canteens or splash some dirt off from our faces and hands. The people we came upon would be happy to trade food for incense. There were even times that the arrival of such a huge group would make a farmer's eyes light up at the prospect of having a huge chore completed within minutes for the cost of some freshly killed and roasted goats. There was always some manner in which we could trade for some comforts that would make both parties happy.

As dusk would fall we would make camp, either on the outskirts of a town or in a clearing by the roadside. Our swordsmen would place themselves around us, fires would be made and beds would be set up. It was impeccably organised and orchestrated.

As the sky lit up each night, we would watch as Jupiter continued on its way to Venus.

"It is as though Jupiter is getting brighter," Melchior said one night.

"Is that even possible?" I asked.

"Who are we to question what is and isn't possible anymore," said Gaspar quietly.

He was right. We had witnessed a phenomenon between Jupiter and Sharu that had never been seen before. We had accepted that a new era was to be birthed with our witness. To stop and question anything right now was almost ludicrous.

So the first week went smoothly. There was still some bickering amongst the men but it was always trivial and smoothed over quickly. It was one of the bonuses of having so many priests along with us; that when a harsh word was spoken, there was always one close by to provide counsel. Many of the priests also took it upon themselves to oversee different facets of the caravan so that Gaspar, Melchior and I could focus upon the actual reason for the journey.

This did not mean they were simply there as glorified servants or as our sidekicks though. As we had at the temple, we gathered each day before we began to ride, to share any dreams or insights that had opened during our rest.

Many spoke about dreaming of the man again but now as a young child. The lion and lamb remained as always. He did not speak but always ran to the priests with open arms, inviting an embrace.

"I feel he knows we are coming," one priest said and we all nodded.

To Gaspar though, he appeared older. He was fully matured though not old. The man would sit running his hands through the lion's mane while the lamb sat beside him.

"You need to accept whatever happens," the man said to him with a smile.

"Why would I question anything?" Gaspar had asked completely perplexed.

"This will not be as you imagine. I will not be as you imagine. This era will not be as you all imagine," the man looked down to the lion and paused. Then he smiled and looked back up again. "I will be the beginning without end. Release me from your dreams of the awakening, and I will be free to do what is needed."

The dream had ended there and when Gaspar woke the next morning he did not share what had been said to him. He knew in his heart the words had been just for him. Gaspar sat up in his camp bed and looked out the opening of the tent. It was set up to face the sunrise and he could tell by the colour of the sky that dawn was over an hour away.

Gaspar lay back down and replayed the words spoken to him.

"If I release you, then what will be of my life?" he asked.

"Then your life will be yours," came the answer and it was the voice of the man.

Gaspar closed his eyes as tears fell down the sides of his face and to his neck.

"This is the only life I know," he thought. "What would I be without this purpose?"

"That is for you to choose," came the voice again.

The tears stopped. Gaspar was now confused. There was nothing of his life that he felt was not his choice. He loved his studies and even more he loved his quest and this search for the new prophet. It was everything he had decided his life should be.

"This is who I am!" he declared to himself.

"And so it is..." was the answer.

CHAPTER TWENTY-EIGHT

Each night Melchior would set up a small table with his instruments. Beside him would sit one of the acolytes of his temple with a quill and blank parchment.

"I will call out a measurement, but do not write it down unless I say it twice," was Melchior's one and only instruction. The acolyte nodded.

Melchior would look up at Jupiter and though his eyes would confirm that all was unfolding as he predicted, he would not feel any calm until his measurements confirmed it.

The fact that the trip had been decided upon based on his projections about Jupiter weighed heavily upon him. Each day he would look upon the group of men and a voice inside would say "they are all here at risk because of you."

In his heart Melchior knew this was not entirely true. Several other of the most talented astronomers had confirmed, and continued to confirm, all that he said. Yet each night his heart would quicken until those numbers were scratched upon the paper.

One evening I went and sat upon a large rock near him. I pulled my feet up and hugged my knees to my chest as I watched him work.

"Do you remember that first time we met? I tried so hard to tease you and you would not bite," I said with a laugh.

Melchior let the instrument he was holding swing to his side. I saw his other hand clench and then loosen. He looked down to the ground and I saw him swallow. Then finally he turned to me.

"I wanted to bite, Balthasar. I thought you were a fool and wanted to inform you of how much of a fool you were ... but I had always been told that to entertain a fool with my wisdom only shows me to be a fool as well. I stated my belief though because I did not think I should suffer you entirely, and that showed me that you were far from a fool," he said and smiled at me. "That next night when you spoke and I knew that I had your respect changed something within me. From that night I knew I was no longer a boy playing at being a priest. I knew my place, my calling and my role in the awakening. Tonight my friend, you have reminded me of that again."

That was the last day that Melchior heard the voice of doubt within him.

As my qualms had been erased during my last meal with my family, I had other things to occupy my thoughts. I too would look upon the group with a sense of responsibility, but this was outweighed by pride and excitement. This would become more so as a dream was relayed or I saw my fellow travellers smiling simply for the joy of being a part of this grand adventure.

Each day Jupiter moved closer to Venus and each day we were closer to our prophet. We were safe and well fed. There was hardly anything that we could have wished more for.

Then that graceful first week ended. It was after that we moved out of our beloved region and land of Babylonia. We were still safe and well fed, but now some dynamics would change. We were in foreign lands run by foreign religions with the watchful eye of Rome ever present. Now we would need all the diplomacy skills we could muster.

Our daily plans were adjusted somewhat. We would rise to be ready to travel soon after dawn, but not before one of our swordsmen would ride ahead as a scout and then return to report on what lay ahead.

"There are no villages for miles," would mean we had a day of simple travel with our stored resources as our food and fuel.

"There is a small village ahead," would mean a small envoy would travel ahead to introduce ourselves and see what the village might trade with us.

"There is a large town ahead." Well, that was a whole other scenario that required more than a simple introduction.

Of the three of us, we would take turns as to who would lead these expeditions into a town or city. We would take several swordsmen, a few elder priests as well as some servants. We would present at the town limits or the city walls and ask who their king or tribal leader was, then request audience with them.

Mostly this went well, sometimes it went less so.

We would often be greeted with a tepid and suspicious hospitality. They would listen politely to our story of the search for our prophet. They would nod amiably but all the while they and their closest men would be weighing and measuring our every word.

When we finished the questions would start and each one was spoken not from interest so much as to test us. For many leaders, the very origin of our men and the very nature of our religion made us no threat whatsoever, but to encounter us far from our home in a time of conquests from the west made things different. In our times everyone was a threat until proven otherwise.

"How do I know Herod is not paying you to spy on us?" one of them asked.

"Spying is of no interest to us. We have nothing to gain from an alliance with Herod," spoke Melchior and the truth of this could not be denied.

"Why would holy men need to travel with swordsmen?" asked another.

"Because even holy men bleed when cut with a knife," I answered. "We would love to arrive to our prophet whole and complete."

Our host chuckled at my answer. "You do understand that in such times we must be certain of who we welcome into our walls," he continued.

"Of course we do. That is why we promise you our peace and honour as we pass through," I replied.

Only one tribal king refused us welcome. We never even made it into his walls.

"Sire says he cannot compromise the town safety without endorsement from Herod himself," was our response.

Gaspar sighed but nodded as he turned his camel away. "And I too would not risk offending the man who killed his own heirs."

That day and night we made camp in a nearby field, with the shelter of a small mountain to our side. Gaspar's initial acceptance of the nearby city's refusal of us wore thinner as the day went on.

"You know we will probably get more refusals as we get closer to Jerusalem. The word of our caravan would be ahead of us now. Other cities are probably preparing to refuse us even as we sit here," he spat as we sat by the fire that night after our evening meal.

"No, I don't believe that is so at all. They may hear of us, but they will also be hearing that we are travelling in peace and honour. That will offer us much favour," I replied.

"Still, how much food do we have? Are the animals rested enough if we need to flee a distance from a town?" Gaspar went on as he rubbed his temples with his palms.

"Brother, you are tired and this refusal is weighing upon you more than it should have," said Melchior with concern.

"More than it should have!" Gaspar flung his hands to his knees. "How can you both be so relaxed at today's outcome? We are only half-way to our finish—what if this continues?"

"It is but one refusal!" Melchior said.

"Gaspar, have you lost faith after one denial of hospitality?" I asked him.

At this Gaspar stood. He clenched his right hand into a fist and shook it at both of us.

"How dare you question my faith! How dare you!" he yelled and I saw everyone close by turn to look at him. "Me—the one with the greatest faith of us all! This…" he pointed to the sky. "This is all I ever thought about. All I have ever dreamt about. I would die before I see us fail and you dare to question my faith!"

"Gaspar, you have either had too much wine—or not enough! You know we respect you as much as we respect our fathers. Please, go and rest. We will talk more in the morning. You know as well as I do that we are all tired from travelling. We will all be clearer after a night's sleep," I said gently and stood to take his arm to walk him to his tent.

Gaspar shrugged it off and grunted before storming off. He did not go to his tent immediately, instead wandering to the outskirts of the campsite.

As he wandered past the swordsmen on guard, the man called out to him.

"Sire, this is the boundary of our watch…"

Gaspar ignored him and walked to the mountainside. Once there he stumbled in the darkness, but soon found a place a little way up where he could look down upon the tents, animals and men.

He thought about crying. That would help release what was within him right now but that was also very juvenile and feminine.

"I won't let myself be reduced to a crying girl," he thought. "Why don't they understand me?"

He sat for a while longer and then looked up at Jupiter. It was getting so close to Venus now. He lifted his hand and pulled his fingers onto his palm so only his thumb was extended. That width of his thumb covered the two with no problem.

"That my son is about as close as any two planets will get. When they get this close, you know something special is being told by Mazda," his father had told him so many years ago as they watched another conjunction.

At the thought of his father, Gaspar allowed some slow, quiet tears to fall as he wished that he was with him now.

"He always understood me," Gaspar thought then looked back upon the campsite. "These men never truly will but I will do my work regardless."

With that he stood, brushed the dust off his robes and began to walk back. Gaspar was far from calmed but then this was a normal state of being for him. To be calm would have frightened and confused him as much as his state of tension would to me. His manner had settled though as he walked back and he resolved to not be so emotive when he spoke. It was one of the agreements as a group and so he must abide.

Gaspar made way to his tent. He did not see it necessary to make amends tonight. He would be clearer in the morning and to sleep now after his mini retreat without any other words spoken would take him into a wonderful dream space. That much he was certain of right now.

As he entered into camp he passed through where the servants' camels were hobbled for the night and he saw Mahesh taking a silver box from one of my camels. It was not small or large but sizeable, engraved with spirals and roses entwined. From the way Mahesh handled it, Gaspar knew what was inside was precious and delicate. Gaspar also knew he had not seen it before.

He was behind my servant before Mahesh could hear him approach.

"What is inside that?" Gaspar demanded.

Mahesh turned and saw Gaspar's dark eyes and instinctively pulled the box to his chest. "It—it—it is some personal effects for my master," he stuttered, hoping that would end this but knowing it wouldn't.

"Open it!" bellowed Gaspar.

"Sire, with respect, I do not think I can..." Mahesh reasoned.

"OPEN IT!" screamed Gaspar and even the camels turned their heads to see what was happening.

Mahesh took a breath and looked down at the box.

"If you do not open it, I will," hissed Gaspar and he reached for the box.

Mahesh pulled it against him again and slowly slipped the catch open, then lifted the hinged lid. Inside was revealed rows of Elana's honey cakes. Once they had filled the box but there was space where some had been taken.

Inside that box was my parting gift from my wife.

"Here, it is not much but I know any small comfort will make your days easier," she had said as she handed them to me. "Perhaps when you eat one you can imagine me giving you a kiss goodnight."

That was exactly what I did. Each night in the privacy of my room or tent, when I finally had time and space to myself, Mahesh would bring me the box and open it. I would gently take one out and slowly eat it. With each bite I would think about my beloved. Some nights I would go back to when she first came to temple. Other nights I would see her holding each of our daughters as they were born. Most nights I thought about her strength and how she had travelled so far with only her faith in her bah-ra'an to comfort her.

It was my kiss goodnight from her in more ways than I can describe. When Gaspar looked into the box he saw something else. He saw selfish-ness. He saw deception. He saw everything that he feared would destroy the very essence of our journey. Gaspar stepped away from Mahesh and stormed into the campsite.

"Balthasar!" he screamed my name as he made way to my tent. "Balthasar! Come out here!"

From inside I could hear the urgency in Gaspar's voice and rose im-mediately, pushing through the flaps of the tent. As I straightened I saw him walking to me, his fists swinging by his sides. Gaspar walked so fast his robes clung to his legs.

He was before me within seconds. I opened my mouth to speak but before the first word came out, Gaspar's right fist collided with my face. As the ground hit the back of my head, all went black.

I am not sure how long I was unconscious. I was told later it was mere seconds, yet when I opened my eyes an entirely different scene of camp was before me. Kneeling over me was Mahesh and my grandson Erasmus.

"Sire, Sire..." Mahesh kept saying until he saw within me some life.

To my other side Erasmus watched me with a look of sheer terror. My eyes regained more focus and beyond the two faces above me I saw Gaspar, restrained by two of his priests. One of his legs flailed and I realised that not content with his one superb punch he now wanted to kick me as well. The two men struggled to hold him and I saw a third join them.

Around us every priest with us had run to see what was happening. Some were yelling at Gaspar to compose himself. Others were calling to me to see that I was alright. Mahesh yelled to my other servants to get some water and cloths to wipe my face. I could even hear horses crying out in the confusion.

It was the most chaos and drama I had ever encountered. It even made the most intense days of our grand meeting seem mild. One of our physicians came and knelt by me and I closed my eyes to shut at least some of the bedlam out. The worst part was that I did not even know why I had been struck. I thought back to our conversation at the fire as my face was dabbed and washed.

Melchior stood to one side of this scene and watched in stillness. Beside him stood his butler and two other of his priests. Melchior looked as Gaspar still struggled against the arms that held him. He shook his head and walked towards Gaspar, even as he still threw a foot towards me.

"Gaspar! Please, show some decorum," he said with an authority that no one had heard before. Even Gaspar paused as he heard the energy in his voice.

"Do you know what he has done? He has deceived us!" shouted Gaspar.

Melchior screwed up his face. "Who? Balthasar?"

"Yes! He hides food from the rest of us!" shouted Gaspar so that as many people as possible could hear and he looked around to see just what an audience had gathered.

I was sitting up now and looked at Gaspar. "That is what this is about? What food?"

Gaspar stopped his struggle, though the men would not let him go just yet.

"I saw your Kshatrapa getting the box from one of your camels. Filled with sweets that you do not share!" he spat at me. "Go Kshatrapa! Get the box so your master can show everyone!"

Mahesh looked at me and I nodded. "Go, get the box, Mahesh." I looked to Melchior and I have to admit there was some shame on my face and within me. We had all made such agreements to unite and be as one that my little secret now seemed so much larger. Melchior looked at me and I could see a plea in his eyes as though he was almost begging for all of this to be a lie.

Mahesh was back quickly with the box. "Open it," I asked of him and he did, walking up to Melchior and lifting the lid once more.

Melchior sighed and closed his eyes. When he opened them a second later, he looked to Gaspar. "This is the reason for your violence?"

"What else does he have? What else does he hide? We may suffer more refusals and go without fresh food, and he keeps secret stores." Gaspar spoke like a magistrate would at a trial.

"These are Elana's honey cakes are they not?" Melchior asked me.

"Yes," I said as I put my hand up to my face. It felt like it was on fire where Gaspar's hand had connected with it. In an instant a fresh cool cloth was being pressed against it. This stopped me from saying more and Gaspar snickered.

"No other words to even make excuse for yourself. That is how little regard he has for us," Gaspar spat.

There have been few times in my life that I truly angered and this moment was the greatest of them all. I stood myself up and would have made way to Gaspar but I faltered as I found my feet, making Mahesh and the physician rush to my side.

"Give me the box," I asked and put out my hands. Mahesh placed the box within them. "These were the last thing my wife gave to me. They may look like food, but they are more than that to me. I do not think I can excuse what seems to look like something else to others, but know I did not hide them with any malicious intent." I held the box out towards Melchior. "Here take them. Let everyone have them."

"Take them Melchior," said Gaspar who I am sure would have if his arms were not still held.

Melchior shook his head and I saw some red come into his face. Then through gritted teeth he spoke.

"I cannot believe that we have been made to suffer such a—a farce because of some cakes." Melchior looked around at all the men who gathered around us. "Who amongst you is truly hungry? I do not mean that sensation where you seek comfort, but that which your body is crying out for nutrition. Raise your hand or speak now!"

Everyone remained silent and not one hand lifted in the air. Melchior watched Gaspar's face as this happened and he saw something shift and change. When Gaspar looked back towards him, his eyes had lost their wildness and his body was finally soft. The men holding him let their hands fall away.

"We are far from destitute or struggling. Our stores are more than abundant and I know with all my heart that Mazda would never desert us or make us want for what we need to survive. So one man holds a gift from his wife for his personal indulgence. When we ride how many of you have bread tucked in a sleeve should you not want to wait for the next meal?"

Melchior looked around and saw not one person ready to challenge what he said. Then he walked to me, pushing the box back against me.

"Brother, keep your gift. You have every right to it. You provide us with all we need in other ways every day," he said to me with his voice still strong though I thought I saw his lip shake.

Melchior turned to everyone around us. "I suggest you all now go to your tents and shelters for the night. We will not travel tomorrow but take a day of rest. Our bodies and spirits need some time to recuperate before we get closer to Jerusalem."

Not one person, not even Gaspar could argue with this. We had pushed ahead each day with a determined and even mindless dedication to our goal. It had worn on us physically but not come out in us emotionally until tonight. I looked down at the silver box and wondered just how something so simple had made us have such a dramatic event. I was thankful for this though. Better a box of cakes to make us stop and take stock of ourselves than something more damaging or disruptive.

Everyone now made way to his space for the night. They did so quietly and slowly, still in some shock at what they had witnessed. Gaspar was left alone to walk by himself. Even when in his tent, his butler made little conversation for which he was glad. He lay upon the blankets that formed his mattress and closed his eyes.

Gaspar knew sleep was far away as he could feel his heart pounding still. He soon drifted off though and was within his dreams.

He was standing in a room that had a long table down the centre. It was filled with a feast but only the man was sitting at the table. He was now the oldest that Gaspar had seen him; around thirty years or slightly more, his skin deep brown from the sun, his hair even longer than before.

The man looked up and beckoned Gaspar to come sit with him. Then he broke some bread and offered it to Gaspar along with a cup of wine.

"Eat this, and know I will never let you go hungry," he said to Gaspar.

CHAPTER TWENTY-NINE

When Gaspar woke it was as though the events of the night before were as much of a dream as that of sitting with the man at the table. The longer he lay in his bed thinking about what he had done to me and the group, the more shame he felt. Gaspar was glad that his father was no longer alive to be able to hear about this.

He called out to his butler who entered the tent with a skin of water and a cloth, ready to bathe him. The butler began, pouring water upon the cloth and wiping down Gaspar's legs and feet.

"It will be nice for both us when we can next bathe near a river or even better, in a home," Gaspar said awkwardly trying to start conversation.

"Yes, Sire," was the simple response.

"Onom, what was spoken of me last night after the ... incident?" Gaspar asked.

Onom stopped moving the cloth and looked up at Gaspar. He looked straight into his master's eyes and without any fear, but immense love and honour he spoke.

"Sire, we are truly concerned for you; especially the men from your temple. We have never seen you act so," Onom said.

Gaspar nodded. "You never will again."

I had risen some time earlier. I was sitting outside after slowly eating some breakfast. I was eternally grateful for Melchior declaring a day of no travel. My face was still on fire despite the salves placed upon it. My head ached and even my neck was tender. A day of bouncing upon a camel would have been torture in this condition.

As Gaspar walked towards me he saw I was cradling my right cheek in my hand. When I lowered my hand he gasped. My face was now a deep red with shades of black appearing. My right eye was half closed due to the swelling across my cheekbone where his fist had landed. He shook his head and clenched his jaw.

I saw him open and close his hands by his side and part of me flinched imagining him preparing another blow to my body. Of course this would never happen. Instead Gaspar walked to me and bent down, kissing me upon the wounded right cheek, then upon the left.

"Forgive me, brother," he said.

"Of course," I replied.

Our morning meeting was called, led by Melchior.

"Who would like to begin? Any dreams or ideas to share?" he said.

Gaspar looked down, knowing that many would be expecting some official apology but this was far from the truth. Over half of us had dreamt of the man the previous night. Some like Gaspar had seen him at a long table set for a feast, and then been offered bread and wine. For others he simply sat and held their hand, inviting the dreamer to pray with him.

"He was offering me comfort, for the parts within me that are still scared of what lies ahead, not just with this journey but for my spirit," one priest said with such honesty.

It was the underlying theme of all the dreams; an offering of security, a promise of protection and the clearing of our doubts. No man held a grudge against Gaspar for what had occurred. In retrospect he had been somewhat the sacrificial lamb for us. Gaspar had allowed his anger and fear to surface for us all. We didn't understand it so much at the time, but each of the men with us had gone to their sleep that night reflecting upon what was within them at the moment.

For some it was their own anger at elements of the journey. For others it was the fear of being killed by a Roman. Each one of us had looked into what was pulling us from our faith and why we were travelling. The monotony of riding and pushing into a new land had washed our focus into a grey hue. Gaspar had helped us get back to some colour.

A day of rest was perfect for resetting and allowing the messages of our dreams to take hold in our spirits, and we had chosen well for our location. Nearby was a fabulous well for gathering water that was crisp and fresh. We emptied out canteens and filled them new. Our animals feasted on some shrubs or slept and let their limbs rest. Their carers took the time to examine them thoroughly for scratches, marks or swelling that needed tending to. The well offered them plenty of water to wash the animals also.

Our swordsmen took extra sleep. Our butlers washed clothes. Our cooks sorted and refreshed our food. Acolytes arranged scrolls. Priests wrote more scrolls. It was productive as much as it was relaxed.

Nearby the mountain looked over us. I sat during the early afternoon looking at it, and something about it seemed familiar. I imagined walking to it and climbing up to see if there were any caves that might be used for retreat. Then I laughed. Every mountain was a reminder of the one my father had left me upon all those years ago.

I thought back to that night and the boy I had been. For a moment I didn't feel so different despite there being over forty years between us. I closed my eyes and returned to when I had lay there, too scared to sleep and aching to be home with my family. Then I opened my eyes and looked around me, now surrounded by all these men who were family, friends and so much more.

I had never had another dream so vivid or meaningful as the one I had upon returning home. Others had taken on the mantle of dreamers in my place. I closed my eyes once more and tried to feel into what it had been like to wake and remember what I had been shown: the star leading me home had been so different to what we were seeing now. It was not the same at all. I did not feel lost or dependent upon its glow to lead me.

Now the star was like a friend reminding me of my faith and the promise of the awakening. When I was that little boy standing before the priests at temple, watching their reaction to what I told them, I could never have imagined that one dream would have led to this nor that it would have taken that long to manifest such a result.

I took a deep breath and called to my bah-ra'an. I did not hear any words. The only sensation I felt was some music that danced within me. I could not help but smile.

The next day we continued on. No other village or town refused us. As we had hoped, the news of our journey was travelling well ahead of us as well as the manner in which we behaved. You have the saying that "actions speak louder than words" and in our time we had something similar; "act as your truth and no lies of you will be believed." This was serving us well.

As we got closer to Jerusalem the presence of Roman centurions grew. They patrolled throughout the region of Judea to keep a presence through intimidation and threats. Even a declaration from Herod read aloud while the soldier sat upon his horse could send shivers down a spine.

"I have never met any men like this in all my travels," whispered Mahesh to me after one experience with them.

He was right - there had never been any men like this in this region. Even the Egyptian patrols under Thutmose III were never this dark.

"A delicate claim of power needs all the control it can muster," I replied.

They were no concern to us at all. Most encounters were more than pleasant, with the chief centurion greeting us with full knowledge of who we were and why we travelled.

Then one day we saw ahead of us a troop of around twenty centurions approaching us. We had never met with so large a contingent and our swordsmen drew in tight, ready for them.

I put my hand up. "Remain calm," I turned and called to our men. I heard it being repeated along the line to the ones out of earshot.

The Romans were soon upon us and I waved Mahesh and another one who could understand their language to my side to interpret in case my

Latin would fail me.

"Good day to you travellers. We have heard much of your journey and Herod sends us ahead to greet you!" the chief said with the most forced diplomatic smile I had ever seen.

"Tell Herod that we thank him for the welcome ... but that we thought Jerusalem was some days travel in the distance?" I said.

The chief laughed at this.

"All of Judea is Jerusalem to Herod," he replied and nodded his head to the land behind us. "You entered his home some days ago."

"Thank him for the correction and we hope the welcome will continue," I said.

"But of course! Herod awaits you in the city. In the meantime I will be leaving five of my men to ensure you safe escort to him," the chief replied.

Something in my spine tingled as I heard those words. Afterwards Melchior, Gaspar and anyone who caught them said the same was felt in them. Here was the perfect way for Herod to truly measure us before we arrived upon his doorstep.

If we said no, then we would seem to want to conceal something and truly we had nothing to hide. To say no would be the ultimate insult to Herod and in short an act of aggression. Even with our swordsmen, we were no match for twenty well trained and well armed centurions. The journey would have ended there and then.

If we said yes, then we were offered extra safety and sure passage to Jerusalem. It was a very straightforward decision. I looked to Gaspar and Melchior who both nodded.

"It would be an honour to have Herod's escort," I said with my hand on my heart.

The chief waved his hand towards us and five of his men rode forward. Two took their place before us, one to each side while the fifth rode to the back of the caravan.

"These men are now your servants," the chief said as he bowed his head. "We look forward to seeing you in Jerusalem. With that he turned his horse and led his remaining entourage away.

"Oh wonderful," sighed Gaspar. "Five men to protect sixty, who cannot speak our language and who know nothing of our beliefs."

"I know - it is perfect. They will keep to themselves, as will we. Let us just see this as the token act of approval we need from Herod," I replied.

"Oh Mazda, you truly work in mysterious ways," said Gaspar to the sky and we all held back our laughter.

Later we made camp as dusk fell. We had pushed our riding that day for as long as we could until we found the best possible place for camp. Tonight was special. Tonight was the night that Jupiter would touch Venus. It had been getting closer just as we ventured closer to our prophet. The previous night they had been so close that it was beyond words. Jupiter had sat to the top right of Venus, with the tiniest line of sky between them. As our servants moved about us setting up our tents, starting fires and preparing food, we priests could not help but look upwards.

The two planets were the first to light up that night and grew brighter as the rest of the sky darkened. I believe that we all stood for over an hour in silence, taking it in, hardly believing what we saw. I could feel every magus in our homeland watching as well. In fact I could feel every astronomer everywhere who was watching.

As chores were completed, even the servants gathered to watch as well. I looked across to Melchior and saw he had tears streaming down his face. Gaspar had a grin from ear to ear. I saw other priests also in tears and smiles or both. Some had dropped to their knees and were moving their lips in prayer.

I put my hand upon my heart and called out to Mazda. In return I heard my bah-ra'an.

"Peace be with you" was what I heard and I understood that beyond the words.

As Jupiter now touched Venus we were all witnessing not just a unique event, we were also welcoming a unique era.

I looked once more to Melchior. He was tracing a line from the conjunction to the horizon.

"The road to Jerusalem is north of the star. We will need to be just south of the city," he said.

"It's not Jerusalem then, you are certain?" asked Gaspar quietly.

Melchior nodded.

CHAPTER THIRTY

In Bethlehem, Joseph walked outside and leant his back heavily upon the wall beside the doorway. He closed his eyes and began to pray to Yahweh.

"You have delivered us this far, do not leave us now," he said to his god.

Joseph was so hot even though the sun had dropped and night was upon them. His brow was wet with sweat and he wiped at it with his shirt. The journey to Bethlehem had been a trial filled with blessings. Each day he would travel with a heavy heart as he watched Mary with her huge belly rocking upon the donkey. Yet each day they would be sent someone to offer them food, fresh water or even somewhere shaded for her to rest. Each day Joseph would pray anew for another day filled with miracles to keep Mary and the baby alive.

As they had made way along the road that approached Bethlehem he had seen Mary wince and grab at her stomach. He had stopped walking and turned to her.

"My beloved, we are almost there. Please stay strong and soon we will be at my uncle's home," he had said to her as much to convince himself they had not much further to go.

Mary nodded. The pains had started some time ago but she had tried to hide them. She too wanted to make it to the sanctity of Bethlehem and had every faith they would before the baby's time.

Each day when she would feel the weakest she would call out to Yahweh. "Please take care of us," she would ask simply. It was at those times that an angel would appear by her side. Now as her pains grew she saw the angel was joined by two others; one was walking ahead while the other walked on the opposite side.

Mary knew there was nothing to worry about and now when she looked up she saw the buildings of Bethlehem grow even closer.

"Blessed be to my god," she thought and rubbed her stomach, but within a moment she was overtaken by the worst of all her pains. Mary doubled over and grabbed at the saddle of the donkey fearing she would fall off. She could not help but cry out.

"Mary!" Joseph was by her side in an instant. He could see in her face they could not ride for much longer. They were almost upon the town but his uncle's home was on the far side, almost another hour of riding up and over the hill.

"There is an inn not far. We will stop there for the night until we know you are settled."

The use of the word 'settled' was quite futile. They both knew Mary was in labour and needed somewhere safe and clean for her to deliver.

"Hold tight Mary. We have been watched over for the journey, Yahweh will not forsake us now," he said and truly believed it.

Mary looked up and behind Joseph she could see the three angels walking ahead of them. One stopped and turned to look at her with a smile. She smiled back knowing they would make sure all was arranged for them.

When the next pain came, Mary bit hard into her lip to stop crying out so she wouldn't distract Joseph. They were soon at the door of the inn. Mary looked up at the windows wondering which room their child would arrive within.

"Oh my son, I have no rooms. We are full because of the census. Have you no family here?" the innkeeper asked.

"I do Sir, but they are out towards the fields on the south. My wife—my wife is with child. It is soon to arrive. Her pains are strong. We just need one night for her and the baby," Joseph explained.

The innkeeper looked past Joseph to Mary and saw the look on her face. He had seven children and had seen that look seven times upon his wife's face. This woman was closer than either she or her husband realised. He could not send them on to another inn—they were all full too. The innkeeper rubbed his forehead, then he pulled Joseph close to him and spoke quietly so Mary could not hear.

"Son, your wife has only hours. Go to my stables. It is not the best I can offer but it is all I can offer. It is safe and there is fresh hay. Make her a bed and keep her calm. I will get my wife to gather the midwife," he said urgently and pointed to the wooden doors to the left of the inn. He then feigned a smile as he looked at Mary while Joseph made his way back to her.

"Mary, he has no rooms but has offered us his stable for the night. He will also send some women to care for you," Joseph explained.

Mary nodded. Right now all she heard was that there was somewhere to stop and rest with shelter. A palace would not have sounded any better.

As Joseph walked her into the stable he looked around and saw a cow tied in one corner. A donkey was also roped nearby. They both looked at him with big eyes and then turned away. He stood Mary near the opposite wall so she would have something to hold onto while he gathered a fresh bale of hay to break up. Over this he spread their blanket, then he helped Mary to lie down. Joseph rolled up his satchel to act as a pillow.

"Thank you," Mary said softly and closed her eyes, instinctively try-ing to rest between her pains.

Joseph looked away. When he looked into Mary's eyes he saw wis-dom beyond her years that made him trust and keep his faith in this child. Yet when she closed her eyes all he saw was a young girl in pain and that tore at his heart. He took her hand in his and kissed it gently.

"All will be well," he said tenderly.

Mary opened her eyes and looked at Joseph with a smile. Behind him she could see the three angels now standing and they too smiled and nod-ded, as though repeating Joseph's words.

Joseph turned to see what Mary was looking at and he too saw three figures standing there in the stable. It was the innkeeper's wife with two other women from the town. The innkeeper's wife held fresh swaddling to wrap the child when they were born. The second woman, a midwife, held a basket within which were twine, scissors, a knife and herbal salve. The third had empty hands but a bosom full of milk ready for the baby's first drink.

The midwife put the basket down and then came and knelt by Mary. She placed her hands upon Mary's belly just as Mary had another contraction.

"My dear, my name is Anna. I will help bring your child. We don't have too long to go. Let me feel your opening," she said with a clarity and calm gained from attending dozens of births.

"Anna is my mother's name," said Mary as her skirts were pulled up.

"Well that is a fine start for us to be together then," said Anna as she expertly pushed her fingers between Mary's legs. "You are close but we will have some time to truly ready you."

Anna looked to Joseph. "You have done your part. Why not go and find yourself a meal while we do our work."

Joseph shook his head. "No. I cannot leave her," he said bluntly.

The innkeeper's wife put her hand upon his shoulder. "Then go sit outside in the fresh air. You can be close by but this is a time for women."

Joseph had nodded and got up to walk outside but not before stopping and looking at Mary one last time.

"All will be well," Mary said and Joseph nodded.

So Joseph looked up at the sky and continued to pray. He knew nothing of the stars and the story they were telling to hundreds of men. All he knew now was that he wanted his wife and child to be safe.

That he had risked Mary and the child for the sake of being counted in a census weighed heavy within him. He finished his prayers with a curse for Herod.

Then he sat upon the ground, pulled his knees to his chest and rested his head upon them. Joseph was exhausted in every way possible. He had walked six days to be here. He had spent every moment worried about Mary and now his heart ached to have left her in the hands of these wom-

248

en, no matter how trusted they were.

Joseph closed his eyes and before he knew it, he was asleep and dreaming.

In his dream Joseph looked up from where he sat to see three men upon camels looking down at him.

"Who are you?" he asked but before they could answer a hand upon his shoulder woke him. It was the midwife.

"The child is here," she said quietly.

Joseph had been asleep much longer than he could have guessed. When he walked back inside the stable the wet nurse was folding her dress over her bosom as the innkeeper's wife was placing the baby back into Mary's arms. Mary had been washed and the salve placed upon her. The afterbirth had been gathered within a sheet ready to be carried away.

Mary's face was still red from her efforts though; the only indicator in this moment of what had just been completed. She smiled upon the baby with such adoration and love that Joseph could do nothing but watch them in silent awe. He put his hand upon his heart and felt it finally slow down for the first time in over a week.

It was done. The child was here. The surroundings were of no matter. Mary was alive as was the child.

The three women walked to the door but not before the innkeeper's wife spoke one last time.

"This is a blessed birth. He may not be born in rich surrounds but he is born of much fortune," she said.

Joseph nodded. "Indeed he is," he responded.

As they had travelled Joseph had imagined the worst of scenarios and not one had manifested. Instead their timing and circumstance had been of the greatest fate he could have hoped for.

Joseph reached out to touch the arm of Anna as she passed him by on her way out.

"Thank you," he said and tears filled his eyes as he looked at the other women hoping they knew the acknowledgement was for them as well. He could not say anymore and he did not need to; they knew too well what was in his heart.

The women nodded, gave a gentle smile and were on their way.

Joseph went to Mary who had not taken her eyes off her new babe. He knelt down kissing her on the forehead and then kissing the child in her arms.

"Were you told of his name?" Joseph asked her.

Mary nodded and looked to Joseph. "He is Yeshua."

CHAPTER THIRTY-ONE

The next night Jupiter remained upon Venus and once more we all watched this miracle with wonder and joy. In Jerusalem, Herod met with his astronomers as they spun more incredible stories of this event speaking of his glory.

Herod sat with his shoulders squared, his hands held in fists and his teeth locked tight against each other. He listened with an angry and silent impatience that made his eyes burn into yours if you dared look into them. Thankfully the astronomers knew better than to do this. It was his advisors who risked a glance every few minutes to measure their king who saw it.

When the astronomers finished Herod did not speak or move for several minutes. The astronomers looked to the advisors who watched and waited upon their king: their concern growing every second. Still Herod did not move. It was as though he could not see anyone around him.

As the glances between the men around him grew more anxious, his most senior advisor finally stepped toward Herod.

"Sire…" he said in a low voice hoping to break the trance Herod seemed to be locked in. The advisor called out several times more and was about to touch Herod's arm when the king turned to look at him.

"Send them away," he muttered.

The advisor turned to the astronomers, who looked to him curious as to what had been said.

"The king thanks you for your presentation. You are dismissed."

The men looked at him as though expecting something more to be said, only to have the advisor scowl at them and wave his hand to the door.

"Leave! Now!" he yelled and the men left as quickly as they could.

The senior advisor turned back to Herod who was once more blankly staring ahead. The other advisors now drew in close also and waited for Herod to speak. Without moving a muscle, not even his eyes, Herod formed his words slowly, calmly and quietly.

"I want you to speak to every astronomer in Judea. I want each story there is of this star. Do not tell them you are from the palace. Do not threaten or harm them. I need to know what else this star is telling."

The advisors sent out palace employees dressed as commonly as they could. They were given a script and the very barest of information to act upon.

"You just need to sound interested. That you have noted this in the sky and wonder what the gods—or god is trying to tell us," was what they were told. "If you are asked where you are from, state a village some distance away. Say you have been travelling because of the census."

This was the line each of the ten men stuck to. Some said they were merchants: others had a trade. No one would have suspected them at all and they all returned to Jerusalem with the same story.

"The Jews are waiting for their new king. The one who will restore their kingdom. He is due in the sixty-sixth generation which is now being born. The bright star sits in the house of Judea and speaks of a new king."

Herod felt a rush of heat hit his chest and his heart jumped within its space making him catch his breath as the words went into him. He looked down and desperately tried to slow his breath so as to appear calm and gathered before his advisors. There were a thousand voices inside him all calling out with a different story.

"You have nothing to fear..."

"These are simple astronomers playing with hundreds of years of silly beliefs..."

"You have an army..."

Every voice clamoured to slow the one voice that spoke the loudest, that made his heart race and that made his breath quicken.

"You fool!" it cried out. "You sit here and wait for something or some-one to save you!"

"I have nothing to act upon," he called back to it.

"Oh yes you do!" was the reply.

Herod looked up at his advisors. His eyes wide and his breath finally slowed.

"Where are the Babylonians?" he asked.

"They are but a few days travel from us, Sire," one responded.

Herod nodded and a smile crossed his face for the first time in weeks.

"Make sure they are given the grandest of welcomes. I will take audi-ence with them as soon as they arrive," he directed.

Back at our camp we could see Jerusalem in the distance. Melchior took his measurements again.

"Now we are even closer I am more sure of where we should go," he said and looked just south of the city.

I nodded and put my hand upon my belly.

"Do you have stomach troubles?" Melchior asked me.

"No—I am feeling a new sensation within me that I have never felt before," I explained.

We were all feeling it. It was a weird combination of excitement and fear. Yes we had all felt something like that before but now as we stood so close to Jerusalem and the other town it amplified. Overlaying it was a sur-real calm. Even now as I tell you this I cannot put it fully into words but I know anyone reading this has felt something similar.

It is that sensation when things are about to change, when you are about to take that leap of faith with something within your life. You feel the excitement of heading into a new phase and era of your experience. Yet parts of you mourn what will be left behind and released. There is the exhilaration of bringing in the new, plus the fear of the very same.

It builds up, and within you this silent, and sometimes not so silent, battle plays out. You give yourself exit points, excuses and reasons to stay the same or turn back to the old. Then comes the point where every fibre of you knows that there is no way but to go forward. The fears do not fall away, but a new sense of acceptance and resignation sets in.

There is no other sensation that is so filled with its own contradictions and trials. Over my other lifetimes I grew to know that when I felt this I was indeed upon a huge key to expanding my soul connection regardless of the outcome, even when it cost me my life. That sensation is so human, yet so soulful at the same time.

What other choice is there but to dive even deeper within it?

So as I stood there with this mix churning within me I took a deep breath and called out to my bah-ra'an. As always it would rise above the chaos and show me clarity.

"Oh the wonders that will unfold..." it said to me and faded into the night.

Gaspar had been somewhat quiet since the incident with the honey cakes. Not that he had been completely silent; he still participated in our morning discussions or any other meetings with the group. Outside of these his contributions were minimal and measured.

It was not from shame, guilt or even being self-conscious. Gaspar had found a new connection with Yeshua in his dreams and it seemed the less he spoke in his waking hours, the stronger he could communicate in his sleep.

His dreams grew. They were no longer simple conversations with the young man; he could now see full tableaus of the man's life.

Gaspar saw him speaking before groups of people. He saw him being questioned and how he remained poised and clear in responding. Gaspar looked amongst the people who listened to Yeshua and he saw something within them open and blossom as they listened to his words.

On the night that the Venus and Jupiter conjunction was its brightest, Gaspar saw the entire scene of Yeshua's birth. It was as though he had stood within the body of another within the stable, watching with their eyes.

When he woke the next day a new calm was upon him, even though he was baffled at the location of the birth. He told us the story of what he had seen and we all listened enthralled. No one could speak for minutes when he finished.

"It seems to fit that the prophet should be a common man," he added after some time and we all nodded, still unable to say any words.

Others too had their dreams of Yeshua. They too now saw his teaching and sharing. Some even saw him healing.

"I feel he will be beyond any measure we have of a teacher," one priest said when he shared his dream.

As we got closer to Jerusalem the dreams magnified. We now knew this man would be more than we had ever imagined. As I stood there looking at Jerusalem with my hand on my stomach, that knowledge added to the fire within me.

Zarathustra has never been questioned or persecuted for his teachings—that we had known of. Our history had recorded him as a noble man, loved and revered, who brought us teachings when we needed them most. His story had been passed from generation to generation with respect and worship. Now all that he had been was just that; a story. There was no proof that he had even existed. No tomb, nor even his original writings, both of which would have decayed and gone out of existence centuries before even I was born.

We had clung onto the beauty of our prophet though. We had continued his story because within it we saw truths and values that were worth living our life by and that had proved themselves over and over. That had given us hope for this awakening. That had given us the faith to travel and to welcome our new prophet.

I will admit to you now that as I stood there feeling my emotions churn against each other, something within hesitated at the thought of being here in the reality of the story of our new prophet. Would it be as glorious as that of Zarathustra? Or would we see the more brutal truth of the life of a prophet?

Further to this what responsibility would we have in recording his story and *how* would we record it?

As this played in my mind I was pulled to look to the stars and breathe beyond what I could see. I went into the space I had known from my youth that took me past the limited and distracting thoughts of my mind. I felt what would unfold.

"His story will be magnificent" was what I heard and I knew this was the truth that would be remembered for eons to come.

CHAPTER THIRTY-TWO

Within Gaspar's dreams he kept seeing the events in Bethlehem unfold with such clarity that he had no doubt he was seeing a reality and not some symbology. He was correct.

Mary slept for most of the first day after the birth, waking only to feed Yeshua. Her milk flowed easily and readily. Joseph watched over them. His relief grew with each hour as he watched Mary regain her strength and he saw the baby eat with vigour.

"I have done well," he thought to himself and the grief at not getting Mary to his uncle's home in time slipped away.

Each day the midwife returned with fresh salve, a tincture to help Mary's milk and to massage her belly.

"When can we go to my uncle's?" Joseph asked.

"Not for a week," was the reply from the midwife. "Can you imagine being bounced upon a donkey after being through this?" she added with a laugh.

Joseph could not. He sent word through to his uncle to let them know of their circumstance. His uncle Ben and his wife Rachel arrived soon after to visit. Rachel ran into the stable, tears streaming down her face.

"Oh my, oh my," she said over and over, gathering Yeshua into her arms.

Ben looked about the stable with a plain expression that said more than any words needed. "Well I suppose that this was better than the roadside..." he muttered.

They left behind fresh clothes for them all as well as a basket of bread and fruit. When Ben placed it within the stable he saw empty baskets and a small pile of swaddling already there.

"The innkeeper and others have been most generous to us," replied

Joseph.

They had been incredibly generous. Every few hours someone arrived who had heard of their story. They came with fresh wrappings and diapers for Yeshua, and took soiled ones away to wash. They came with food, water and wine. Mary, Joseph and Yeshua wanted for nothing.

It had been a week from their arrival when Mary looked to Joseph. "I am ready for us to go to your uncle's," she said.

Joseph sent word and Ben came with two donkeys leading a cart large enough for Mary and Yeshua to lie within. The innkeeper and his wife came to farewell them.

"I hope one day we can repay you," Joseph said.

"There is no need," replied the innkeeper, putting his hand upon Joseph's shoulder.

Then with Ben and Joseph leading the animals they made way for Ben's farm.

"It almost feels odd to be in a bed," said Mary as she settled into their room.

"It almost feels odd to not have animals stare at us as we sleep," laughed Joseph.

Mary had Yeshua in her arms and gently kissed his forehead.

"I have had no more word as to what will happen," she said concerned and looked to Joseph.

"They know you need rest. I have been seeing things in my sleep," Joseph said.

"Why have you not said anything?"

"Because I too know that you need to rest."

Mary nodded. "Will you tell me what you see?" she asked.

Joseph closed his eyes and began.

There were three men, always three, no more, no less. They rode upon camels and seemed to be kings but they wore no crowns. One was quiet and calm, the second was smiling while the third was the one who spoke.

"We know of you. You are safe. You are the bringer of the new teacher of humanity. We are coming to welcome him."

He said the same thing every time while the others simply looked upon Joseph.

Within Gaspar's dreams this too was what he always chose to say when he saw this man standing over the baby and his mother. Gaspar saw them move to the uncle's home and knew they were now within more comfort.

He shared this with the meeting.

"This becomes more curious as we progress," I said.

"It is only fitting that he should have such a story," answered a priest. "Imagine a prophet with a boring story!"

We all laughed at this, even Gaspar. "Perhaps we should make better speed so that we reach him before he moves to Egypt."

Though it was a joke, we all knew we needed to make better time just as he suggested.

CHAPTER THIRTY-THREE

The following day we reached the outskirts of Jerusalem. As we made way on the road leading to the city's eastern gates a party of soldiers rode upon horses to greet us. There were at least fifty of them and they surrounded us within minutes. Their general came to us and smiled. His sword was within its sheath at his side but his hand was upon it.

"King Herod welcomes you to Jerusalem," he said with all the glory he could muster and he bowed as he sat in his saddle. "He asks that we escort you to the palace, for audience and certainly for a meal."

"But of course," I responded and returned the bow. "It is an honour to be welcomed like this and we look forward to meeting the king."

With that the general turned his horse to lead the way, calling out to his men to do likewise.

"I do not like this," muttered Gaspar beside me.

Neither did I but we rode to make good with Herod; to show him that we were men of peace and no threat. Sometimes you must do the things you have no desire for in order to achieve those you do. A meal and conversation with a king would seem nothing as part of our journey to meet our prophet.

The city gates opened and we heard a trumpet fanfare which was followed by the sound of flutes and drums. I looked beyond the gates to see a group of dancers moving to the music, the musicians were just ahead of them. The dancers jumped and pranced; some were waving ribbons as they moved while others had baskets of rose petals that they scattered.

I bit my lip to stop from laughing. It seemed so funny to see such a sight after weeks upon the road and it was also quite overwhelming. I turned to look at Gaspar whose face remained in a steely resolve. Melchior to my other side seemed amused and intrigued.

261

"Well this is certainly like no other welcome we have encountered," said Melchior as he smiled.

"I still do not like it," said Gaspar with his jaw clenched.

In-between them both I felt the extremes of what each of my brothers were experiencing. My stomach made itself known as once again that sensation that had taken residence there called out to me. I placed my hand upon my belly, took the deepest breath I could and called to my bah-ra'an.

"Let us remember who we are and why we are here," was all I could think to say. Then I squared my shoulders, nodded to each of my brothers and made way into the gates.

The spectacle of the musicians and dancers had attracted commoners who flocked to see us being led to the palace. I wondered what they had been told of us. Herod had in fact spun a fantastic tale; we were tribal kings visiting from the East who had come to see the wonder of Jerusalem in hope they could take some of Herod's knowledge to their homeland. To them we were a political pilgrimage and they ran to see what we looked like.

I glanced behind me to see how the rest of our caravan was doing. They were all smiles and laughter; enjoying the attention and the show that the people were putting on. Hands were waved at us, people called out words we could not understand and children weaved in and out of the animals to get as close as they could to us.

It was soon as much mayhem as any festivity and I even caught Gaspar finally smile at how ridiculous it all was.

In no time we were at another set of gates. These were the gates to the palace and before them was another contingent of thirty or so guards on foot. As we approached one turned and though I saw him yell a command I did not hear the words. The men parted to clear the way as the gates slowly opened.

The dancers and musicians fell to the sides of our caravan. It seemed they were not welcome within the palace, but they would now serve another purpose, providing an extra barrier for the commoners to have to get through in order to enter the gates. The razor sharp eyes of the palace guards watched as each one of us rode or walked through, knowing exactly who should be there or not.

As we entered the courtyard the sounds of the crowd and the music fell away. Soon the courtyard was filled with our entire group as well as the soldiers who had greeted us outside the city. Not one of us spoke a word. I looked to Gaspar whose face had an expression I had never seen before and it was what I was feeling for the first time since leaving home. It was fear.

The general from our escort appeared at the top of some stairs before us.

"Servants," he yelled. "Your quarters are to the north." He gestured to his left and a laneway that led off from the courtyard.

"Our servants remain with us," Gaspar called out.

"Oh please," the general put his hand upon his heart and feigned a smile. "Whilst you are guests of the palace, our servants will serve you. Let yours rest after their journey."

Gaspar leant forward to respond but I lifted my hand to stop him. I knew that now within the palace walls we were not at liberty to challenge anything, even when presented as hospitality.

Mahesh was at my side in an instant. "Sire..." he began, but my raised hand was now directed to him.

"Mahesh, please lead the servants to the quarters to rest and bathe," I said as calmly as I could.

Mahesh looked at me wide-eyed, but I simply nodded and with that he walked away and called out to all the servants to follow him. Some stayed mounted while others walked; the stables would also be down this alley-way.

Soon all that remained were the priests and our guardsmen. The general now looked directly at me.

"Tell your guards to relinquish their weapons," he said with a broad smile.

"That is outrageous!" yelled Gaspar.

"Oh please," the general said once more. "If we had planned an assassination we would have done so long ago and before you were within our walls. Besides look around you; our soldiers outnumber yours four to one. Taking your weapons is a mere gesture to show that you come in peace. Or does our king have this incorrect?"

"Of course he does not," said Melchior. "Conflict is the furthest thing from our intentions."

Behind me I heard our guards unsheathe their swords and daggers, and then there was the sound of their metal clinking together as the palace guards gathered them.

"So with those formalities aside, I ask you now to dismount. Your animals shall be watered and fed while you bathe and make ready for your audience with Herod."

Within minutes we were standing upon the ground, our animals were led away, and we stood silent once more waiting to be shown the way. Our servants were gone, our protection stripped. The only way we could have felt more naked was to have our clothes taken from us and now as we were led to the baths this was exactly what was to happen.

Bathed and with fresh clothes upon us we were led by the palace butlers into the hugest and most grand hallway any of us had ever been in. Two massive doors closed off the end before which we stood. Gaspar looked back upon the group of priests and without an ounce of fear, concern for consequence or regard for the palace staff he called out to them all.

"Remember who you are and why you are here. Let Balthasar, Melchior and I speak for you with your absolute trust and faith."

There were mumbles of agreement and heads were nodded amongst our brothers. To the sides of the hallway the palace butlers and servants glanced between them with looks of concern even though they had not understood one word.

I looked to Gaspar to my right with Melchior to his other side and nodded.

"You still do not like this do you?" I said to Gaspar.

"No," he replied softly. "And I am quite certain neither of you do either."

I looked to Melchior who was looking ahead stoically but I could see a flush of red upon his face that I knew could not be residual from the hot bath just taken. Turning to Gaspar I let out my breath.

"Indeed we do not," was all I could say and then the doors before us began to open.

They parted slowly as though for some more drama which we were quite expecting now. There was no music or dancers this time though. Beyond the open doors was revealed a spectacular room, every inch of which was adorned with gold leaf, or painted scenes or finely woven rugs. Four massive columns propped up each corner, carved and painted with victory scenes. There was scant furniture against the walls; some chairs, small tables and the odd stand holding a vase or urn.

It was essentially a huge open space, with its focus being a stage against the back wall. Several steps led upwards and upon it was a gold throne, embedded with jewels and lined with silk cushions. To the side of the throne were some lesser chairs, also of gold but not so decorated. These smaller chairs were empty with the ministers who would fill them instead standing before them, flanking Herod who sat upon the throne in all his majesty.

Herod was dressed in full regalia.

"Bring me my coronation robes," he had ordered. "And my finest crown and jewels."

He had been so laden in silk, gold and gems that he could hardly move once he sat within the throne. Beneath the layers of silk and cotton

Herod was wet with sweat making his underclothes stick to him like a second skin. To those around him he appeared as majestic as any ruler to have lived and that was certainly how he looked to us as we walked towards him.

I remember as we entered that I took in the room and the way Herod was waiting, that this was how I imagined entering a Pharaoh's court. I had heard though that the Egyptians had much better taste in their decorations and attire.

We entered in silence, carrying ourselves with all the dignity we could muster. We were entirely at Herod's mercy and will, so to walk with grace was all we could do. When we were halfway to Herod's stage, his chief minister, standing to the right of the king, stepped forward and lifted his right hand towards us.

"Sire, I present to you the magi of Babylonia, here on their pilgrimage to find their new prophet," he announced in a booming voice so that even our youngest acolyte at the back of the group heard him.

When we were within several feet of the stage we stopped and bowed. I was about to speak when Herod clapped his hands.

"Get these men some chairs!" he barked, looking at no one in particular.

Within seconds there was a servant behind each of the elders with a chair from the side of the room. The youngest knew to make do upon the rugs and settled into crossing their legs or sitting upon their haunches.

Herod smiled as we adjusted our robes to sit and took in each and every one of us. Even as I spoke my customary gratitude to being received in peace I could tell he was measuring every facial expression and gesture. This he did over and over as Gaspar and Melchior also spoke. He smiled but it was such a staged expression that it often lapsed into a poorly hidden sneer.

Herod's words were beautifully scripted. To a young inexperienced ear his speech was regal and diplomatic. To the ears of aged magi with decades of counselling and meditation, it was easy to see when he was gathering information and testing us.

He already knew our story but he asked for it to be retold.

"To hear a story from the original storyteller is a blessing and delight as it has not been diluted or curved," he said and his mocking was all too clear.

So I told our story once more. I spoke it as I had always done. There was no need to change, hide or alter anything.

"So you believe this teacher will bring in a new era of humanity?" he questioned and his smile finally slid off his face.

"Yes," I replied with a smile and then put my hand upon my heart. "Our people have been waiting for this for thousands of years and the world is ready."

Something caught in Herod and I saw him adjust his body in his seat, as he looked away, dropping eye contact with us for the first time since we came in the room. Just as quickly he regained his composure and looked back to us.

"And—and where do you believe him to be? You have travelled very decidedly to the East, surely you are not just travelling on assumptions and faith?" Herod added a slight laugh.

"We believe we will find him just to the south of Jerusalem. The meeting of the planets indicates this," Melchior answered and we could hear a tremor in his voice. I sensed Gaspar stiffen in his seat.

It had been a simple and honest answer but something in the exchange seemed entirely wrong. Herod laughed out loud, startling many of us.

"To the south? There are only poor villages to the south filled with farmers. That does not seem like the place for a prophet to be born!" Herod comfortable in finally finding something to openly ridicule us with was in his element. He turned to look to his ministers and continued laughing.

I saw Gaspar clench a fist while Melchior shrank back in his seat. Behind me I felt the bah-ra'an of every magi and acolyte rise up. I looked up and with the strength of every one of my brothers I spoke clearly and calmly.

"A man's beginnings do not determine his endings," I said.

It was few words but enough to stop Herod's gloating. My voice carried to him, dragging the smile from his face and setting off all the voices inside his head.

"You were nothing but a general's son..."

"Rome could replace you tomorrow..."

"What if this prophet is the king that the Jews are waiting for..."

It took all of Herod's strength and self-control to remain calm, as well as not order me struck down. I knew those words were not just to support Yeshua, they were also to let Herod know we knew his follies.

It was the most powerful and yet foolish thing I would ever say. I regret not one word of it. At the time though the tension it had layered within the room could not be ignored. Herod kept his eyes locked upon me. Beneath his clothes his body was sweating so much now the wet was making its way through the layers of clothing.

Melchior leant forward within his chair and spoke, breaking the strain with perfect grace.

"What my brother meant to say, Your Highness, is that our beloved prophet Zarathustra came from humble beginnings. He was but a common man and yet he showed us the glory of the creator and the beauty of a virtuous life. We have faith that another such man will show us more of such teachings."

"But of course," Herod once more installed his diplomatic grin. "I fear we have spoken enough for now. Let us dine now. I wish to show you the delights of my cooks and gardens."

With that Herod waved to the minister who stood to his right. The man jumped from his seat and yelled out to the entire room.

"Stand for the King!"

We all stood immediately for no man remained seated while a king was standing. Herod was escorted from the room and the same minister turned to us.

"You will wait here until the dining hall is ready."

Then he too left with the remaining ministers. Once again we were alone apart from the palace butlers.

"That was dreadful," muttered Gaspar.

Melchior looked down at the floor and I simply fell back into my chair.

CHAPTER THIRTY-FOUR

Thankfully the rest of our stay was not so dramatic. Our dinner was elaborate and delicious. We ate things we never imagined existed; fruits from the coast, spices from the deep south of Egypt and exotic meats such as pheasants. Music played, dancers swirled and wine flowed. We indulged and relaxed and it even seemed Herod did too. It was as though the meeting had been nothing like what it had actually been.

Herod sat at a table that was raised upon a platform. As always he was above the general gathering, able to look down on each and every one of us. Gaspar, Melchior and I were asked to join him at his table and I have to say it was a delight to look upon the other magi and acolytes enjoying the meal of a lifetime.

However sitting directly to Herod's right I also knew to keep my wits sharp and alive. I sipped lightly upon my wine and ate sparingly as well. I tasted but did not indulge, lest my senses be dulled and dampen my awareness, for as the night wore on Herod began exactly what I expected of him. Now with a more casual setting and the hope of the influence of alcohol and a swollen stomach, he began his dialogue once more.

"So my dear friend," he began, leaning in so close I could smell the last dish he tasted. "What do you think you will find when you get to your teacher? Will he be grown? Will he be a toddler, just finding his words? What do you think he will look like?"

I took a deep breath, buying some time before I could answer diplomatically but without saying too much. Thankfully Gaspar to my other side heard all of this and leant forward and across me in an instant.

"We will find what we find. Who are we to put expectations upon the teacher our creator will send to us," he answered firmly.

Herod leant in even closer across me, so that his hair brushed my face.

"But how will you know it is him?" he spat.

"Our souls will let us know," replied Gaspar also leaning forward even more so that I was pushed back in my chair.

They both finally returned to sitting straight in their chairs, taking their food-laden breaths with them.

"Your souls!" Herod muttered. "What good is the voice of a soul?"

I did not answer, not that Herod was looking for an answer. Instead I prayed for the night to be over and the morning sun to be risen so we could make way to Bethlehem.

"Souls!" spat Herod as his butler undressed him. "Does your soul speak to you?" he asked the man as he pulled his robes off.

"No, Sire," came the expected response.

"Souls... " muttered Herod as he collapsed into bed and fell asleep.

Herod rarely dreamed so when he did he took notice of them. That night as he slept he watched as we rode into Bethlehem; there waiting for us was Yeshua, with the lion and lamb beside him. Yeshua was fully grown, around thirty years old, and smiled at the magi. He saw that they all spoke to each other but not one word was said out loud.

That was all he remembered when he woke.

Gaspar did not sleep so well that night as did any of us. He slept for short periods though, just an hour or two at a time and when he did the same scenes played out. They would make it into Bethlehem and find their teacher, only to turn and see Herod standing behind them.

He remembered every detail when he woke.

The next morning we gathered in the courtyard where we had entered the palace grounds. Our servants and animals were waiting for us, including Mahesh holding the reins of my camel. Never had I been so happy to see them both.

Melchior walked beside me. "Do you suppose the escort will follow us south?"

"I doubt it," I said. "I think he has had his fun with us."

Gaspar heard but did not answer. He knew he could not share his dream while we were within Jerusalem, let alone the palace walls.

Herod arrived to farewell us, dressed as majestically as he could and still be able to walk. His red eyes were the only indicator of his indulgence at the dinner the night before. I thanked myself for choosing not to do so. As Herod walked to us he threw his hands up in the air.

"Ah my brothers! I hope you do not mind me calling you such but I feel we have such a—a—a connection now since our visit. It pains my heart to see you leave so soon but I understand your work is so important," he said with the most elaborate expressions he could muster.

Each one of us stayed in place wondering just who this king was who spoke to us now. It was nothing like the man who had sneered at us during the audience or the meal. Now it was as though we had been friends our entire lives.

I bowed deeply, leading the way for all the magi to do so also. Mahesh brought to me a small chest.

"Our dear King Herod, we thank you for your hospitality and grace," I took the chest from Mahesh and held it out for Herod. "We pray you will accept this small gift as way of thanks knowing it is but a token of our appreciation. We will forever be grateful for your part in our grand journey."

Herod did not move. His hands were pulled back by his side and that is where they stayed. He looked to one of his ministers and jerked his head towards me. The man stepped quickly to take the small chest and carried it to Herod, opening it so the king could see inside.

Herod looked inside to see it filled with a small bag of frankincense and a small jar of myrrh oil. He surely knew that we may as well as given him gold. This was the finest sample of either he would ever receive. He nodded his head in recognition of the gift but did not say a word. Instead he just waved his hand at the minister, signalling for the chest to be closed and taken away, then he looked back to me and my brothers.

"I wish you safe journey," was all he would say to us now.

"You may mount and leave," we were told by another minister and within minutes we were all upon our animals and ready to depart.

The gates opened once more. There was no music, no dancers and no rose petals being strewn as we made our way back out into the city. We rode silently. A few passersby looked to us but only briefly as they went on with their day.

I looked back as the last of our group left the palace. Herod was small in the distance but he stood and watched as the entire party left. Now the gates began to close and I saw him turn and leave. Never was I so glad to see the last of someone.

When we reached the city limits the gates here too were opened but before we made way through the general who had greeted us on our arrival approached me.

"Our king apologises but we cannot spare men to escort you south. He feels you will be safe and secure regardless of this," he announced.

I saw Gaspar and others raise their eyebrows and inside my stomach knotted. We all knew that this was some ploy but we could not say anything.

"Indeed. We are most grateful for what has been provided thus far. Our swordsmen will do their duty I am sure," I responded and turned my camel away. I was done with the pleasantries of being a politician. All I wanted now was to be a magus once more.

When we were a distance from Jerusalem's walls Gaspar rode close to my side and put his hand up for me to stop. Then he beckoned Melchior to come to us.

"We may have left Herod and his guards behind but we both know that his eyes will still be upon us. I am sure he thinks that withdrawing an official escort will leave us complacent. His interest in this birth is far greater than he makes of it," he said strong and clear.

"I agree," answered Melchior. "That man is the most calculating and layered being I have met. He is like five men operating within one body."

I knew just what Melchior meant, as did Gaspar. One person seemed to speak to you while another looked at you and yet another planned a response.

"So what do we do?" I asked of them.

I knew what we needed to do. We would simply carry on regardless. To come this far and not meet our teacher would be foolish in all measures.

"We continue on. We find the child but we make no great news of who he is. Time will reveal his truth and strength. Herod will be long gone when the child becomes the man we are expecting," Gaspar proposed and I saw Melchior nod.

"Let us continue on our way then." I flicked my reins and rode once more.

✳ CHAPTER THIRTY-FIVE

The town of Bethlehem was waiting for us. As we passed through the fields that flanked the road leading to the town, shepherds stood from their midday rest under trees to watch us ride by. I looked upon them and wondered what they had made of the meeting of Jupiter and Venus.

Shepherds knew the night sky as well as any magus; not from necessity or scrolls stored in a library as we did. They watched the sky because at night when they tended the flocks there was little else to look at. Their elders would point out major stars and planets, the rest they would discover on their own; the dance of the moon, the flash of a falling star and the burn of a comet.

The shepherds had watched as Jupiter played with Sharu and then sat upon Venus. It had been like nothing they had ever seen or been told of.

"What do you suppose it means?" one asked another.

"Does it have to mean anything?" was the reply.

The first shepherd though could feel it did. Why would the sky put on such a show for no reason? Now as he watched our caravan making its way into the town he knew we too were part of this. He ran to the roadside, causing a swordsman to race his horse to meet him.

"Halt!! Who are you? What do you want?" the swordsmen yelled, pulling his sword from its holder and pointing it at the shepherd.

The young boy stopped in his tracks and threw his open hands out to his sides in peace.

"I just want to know who these men are and why they come to Bethlehem," he said.

"These are the grand magi of Babylonia. They come to greet their new prophet."

The shepherd nodded. "Thank you."

He had heard all he needed or wanted.

On the outskirts of the town we made camp. There was no way that our entire entourage could make way into the small town. We would have choked the streets. So only the most senior magi and some guards rode into Bethlehem while the rest settled upon a grass field near the shepherds.

There were no gates or walls around Bethlehem. There never had been. This was a modest town filled with people living simple lives. There were travellers who passed through on their way or returning from Jerusalem but not much else of note occurred here. So to have a huge group of foreigners arrive, with our story as an extra flourish, made us well worthy of curiosity.

There was no formal greeting though, nor were there any dancers and musicians. As we began to climb the road that led into the town centre, people who were out in the streets stopped and gestured a welcome. People within the homes we passed leant out of windows or opened doors to look out. They too made their greetings to us.

We were before the inn where Yeshua was born, making our way still when the innkeeper signalled for us to stop.

"Sires, would you care to stop and rest here. Perhaps even for a meal and wine before you continue on?" he offered.

The busy time of the census had passed and the innkeeper had grown accustomed to the extra money he had made. To see a party like this and miss the opportunity for some business was simply not an option.

We looked amongst ourselves and I nodded.

"That sounds very pleasant indeed," I said.

The inn was as far from the grandeur of the palace that you could imagine. We had to lower our heads to enter the front door and I even felt like I should stay stooped once inside. Tables were arranged with barely room to walk between them and every few feet there was a wooden pole supporting the ceiling which was also the floor for the sleeping rooms above.

I looked up and could see between the floorboards into the bedroom above me as I sat at a table.

We filled all the tables, with our backs leaning against each other as we sat upon the benches that served as seats. Within minutes the tables were crammed with platters and cups were being filled with wine. The innkeeper joined by his wife and his daughters served us with broad smiles and invitations to enjoy our meals. All the while the innkeeper spoke continuously telling stories of all the travellers who had stayed in his inn.

"They came from everywhere for the census!" he said, his voice booming throughout the small room and I hoped that no one was trying to rest above us. "Even from near the Egyptian border! Can you imagine that? One night last week I had no rooms left. Now that only happens for the feast of the harvest and only when our lambs are especially abundant. Every room in town was full. Every room!" he repeated this and even louder to make sure we knew just how significant this was.

I heard Gaspar sigh. The only thing I had seen Gaspar show more disdain for than small talk was Herod and Jerusalem. The innkeeper was oblivious to this though. All he cared for was sharing his stories to a somewhat captive audience.

"Then just as the sun was setting, this young man arrives with his wife. She was about to give birth. How she had not done so on the road is a miracle. They could not go further. All I could do was let them stay in the stable and call the midwife."

Every noise in the room stopped. There was no chewing, no slurping, no grunts or sighs of enjoyment. Every man was looking at the innkeeper.

"Did the child survive?" I asked hardly breathing as Gaspar stiffened in his chair across from me.

"Oh yes! They had plenty of time after all."

"What was it?" hissed Gaspar.

"A boy. Healthy as any first child could be thanks to our midwife. She truly is a wonder. Never loses a child that does not need to be lost—or a mother come to think about it..."

The innkeeper spoke much more about the midwife but we were not listening. Instead we looked amongst ourselves and one by one each of us now had smiles as wide as those of the family serving us.

"Where are they now?" I asked.

"Oh they moved onto the uncle's farm across town as soon as the mother could be moved. Mary was her name, like my own mother. The father Josephus left here to learn carpentry with a cousin in Galilee many years ago..."

Once more the innkeeper trailed off into another story. I looked to Gaspar and Melchior. There was nothing I could say. I simply raised my glass to each one of them and sipped my wine.

We ate and drank some more, as the innkeeper kept telling his stories. My mind was racing as was every magi in the room. Not one of us spoke but within our heads a thousand conversations were happening.

"We have to keep going," whispered Gaspar across the table to me and Melchior nodded.

"We need to go back to camp first," said Melchior as quietly as he could.

"What for?" snapped Gaspar.

"If we head straight to the child, Herod will be there tomorrow. You do realise that he will have people watching us. He may even be paying one of our own," Melchior said.

Gaspar looked around the room. He knew it would not be one of the magi but one of the servants or even a guard? That was entirely possible. They had been taken away from them at the palace for a reason.

"We cannot act like we would know that though," Melchior suggested.

"I agree. Let us go back to camp and plan how we will do this," I added.

If the townspeople thought it odd that we left as quickly as we arrived was of no consequence to us. Back at our camp we gathered the most senior of the magi who had been with us at the inn.

"We need to do this with no clear indicator of who the prophet is," Melchior began.

It was Rafeem who came up with the perfect plan.

"We visit every newborn male, and even those within the timing of all the events that have brought us here."

"That would cover any male born within the last ten months or so," I realised and knew this was perfect.

Not only would we not target one child but we would also make sure we did not miss any possibility of who it might be. It was the perfect insurance for us and the child.

"Keep your words simple and low. We do not need anyone apart from our brotherhood to know the truth of what we do," finished Gaspar.

The next morning we divided the senior brothers into four groups. We would work our way through Bethlehem visiting any newborn or infant males. Our story became this; we were told through the stars of the birth of a new prophet and that we would find him south of Jerusalem. Though we had no more information to know who exactly he was, we knew he would reveal himself as he grew into manhood. For now we were visiting to honour any possible child that he may be.

We wound through the streets, taking time at the homes with the young boys as tea or wine was poured for us. Even the most humble of homes gave us what they could to show some hospitality. In return we prayed over their sons, giving them a Zoroastrian blessing for a meaningful and productive life. Then we also gave them a gold coin, a small bag of frankincense and a vial of myrrh.

It did not take us as long as we thought, and we gathered together at the southern edge of Bethlehem. I took a deep breath as the last of us arrived.

"Did you see any child that made you question who he might truly be?" I asked and every man shook his head except for Izrael.

"There was one, born during the first conjunction. He had such a beauty to him," then Izrael stopped and shook his head. "But I sensed an illness that will not let him even see his early manhood. That just does not seem to be the story we are looking for."

We all shook our heads knowing this to be true.

"So we move onto the farm then. Let us make haste so we do not travel back to camp in darkness," I said and led my camel onwards.

CHAPTER THIRTY-SIX

Joseph saw us approaching and smiled. We looked nothing like how his dreams had shown us but he knew who we were. He had been walking a cow to the stables and he tied her to a post and watched us head to the farm gates. When we stopped and waved, our way to ask for entrance, he walked to us smiling.

As he opened the gate he looked up at us and I saw his eyes were filled with tears.

"I have been waiting for you," he said.

I laughed as I rode my camel past him and into the farm.

Our first instincts upon hearing the innkeeper's story that Yeshua was the child we were looking for were confirmed in every moment of our visit.

It began with Joseph's greeting and then as we walked with him to the house, he continued to speak.

"I kept seeing three of you in my dreams. You told me you were coming," he went on and I saw Gaspar smile broadly.

"What did we say to you?" Gaspar asked and Joseph recited the words that Gaspar spoke in his own dreams. Gaspar's smile spread even wider.

"I will take you to see Mary and Yeshua, but I fear my uncle's home is not big enough for you all. It is still warm, I will gather Mary and our son and bring them outdoors," Joseph said with excitement.

We waited beneath a huge cedar tree that was near the home. Our camels were tethered to a fence nearby and the donkeys in the field it enclosed came to see their temporary companions. We heard a cow call out, followed by the bleat of some goats. The low cackle of some chickens played out as well.

I stifled a giggle as the others too delighted in our surrounds. "Well my brothers, it seems our new teacher chooses to be surrounded by the comfort of god's creatures," I said as we waited.

"All that is missing is the grand ark of his ancestors," shot Izrael back.

At that a rooster crowed reminding us of his grandeur and that we were in his domain. To us though, it sounded like the farm was agreeing with our story.

We remained upon our feet as Joseph walked back out from the house, behind him walked the tiniest woman, barely five feet in height, yet she moved with grace and poise. As I looked at the child within her arms I suddenly felt overwhelmed. I fell to my knees, placed my right hand upon my heart and thanked Mazda for this moment. Within seconds every one of my brothers had done the same.

We had not planned such an act of devotion, but within that moment it felt the perfect thing to do. Mary did not act surprised, nor did Joseph. They smiled as they stood before us. Mary looked up at Joseph.

"All is well," she whispered and he nodded.

I finally looked up and Mary was gazing into my eyes with such profound warmth that I felt like I was looking at one of my daughters.

"We are so glad you are here," she said.

A chair was gathered for Mary and she sat upon it with Yeshua still cradled in her arms. Then we all stood and walked one by one to meet our new teacher.

Mary and Joseph told us many stories that showed us the depth of Yeshua's arrival and his being chosen to be here for us all; from the story of Mary's divine conception, to the appearance of the angels and Joseph's dreams. However nothing convinced me more that this was our teacher, than when I looked upon Yeshua's face.

In that moment I felt everything I had sensed or felt about the awakening to be confirmed. As I looked upon him I felt my own inner peace open up, all the fear surrounding Herod fell away, all the questions through the Great Excitement were answered and I felt that everything we had done in travelling here was made true and correct.

Yeshua's eyes were not open. He slept with that depth only a child can know. Yet he saw me and he spoke to me. It was his bah-ra'an and mine there together in that moment. Later each and every one of my brothers spoke of feeling the same thing and we all heard the same words spoken between us and the child.

"You are god also."

We stayed upon the farm as long as we could. I wished we could return to visit another day but that would target everyone there. Instead we made the most of our visit, sharing as many stories of our experiences as we could. This confirmed for us all exactly what the life of the newborn signified.

When we made our farewells, we gifted the family with a small chest filled with frankincense, a large jar of myrrh and all the gold we could spare and still allow us passage back to Babylonia with ease. Then we gave one more gift; a promise.

"Please know that all of us and our brothers and the families of Babylonia offer you our eternal support and love. If you should ever need of anything, send us word, to anyone within our priesthood. We will always honour any message you send us. Our home and hearts are yours," I said as tears fell down my cheeks. Around me every magi present nodded, letting the small family know they echoed my words.

Gaspar stood forward and took Joseph's hand in his. "And you know also we will send news in our dreams as you can with us."

Joseph nodded and smiled. His heart ached to see us all leave now after waiting what seemed so long for us to arrive. It had been almost two weeks now since Yeshua was born; he had been told to wait another four before Mary could ride back to Galilee with him. He knew this time was precious and necessary, especially now in that it allowed us to find them.

I looked upon Yeshua's face one last time before we left. The sun was falling fast and we needed to make our way. The child opened his eyes slightly and but for a moment. I knew we would meet again some day.

Mary watched us ride away and then looked down at the child in her arms.

"I will tell you of these men one day. They are sure to be great teachers to you," she said.

As we approached our camp the young shepherd ran towards us through his field.

"Sires, Sires," he called out and I could not help but stop. "Did you find him?" he asked.

Before I could answer Gaspar snapped at him. "Who has paid you to ask us this? Are you one of Herod's spies?"

The young man was taken aback. "A spy? Why would I be a spy?"

It was an honest question spoken with all his heart.

"Yes we did my son. He rests upon a farm to the south," I told him and turned to Gaspar. "He is the same as us, Brother, let him have his excitement too."

With that we continued on to our camp. We shared with everyone the basic story that we had told the families of Bethlehem. This had also been told to Joseph and everyone at the farm, so they knew it was in place to protect them all. Now everyone could feel as though our journey was of value and complete.

"Tomorrow we make way to our homes and we can do this with the knowing that all we set out to do has been as we imagined. The child is born and welcomed. He has our blessings and prayers. Now we can return to await his maturity and the teachings that will come from it. Know that each one of you has contributed to this amazing time in our history. People will read about you in the eons to come and they will honour all you did at this time," I told them all.

CHAPTER THIRTY-SEVEN

As I went to sleep that night I wondered how our story would be told in the years and even millennia to come. This was not just an event of our lifetime or even a generation. We had been part of welcoming the prophet of new consciousness. His birth would change the world forevermore.

I smiled as I thought of this. That one man would change humanity with his being, with his words and with his bah-ra'an. The story of a group of magi who rode across the lands to greet his birth would seem so small compared to that.

I said this to Gaspar the next day as we ate breakfast before we rode. He looked down the whole time I spoke, contemplating all I said. Then he lifted his eyes and I saw an expression that I am sure he had never shown before.

"If we are meant to be known then our story will stay true and be told to those who will accept its truth. For now I am willing to accept that we did all we could in the purest love and honour that we could. A conqueror's name gains fame and notice for his deeds and actions. Perhaps a magi's name needs not be known but the result of his actions lives on as his tribute."

I smiled at his words. "How true. I would rather know that the new humanity will bloom and prosper as we were promised, than have my story told."

In truth I will tell you that my spirit is now celebrating both.

When we rode away from Bethlehem we did not take the road north as we had arrived. There was no way we could go back through Jerusalem and endure another audience with Herod. We knew he would not believe our story or worse he may hold us hostage until we "surrendered" the truth. We were not obliged to return, that had never been spoken of or agreed to. To head east directly from Bethlehem was not in any way a breach of our pledge to Herod. It would also make it difficult if there was a spy in our midst to send him information. To do so they would actually need to abandon the caravan.

"It seems only right that we travel a new way to return home. All is changed now. To walk the same steps would seem like returning to the old," said Melchior when it was decided.

As we began to ride I looked to Bethlehem one last time, and I did also to the north to Jerusalem. The capital seemed so small from here, yet it had so much power.

Within me I felt a new sensation. Gone was that twist of anticipation and fear. In its place now was elation and wonder at what would unfold. I have to say it sat within me with much more comfort than that with which I had arrived.

You see, we now had no idea as to how Yeshua's life would play out and how his teachings would truly open the new consciousness. Would it be dramatic and sudden? Would it take a thousand years or even two? All I could do now was trust that it would happen.

Gaspar rode close by my side.

"We must write down all we saw and spoke of at the farm as soon as we return," he said looking to see who was riding close by.

"Of course," I replied.

"We cannot send scrolls to each other with this information," he went on. "We must visit all others in our regions and share this in person."

"I agree," said Melchior who was riding behind us. "This is not something to share in a scroll. It must be shared in person."

We were three days of riding away when Herod asked his advisors as to news of our progress.

"We have had no word, Sire," was the answer.

"Have you sent anyone to see what they are doing?" Herod pushed.

"Sire, you told us not to."

Herod's face turned red. "Well now I am telling you to!"

"Yes, Sire."

Ten of Herod's soldiers rode south the next day, giving us even more travelling time to be clear of him. As they rode into Bethlehem, people looked down as they passed and the soldiers heard the sound of doors and shutters being closed. When Romans were about, the less contact you had the better.

They dismounted outside the inn and walked inside.

"Good day, gentlemen," was the simple greeting the innkeeper offered. "What might I serve you?"

The commander pulled out a purse full of coins and threw it upon the table before him.

"I'd like you to tell me all you know about the Babylonians' visit here," he said and everyone was clear it was a demand and not a negotiation.

The innkeeper showed just how wise he was. In that instant he knew how much danger Yeshua was in as well as our caravan. He took a deep breath, smiled and began.

"Oh so much to tell you," he said as he scooped up the purse off the table. "But please I must get you some wine and the cheese my wife makes is superb, not to mention the cured meats her cousin brings to us."

He made way to the kitchen where his wife and daughters were preparing food.

"You will help me serve but you will not say a word or react no matter what you hear me say!" he pleaded and they nodded.

Back in the dining room, carrying a huge jug of wine, the innkeeper began pouring for the soldiers.

"Oh it was so nice to see such a party after the census. They seemed so grand and regal. I have never seen such fabrics, and I have many travellers from many places, as you can imagine…."

He rambled on, knowing that he was essentially saying nothing and hoping the wine and food would distract them enough to not notice. Of course it didn't. The commander let him carry on for several sips of his wine then grew tired of the banter.

"Who did they visit?" he interrupted.

"Oh everyone…" began the innkeeper.

The commander lent forward and grabbed the innkeeper's hand. "Now you know that is not entirely true. Who did they visit?"

"But it is my Lord. They visited all homes to visit all our people. They prayed for us and blessed us. My knees have been wonderful ever since!"

The commander sat back and rubbed his chin. "Do you need more coins or do you need me to be clearer as to what I need to know?"

"I am not sure I understand what you mean," answered the innkeeper.

The commander looked at him closely. It was entirely possible this man was simple enough to not know and he had to at least begin with that assumption. He was after all an innkeeper in a village and not a politician in Jerusalem.

"They came here to witness the arrival of a prophet. Did you hear if and where they found him?"

The innkeeper smiled. "Oh that story! Yes, yes, they visited all the young males. Blessed them and gifted their families with incense and gold. It would seem we have over a dozen prophets awaiting their manhood."

"What?" spat the commander.

"They were all told he would not be truly revealed until he has grown. Which makes sense, how could you decide that of a child who can barely walk or talk?"

The commander had heard enough. He threw back the rest of the wine and grabbed the cheese upon the table before him.

"Thank you for all you have provided…" he muttered and led his men outside.

The innkeeper gathered the plates and cups and made way to the kitchen. He dropped them upon the table there and collapsed into a chair, putting his head into his hands.

His wife walked to him and put her hand upon his shoulder. "You did noble, my love. You know as well as I do that it is Ben's family they seek."

The innkeeper looked up. "Who knew that letting them stay in my stable would become so much?"

The soldiers spoke to more people of the town but all said just what the innkeeper had told them. Even the lure of extra gold coins didn't acquire any new information. They spoke to innkeepers, farmers, bakers and any other variation upon a villager of Bethlehem they could find. Everyone spoke the same story, with hardly a variation.

"If this was not the truth we would have broken or at least bent one to tell us otherwise," reported the commander to Herod on his return.

"You fool," muttered Herod through a sneer. "These men travelled for weeks upon the story of a star to find their messiah and you truly believe they were not clever enough to cast a spell over some simple peasants?"

"Sire—I…" The commander stumbled to defend his findings.

"Oh hush!" laughed Herod and then he went quiet. Herod looked around the room at the men surrounding him. "Perhaps I should pay this town a visit. Maybe find this new hero for myself. Surely a king cannot be outwitted by a babe." He laughed again and then looked at the commander. "Though it seems he can outwit a soldier."

Herod looked the commander over and his eyes stopped at the right hip of the man. "Do you know what cannot be outwitted? A blade!"

The commander gulped hard believing this was to be his demise, then he squared his shoulders determined to meet his end with stoic grace.

"Oh relax," Herod said waving his hand at the man. "Your stupidity is not enough for a death sentence. You did the job you were sent for. Though now I will send you back with another job. You will gather one hundred men, you will ride at first light and you will slaughter any male born within the past year."

The soldier's mouth fell open and his eyes grew wide. "Kill innocents?" he thought to himself.

Herod saw the expression on the man's face. "Just imagine them as fully grown men with a dagger in their hands. And do not waste time to stop and ask how many name days they have had—if they look young enough they die. If someone tries to stop you, they die also. Do you understand?"

The commander nodded.

CHAPTER THIRTY-EIGHT

We had covered great ground in making our way. We avoided towns and villages, stopping at them only to trade when supplies dwindled. This saved the time of any tribal leaders having to hold audience and for having to explain our story yet again as most of the places we passed now were not upon our original route. Instead we made camps in the plains or at bases of mountains to rest each night.

Each day we prayed for Yeshua and our dreams showed him to us as a grand teacher walking the lands with people gathered by his side.

"He speaks with such beauty and love that people want to repeat the words," said one magi during our morning meeting.

"I see him coming through Babylon to seek our counsel," said Rafeem.

Many others spoke of similar scenes and themes but only Gaspar had the dream that would crush our hearts.

The night that Herod ordered the massacre of the innocents our camp had fallen quiet unusually early.

"We need the stillness and rest after leaving the reach of Herod," I thought to myself.

Sleep took some time to come to me that night and when it did it was deep and dreamless. So when the scream reached my ears it was even more of a shock. It was deep and guttural; with so much suffering within it that my first instinct was to check my safety. We were surely under an attack from savages.

The opening to my tent was flung open and I braced myself. It was Mahesh.

"Sire, please. You must come quickly. It is Gaspar, he…"

But I did not wait to hear the explanation. I was past him before he could say any more.

There were men running beside me also as we made way to the sound. Then I saw Gaspar. He was upon his knees, still screaming from the depths of his being. His hands were thrust in the air, and he looked up at the sky.

"Forgive us! Forgive us!" he began to cry out.

I ran to stand before him and saw his face wet with tears. Alongside his tears I saw scratches upon his cheeks and blood at his temples, where he had clawed and pulled at himself in his anguish.

"Gaspar," I said gently. "Gaspar, look at me. Please look at me." Slowly he brought his eyes to look at me. "What is wrong? Please speak to me," I begged him as I lowered myself to kneel upon the ground beside him.

"It is all over. It has all been for nothing," he screamed at me. I looked up at Melchior who was standing behind him. Melchior looked at me as though to ask what was happening.

I reached out to touch Gaspar's shoulder but he pulled away.

"All we have done, from our youth to today, has been destroyed. We can blame Herod but it is our sin to wear as we should never have left Babylonia," Gaspar shouted and fell forward leaning on his hands, crying anew.

"How Gaspar? How?" I asked, desperate to know what he was talking about.

Gaspar sat back upon his legs and wiped at his eyes. "Herod has killed Yeshua. I saw it in my dream."

I looked at Gaspar, hoping upon hope that he was wrong, but we all knew the power of his dreams. I looked at the men gathered around us waiting to make sense of this scene.

How could it be? After everything we had been through. The dreams, the insights, the messages of the stars—but most of all our faith and belief in this birth. How could one man destroy all that? This could not be true.

Gaspar moved his legs from under him so he could sit cross-legged. He put his head into his hands and then began to speak. He told us of his dream. How he had seen the soldiers arriving into Bethlehem, asking questions. Then he saw them draw their swords and begin killing. It was men first, then the women so only the children were left, crying and with no protection. Then they too were slaughtered.

Gaspar's voice became louder as he spoke. When he finished the story, he began to cry again. He looked up at the sky.

"Mazda, forgive us!" he implored.

I wanted to vomit and thanked my stomach for being empty. I looked again to Melchior.

"If he has slaughtered the town he may come for us next," Melchior reasoned.

That made my heart sink even further. Though we had our swordsmen they would be no match for a hundred, even fifty, of Herod's soldiers. We had nothing to fear though. An advisor had even asked this of Herod.

"I do not need that diplomatic nightmare upon me. We need the trade with them. No, no, no. Killing their prophet will kill their hope. That will be punishment enough for the silly old fools!" Herod had laughingly replied.

I simply could not believe that Yeshua had been killed. It made no sense after the messages and protection that had been offered to Mary and Joseph. I took a deep breath and I asked my bah-ra'an. I felt nothing that told me otherwise.

"Gaspar, it is possible he is not harmed. They are a distance from the main village. Ben's farm may have been missed. They may have been warned and escaped into the hills to hide," I reasoned with all my might but Gaspar shook his head.

"My dreams of him have all been correct," he replied sullenly.

This was true. All the dreams that Gaspar had received from his spirit had been as clear and prophetic as if he had been there. There was a difference with this dream that Gaspar had not noted. It was not a dream from his spirit. It was a message sent from Joseph. This was why I had sensed it could not be entirely precise. There was something missing from the story.

That being that Gaspar did not see Yeshua being killed.

When the soldiers came to the farm, it was Ben who greeted them. Yes, the magi had visited. Yes, they had blessed his nephew's newborn and gifted him. Then the magi had left with hope to hear of how he matured. No, he had not been deemed a prophet or teacher.

Ben had been asked to live the same story as all else had. The common hate for the Roman soldiers made such lies easy to speak. The soldiers left and Joseph who had stood watching from behind a corner of a barn took a deep breath.

"You need to leave NOW!" he heard from behind him and turned to see the angel who had told him of Mary's pregnancy.

"Where will we go?" Joseph asked.

The angel said nothing but turned and pointed south. Then he was gone.

Joseph ran to tell Mary who he found folding clothes into her satchel.

"He told you too?"

Mary nodded.

They waited until the first light of the next day. This gave them time to prepare the donkey and to farewell Ben's family with honour.

"Where will you go?" asked Ben.

"We will go as far as we need. That may even be in Egypt. We will be guided," answered Joseph.

"Send word when you are settled," said Ben.

Joseph shook his head. "I will not risk that for either of us. One day we will pass back through here and my son will greet you with his own words. I will tell him all about his first weeks here."

The night before he left though Joseph sat and prayed with Mary.

"Yahweh, you have been kind and generous. Please know we will promise all that we can to protect and nurture this child."

Mary took his hand.

"All will be well," she said once more.

Yes all would be well. Joseph had to hold onto this. They would now be riding into lands he had never been and amongst people he knew little about. His faith in Yahweh and the angels would sustain him. They had the gold and incense for trade. He could find them a home and surely his carpentry would find them income.

Yes all would be well. Joseph was sure of it.

The first night away from the farm they rested beneath a tree on the roadside. Joseph built a small fire and as he looked into the flames he thought about us travelling home.

"I wish I could send you word to know we have moved on and where," Joseph whispered to the fire.

That was enough to send the message in Gaspar's dream.

I am still not sure of the energetics which seemed to scramble how it was received. Perhaps it was entirely perfect that we learnt of the massacre in this way. Though it was hard to accept this as we watched Gaspar struggle to hold onto his sanity.

Gaspar now finally sat quiet. His knees were pulled to his chest and his arms wrapped around them tightly while his head rested forward upon his knees. Slowly he rocked from side to side as though comforting himself.

I stood up and went to Melchior.

"We need to send someone back to see what has happened," I said.

"Should we not all go?" asked Melchior.

I shook my head. "We cannot risk meeting Herod's soldiers again."

Melchior nodded. "Who do we send?"

"None of our brothers," I said. "We will send some servants with a guard. Make it look like some casual travellers. Any of the priests would be recognised and they may be watched to lead them to Yeshua…"

I did not add "if he survived". I still truly believed his death could not be possible. A small party could slip by towns without notice. They would not be reported or stopped. They could ride fast upon horses and return much quicker as well.

"Do you have any ideas as to who?" Melchior asked.

I did indeed. I knew it would be Mahesh. He was sly enough, knew the languages and could be fast enough on his feet to come up with a good story should he be questioned. Now it was just if he was willing to go.

Mahesh was standing nearby; waiting and watching for anything I needed as always. I turned and looked at him and even now I am convinced that he knew what I was going to ask before the words were spoken.

It was a quick conversation. Mahesh would never have said no to me.

"It would be an honour to do this for you," he said and bowed.

Another Kshatrapa chose to go with him as well as a servant who knew the horses. A swordsman rounded out the small party to four. They rode two upon each horse. I wondered if one swordsman would be enough but as Mahesh climbed upon his mount his trousers rode up a little and I saw a dagger strapped upon his calf.

After they galloped off, I gathered everyone for prayers. We prayed for the men we just sent back. We prayed for the spirit of Yeshua and we prayed for the people of Bethlehem.

Then I offered a prayer for Herod.

"What!" hissed Gaspar.

"We pray for the lost spirits as much as any other. If we offer some succour for his ways, then maybe he will find something within himself to come back to a virtuous life."

"No prayers can save a man who slaughters children."

CHAPTER THIRTY-NINE

Mahesh and the others made it back to Bethlehem in less than two days. Four men on fast horses made light travel. They knew not to go straight to Ben's farm. If they were being watched then this would lead Herod's men straight to Yeshua.

So they entered from the eastern side of the town. The same way we had all left.

"Can you hear that?" said the swordsman pulling his blade out of its sheath and holding it forward.

They stopped and the guard slid down from the horse, walking to the front of them.

"What can you hear?" called out the second Kshatrapa.

Mahesh could hear it now also. It was low, deep hum of human voices. It was not an animal; that he was sure of.

"Ride slowly behind me. One of you look to either side, the third look to the rear," said the guard and grasped his sword with both hands.

They moved ahead slowly, watching for anything around them. The sun was starting to fall and make shadows, but there was no one they could see.

As they got closer to the buildings of the town the sound grew louder. Mahesh realised what it was now. It was the moans and cries of those in mourning. Some voices were in prayer, others were in pure guttural grief. It grew louder and louder, becoming one huge mass of sound.

The men looked at each other.

"Do we need to go further?" asked one.

"We have to. We have to know—to know—if…." Mahesh choked on the words but they all knew what he would have said.

They all now dismounted and walked alongside the horses. Mahesh removed his dagger and held it tight.

Two houses marked the eastern edge of Bethlehem and as the four walked between them another sensation washed upon them; the smell of death. Each one knew it in some way but it was nothing like what they were about to witness.

There was red everywhere. It was blood. It was splashed against walls, it covered thresholds and it sat in puddles upon the streets. The homes with the most blood upon them or before them also had the loudest wails from within. No one was upon the streets; there were no other noises.

Then they heard a door shut quickly. The sight of a man with a sword and another with a dagger was enough to warrant your door closed and barred.

As they walked towards the town centre they saw a woman sitting in a doorway. In her arms was a baby. Its swaddling was wet with blood, as was her skirt beneath where it lay.

"Help my son please," she implored them with empty eyes. As she held the baby up its wrappings fell open and Mahesh saw its small body had been cut open. The baby's innards were spilling out. The woman pulled her child back close and wound the cloth back tightly again as though to hold him together.

Mahesh felt his head go light and his balance falter. He grabbed the edge of the doorway, leant away from the woman and tried not to vomit. The guard grabbed him and pulled him along.

"Keep your wits about you or you will end up the same," the guard whispered in his ear.

When they reached the town centre they finally saw some activity. A cart was stopped before the temple and two men silently unloaded small bodies wrapped in shrouds. They stopped when they saw our men and one pulled a knife from his side.

"Who are you? We have had enough trouble. There is no more here for you to take," he shouted and for a moment there was something louder than the cries of grief.

The guard sheathed his sword and Mahesh put away his dagger and raised his open hands.

"We come in peace," Mahesh said.

They helped unload the cart and take the bodies into the temple. The floor was almost full with these tiny bundles all wrapped and tied. In here the smell of blood and death was no more. Now it was the smell of the anointing oils and incense that had been rubbed upon the corpses.

To one side of the temple, the bundles were not so small. There lay the bodies of the mothers who refused to let go of their sons, the fathers who had tried to stop the soldiers, as well as the grandparents, cousins, siblings and whoever else had failed to stop a child from dying.

"Some are the mothers who took their own lives. Grief can do that to you," said one of the town men. "There are some mothers who hold onto their children and will not let the women anoint the dead and prepare them for the crypts."

Mahesh pictured the woman sitting in the doorway and his stomach heaved again.

"So there is even more?" he asked to distract the image.

"Oh yes. We even have to use an inn for the other adult bodies. Our midwife is lying there right now. When they found out who she was they dragged her from door to door, making her name every child she had delivered. If she lied they cut her. Then when they were done they slit her throat so she could never deliver another child."

This was a clever ploy on Herod's part. If the prophet was yet to be born then he would at least make his chances of surviving birth minimal.

"Have you heard any news from Ben's farm?" Mahesh asked.

"To be honest we have not had the time to even get that far out yet. Besides Ben would anoint and bury his own. That is the way of being a farmer. He has his own crypt."

305

They had all heard enough. Mahesh handed a purse of gold to the townsmen.

"Use it for whatever and whoever needs it," was the instruction given. To this Mahesh added, "to ensure a proper burial."

They rode through the town seeing places where even more blood was spilled. Occasionally someone would stare at them from a doorway. It was always the same blank stare. All the while the hum of the moans and prayers were there as a backdrop.

As they made way to the southern limits, they saw some houses with bodies bound and ready for the cart which they could hear now making its way to collect them. Mahesh tried to make note of all he was seeing, taking in every aspect, so he could tell me as much as he could. Now as he saw the homes with bodies waiting to take their last journey, he knew details would never matter with this story.

For Mahesh the cries of the surviving women were all you would ever need to speak of to show the brutality of what had occurred.

"Dear Mazda, let us not find the same at Ben's farm" he prayed as they left behind them the buildings and began on the road that would lead them to Yeshua.

When they arrived they waited at the gate, but there was no sign of a welcome from Ben. The guard jumped down from the horse and opened the gate.

"Pleasantries and manners can be damned right now," he said.

Ben appeared before the farmhouse. In his hand was a knife. The guard lifted his hands above his head.

"We come in peace on behalf of the magi," said the guard.

With that Ben dropped his knife and began to cry. "They are gone.

They rode away days ago. The child lives."

Ben took them inside and poured them some wine.

"Just days after the magi visited, they both had a vision and knew they should head south. When the soldiers arrived they already knew that they were here with a child. When I said they were gone, returned home after the census, they called me a liar and held a knife to my throat. They threatened to burn down the farm. I told them search all they liked, they would find no one here aside from my wife and grown children. So they did search, even out into the mountainside where they found one poor woman hiding with her babe. We heard her scream from here…."

Ben trailed off, as he looked out the window to the mountains.

"I don't know where they are and that is a curse and blessing. I trust they are safe. They left with enough time to have been truly south. The soldiers seemed not to care so much to follow them. One muttered something about him not being truly of the village anyway."

Mahesh laughed slightly. Funny how a man away from his home did not seem to have such importance.

"Thank you Ben, this is truly wonderful news of Yeshua," Mahesh said. "We must make way back to our group."

"You cannot ride in the night. Rest here and ride your horses fresh in the morning. You will make better time," Ben suggested and to the four men the idea to sleep under cover for one night was a perfect temptation that also made sense.

CHAPTER FORTY

We continued on our way knowing the speed of their travel would allow them to catch up to us eventually. It would just be further along. Also if they did not return, we needed to be making sure we were a good distance from the threat of Herod. Besides, the call of home was just too strong.

Gaspar stopped speaking unless he was addressed directly. His eyes were underlined with the darkest of circles and he barely ate. We all made effort to speak with him to at least remind him of where he was but his depression at the events he saw in his dream could not be allayed.

His dreams stopped entirely and even when others spoke of seeing Yeshua within theirs as a grown man, he would not believe them.

"Stop spinning stories to delay what you will all know to be true when the scouts return," he muttered.

Two to three days to get to Bethlehem and the same to return was what we had allowed, as well the extra time to find and join us upon the road. It was only upon the sixth day though that a cloud of dust appeared behind us.

The swordsmen to the rear called out for us to stop and the remainder made sure we were surrounded. It was the two horses with their four riders, galloping as fast as they could once they spotted us upon the road ahead. They tore to the front of the caravan, where I was standing waiting for them.

"Sire," cried out Mahesh as he threw himself from the horse. He ran to stand in front of me and I saw his eyes were as dark as Gaspar's, even with his dark skin I could see the heaviness of what had happened through his complexion. I grabbed at my heart, fearing the worst.

"He is alive," was all Mahesh would say before his eyes rolled back in his head and he collapsed before me.

We could not wake him for hours. The physicians tried to pour teas into him but he could not swallow. They waved oils beneath his nose and rubbed them upon his skin. There was no response.

In the meantime the other three scouts told us everything: the carnage, the temple overflowing with bodies, and how Joseph had taken his family south.

"Oh praise be," whispered Gaspar.

It was somewhat hard to celebrate the news of Yeshua's escape. Instead we thanked Mazda for Joseph's wisdom and then we prayed for the souls of the slain.

That night I looked to the stars and I breathed. I stared until I saw beyond the stars. I breathed until I could hear them. Then I called out to my bah-ra'an to make sense of what Herod had done. It could not answer me with any words that I would make sense of. Instead I knew these souls of the slain had been servants to the new humanity.

"They will live again with you all in paradise. For now they will be the grandest of beings in the heavens…"

I know that was Mazda comforting me.

"Thank Mazda that we lost none of our own," I heard Melchior say beside me.

I closed my eyes and remembered the look on Mahesh's face before he collapsed. I knew Herod's slaughter was not over just yet.

I made way to see how Mahesh was the next morning. He was lying within the tent of our physician, still in the clothes he had ridden to Bethlehem in. Mahesh stared at the roof of the tent. It was a blank, hard stare in which I could sense much brooding.

"Mahesh," I called out softly but he still stared above him.

I walked to stand by his side and called his name again. Mahesh now turned to look at me and for a moment I thought he was someone else. His face was changed completely. I do not mean his features or his structure, but the expression was so unlike anything I had seen of him that he appeared as another. His eyes burned into mine.

"How are you feeling?" I asked.

Mahesh sneered. "I feel nothing."

I lowered myself beside him and began to say some prayers. I knew no other way to respond to his answer.

"Stop!" he cried out.

I looked up at him and could see his face was flushed with red beneath his brown skin.

"Please tell me what is happening within you?" I asked of him. "I cannot imagine the horror you saw…"

"I didn't just see it. I smelt it and I heard it. I cannot close off the cries of the women. I can still hear them from here. They carry across the plains with me. They will follow me back to my homeland. I hear them in my sleep. I hear them now as you speak. They will never leave me," Mahesh finished his words and closed his eyes. I knew he wanted me to leave but I could not.

"Mahesh, call out to your bah-ra'an. Say your prayers and this too shall pass. You will find yourself again. This event will fade…" I began but his eyes flew open and his head turned sharply to look at me.

"I have no bah-ra'an. That ride took it from me as surely as Herod did those he killed. You should have sent someone stronger for such a task. You should not have sent me."

His words were crisp and strong. Each word said with force and conviction. When he finished, his eyes remained locked upon mine and I looked deep within them.

Mahesh was right. His bah-ra'an was gone. Not because his spirit had abandoned him in his trauma, but because he had released it to stop feeling so much of what had happened. It was only a matter of time before he released his body as well.

His contract with himself was clear and there was nothing I could do but honour his choice. My eyes filled with tears that Mahesh did not see. Instead all he saw was me stand, and without a word, turn and walk away from him forever.

I was resting within my tent later that afternoon when the physician informed me of Mahesh's passing. I simply nodded and called for any Kshatrapas in our group to come to me.

They all knew of Mahesh's death before they got to me.

"I need to know how we should honour his body. We still have weeks of travel and cannot take it with us. It needs to be done here and today. We move on tomorrow,"

"We burn our deceased," answered one.

I nodded. "Then you will all have this arranged. We shall do so at dusk."

As the sun fell we all walked to surround the pyre that had been built. Six men carried Mahesh's body and placed it upon it. His body had been wrapped in a sheet and bound with ropes to hold his arms and legs in place. Mahesh's face was uncovered though.

"So he can see his way to the next life," was the explanation I was offered.

We said our Zoroastrians prayers, then the Kshatrapas said theirs, asking for the gods to lead him to a glorious life. Then one began to sing the most heart wrenching song as another lit the pyre.

The flames started to dance at the bottom of the woodpile and I stepped forward to look upon Mahesh's face one more time. He looked so peaceful now. There was no struggle there at all.

Then I said the words that he had hoped to hear at our last meeting.

"I am sorry…"

The next morning as we packed up camp and prepared to leave, I saw the Kshatrapas going through the remains of the pyre. Mahesh's flesh was long gone as were the smaller of his bones. What had escaped the force of the flames though were his larger bones and his countrymen now pushed through the ashes and coals knowing they would be there. I watched as they lifted out his thigh bones which now looked like they had been whittled into batons. Then there was his pelvis, now in two as its ligaments had melted. There were a couple of ribs that had somehow survived, an upper arm bone and of course his skull.

One by one they lifted each bone and looked at it, turning it over as though taking in every detail. Then they gently tapped it upon the ground.

"Oh they are clearing off the ash," I thought as I watched them do this.

Indeed the ash did come away, but then they would tap even harder and I saw edges of the bones come away like dust. Made brittle from the heat, they made sure only the true remains would be lifted. The rest must stay as ash and dust with that of the pyre.

When the true remnants of bone were gathered, they wiped each one delicately and with reverence. Then they were placed within one of the Kshatrapa's satchels.

I walked to them just as they began wiping the skull free of ash.

"Sire," the man said and bowed his head. "We are gathering his bones to return to his home. I trust it is alright to carry bones with us."

"Of course," I answered.

In truth he could have said anything. I was too mesmerised by the skull to listen properly.

I gazed upon the skull and was fascinated as to how only a day earlier it had been filled out with muscle, tendons, ligaments, skin and hair. Within it had sat eyes that had looked at me, and a brain working out everything about his existence.

Now it was nothing but a shell: a cold brittle shell that could belong to anyone. I had always questioned the act of burning a body at death. It was not our way. The body remained, anointed to try and preserve some semblance of the life it had shared. It was stored and prayed upon. Its crypt would be honoured.

I looked upon the funeral pyre. No one would pray over or honour this pile of ashes. Within days it would be scattered by the winds anyway. Mahesh's bones would go back to his family home, but they were but a mere representation of what his body had been. There would be no clothing to declare his status, no carving above his crypt to tell his story.

His family may weep some tears as they lit another fire to heat and dissolve the last of his bones. A priest would grind what remained. Mahesh would become part of the land he had left. There would be nothing to weep over or remind future generations of his existence. Just some stories told by those who knew him and they too would fade with time.

As we rode that day I thought about all this over and over. "Where would his spirit sit now? Where would mine sit when I died?" I had always believed it would stay with my body until the days of paradise began.

Perhaps Mahesh would never return for those days now that he did not have a body to represent him. Perhaps Mazda would create a new one for him.

That would be nice. A new fresh young body to live in paradise for eternity. I laughed out loud at this.

"What is so funny?" called out Melchior to my side.

"How do you picture yourself in paradise, my brother?" I asked him.

Melchior shrugged. "To be honest, I have never imagined that at all. But why would that make you laugh?"

"Well I am wondering now, will Mazda bring me back as I was at my death. Will I live out eternity with an old body or will he create new bodies for us to be within?"

Melchior now laughed. "That is the most curious thing you have ever said, Balthasar."

"What bodies we have will be of no consequence in paradise," called out Gaspar behind us. "It will be our hearts and bah-ra'ans that will decide how we will live it."

I turned and looked at him, offering Gaspar a deep smile. "Thank you, brother, that is the deepest truth I have heard in a long time."

It was indeed true. We so believe our bodies decide our experience. It seems the most real aspect of all we experience in our humanness. Yet it is not the way. If our hearts and souls choose paradise, then our body is of no consequence to that choice. It becomes free of all we believe it controls for our experience.

A cripple, a leper, the blind, the elderly: they could all experience paradise equally when their heart and bah-ra'an desire to know it.

So too a bah-ra'an with no body would know it also. I took a deep breath and knew that Mahesh was now free to enjoy paradise anyway he wanted to.

CHAPTER FORTY-ONE

There was no grander feeling than when we crossed the border into Babylonia and we were upon our homeland once more. We had no majestic cities such as Jerusalem. We had no forts or walls to let a foreigner know he entered our domain.

Instead a small settlement marked our arrival back home. It was dusk and we would have no daylight to set up camp but we didn't care. It had been so wonderful to know we could be back upon our lands that we had pushed on, riding three hours more than we would have or should have for the animals.

It was worth it. Every man from every home came to greet us.

"Our homes are yours. Forget your tents and campfires. You will all rest under roofs and with a full belly tonight."

I could have wept.

There was no grand temple in this village. Instead their one elder magus and his home was the place where people worshipped and it was there that Gaspar, Melchior and I would stay.

"I only have two beds but we will make another," he said and as I looked about I realised the comforts and excess of my own home.

"This is wonderful and most appreciated," Gaspar said.

His dining table was the old style. Low to the floor surrounded by cushions that we sat cross-legged upon.

"This table has been that of the magus here for ten generations. I cannot bear to part with it," he said. "Though I am sure one day it will happily see itself off. There are only so many times you can repair such things."

I looked down at the table and saw how there were dips in the wood where plates had sat over for hundreds, if not thousands, of meals. I saw scratches and wine stains upon the wood and smiled. How many men had sat and what had they spoken of?

"Please, would you tell me of your journey and all that happened?" asked the magus.

That night we added to the stories that table witnessed.

Within another full day of riding we were upon Gaspar's hometown. I looked up at the temple there and ached to see my own. As we climbed the stairs to take prayer and look upon the great fire, I fought to hold back my tears. Once inside though with the magnificence of the great fire before me, my tears flowed freely. To my side Melchior saw my tears and put his hand upon my shoulder.

"I am still far from my temple, yet standing here right now I am there," he said.

I felt the same but I wanted Elana. I wanted my children and theirs. I wanted to tell my father everything that had happened. I was back in Baby-lonia and though I had been so far away, right now every mile seemed like a trial to overcome. Even the one night we stayed in Gaspar's town seemed to take forever.

The next day though I was to experience something I did not expect. We were loaded and ready to ride when Gaspar came forward and said goodbye.

It truly was not until that moment that I really registered that he would not be coming any further. His part of the journey was over. He was home.

I grabbed him and hugged him as tightly as I could.

"I know we say the word "brother" a lot but I truly feel we are," I said.

"I agree," he replied.

"You will visit me sometime," I said and it was not a question.

Gaspar shook his head. "I fear that scrolls and messengers will have to do. I intend to never leave my home again!" He raised one eyebrow as he finished but I knew what he said was no way in jest.

I felt the same. I doubt there would ever be anything that would make me leave my home again. I knew Melchior would feel the same also.

So as I said goodbye and rode away, I looked upon him knowing that would most likely be the last time I would have seen his face or have heard his voice. This did not make me as sad as I thought it would. Though there was an ache in my heart to say goodbye, it also felt right to be closing off this time together in such a way. It made what we had done together complete.

I waved and turned to look to the road ahead.

Another two days of riding west and we reached the beginning of the road that would lead Melchior home to his town.

"Do not dismount. I do not need an embrace or emotional words. Let me say goodbye to you as we have been for all these weeks; upon our camels and ready to keep going," he said.

I shook my head. "That hardly seems sufficient."

Melchior looked back to the east and smiled. "Brother, there are no words or gestures that can match what we have done together and not just on this ride. I am thinking back to your teasing the first time we met!"

We both laughed at this.

"Let me leave while we are laughing. That is how I want to remember you."

With that Melchior and the other priests from the north, their acolytes, servants and half the swordsmen turned upon the northern road. The remainder of us sat still and watched for sometime.

I then turned and looked at who remained: the priests of the west, my grandson, the other acolytes, our servants and the guards. For a moment I thought I saw Mahesh amongst the Kshatrapas. There were barely twenty-five of us now. We would travel quicker and make it back to our towns within a couple of days.

"Let's go home," I said and continued on the road west.

When I could see my town off in the distance I called a swordsman to my side.

"Ride fast ahead. Let the temple know we will be back soon and tell them to send word to my family," I told him and he was off in a cloud of dust soon after.

I would have loved to ride fast too, but my camel did not deserve such lack of consideration after all he had endured. No animal we had ridden or used to travel did.

I leant forward and stroked his neck. "Trust me my friend. You will never wear another saddle or carry another sack in your remaining days. You will rest and eat the sweetest hay I promise you."

There was no need to send word ahead of us. Every town we had passed through had already done so. Not only did they know we were near but they knew when to expect us.

Platters of cheeses, fruits and sweets were being laid out. Chickens were being roasted and huge pots bubbled with lamb and goat stews.

"We have to make all of his favourites," Elana said to the cooks.

As we rode closer, my heart began to swell as I could make out which building was which. I saw our temple rising majestically above all else, with its curl of smoke above it. I could make out some people standing upon the top steps. It was the grandchildren, sent to keep watch and let everyone know when we were almost there.

I could see them now jumping up and down, waving their arms in the air and I assume yelling out to us. Their yells burst through the temple, making my father and the other priests run to see. Below in the village, people came running too to find out what was happening."

"They are here! They are here!" was all that they shouted over and over.

"There is so much to tell," was all I could say when my father had come to greet me.

"We will save that for tomorrow. Tonight we celebrate your return. Tomorrow is for stories," he said.

So we had put aside our adventure to simply be home. We had the grandest feast in the dining hall of the temple. It was the only place where we all could be seated with the other priests and have room for servers as well.

Now walking home with my father and Elana something inside made me feel truly at home. I was with my greatest teacher and my deepest love. I felt safe and whole. It was as though someone else had ridden away to find Yeshua.

Elana helped unwind my robes as I made ready for bed.

"Are you comfortable, my love?" she said as I lay back into the feathers and silk.

"Truly I am," I answered and within minutes I was sound asleep.

CHAPTER FORTY-TWO

I had not had one prophetic dream as we travelled. As I have told you before I had rarely had one since my return from the mountain when I was a boy, and all this had begun. That night I slept so soundly that I slipped away from this world to another one entirely: as far as you could without leaving life.

I sat upon a camel once again and when I realised I was not at my home, my heart broke and I shouted to the heavens.

"I served you. I did all I could. Leave me in my home now. There is nothing else for me to do," I yelled.

There was no answer. So as always, I looked to the stars to figure where I was and hopefully why. There above me I saw within minutes all the celestial events that we had watched the past year or more.

I saw Jupiter sit above Venus, then cross over Sharu three times before making way back to Venus. There they joined together, the mother and the father in the brightest marriage the sky had seen.

I looked around me and saw Gaspar and Melchior upon their camels, but they were young boys, small and unsteady in their saddles. Then within moments I saw them grow into men, holding their reins with strong hands and their eyes full of wisdom.

Before us on the ground was a man; he was tall, his hair grew long and free like the Judeans wore it. His eyes were the brightest green, but it was not the colour that made you want to look into them.

He smiled deeply and held out his hands before him. I saw his wrists had deep wounds within them.

"What happened to you?" I called out.

"What was perfect and amazing," he answered. He looked to Gaspar and Melchior then back to me.

"I'll think of you often and will see you all again as I travel," was all he said before he turned and walked away.

I looked to Gaspar and Melchior but they said nothing and their faces stayed blank.

That was all I could remember when I woke.

That morning all the priests gathered to share what those who travelled had experienced. We spoke of the ease of our travels, the dreams we had along the way, the insights and revelations. We told of the discomfort with Herod and his "escort" to protect us. We spoke of the wisdom and grace that Joseph and Mary held within them.

Mostly we spoke of the undeniable truth that Yeshua was the new prophet.

"You could sense it in him. We all did. We heard his bah-ra'an speak to ours. His message is simple and bold. He wants us all to know of the creator we hold within us. He spoke the words "you are god also" to each and everyone of us. This is the new humanity; that Mazda creates us, and we carry him within us."

When I finished I stood silent and waited for a reaction.

Each priest sat quietly contemplating what I spoke of. Then I saw one nod his head.

"Yes, this must be the new humanity. This is what Mazda had promised us. We live in paradise when we know him. So to carry him within us means to live in paradise here in this life."

Another though shook his head. "How do we take the creator within us? That is like asking a child to carry the mother within them."

"And they do all the time," I laughed. "I carry my mother's love and wisdom within me as part of my life, as I do my father's. If we embody Mazda's love and wisdom then too we become him."

I could see minds churning and many more thoughts and beliefs being challenged. I knew this would take more than one conversation for us to know the truth of the words.

"So starting tomorrow, when a farmer comes calling for counsel about his troubles I am to tell him that he is Mazda and to act like it?" one of the younger priests asked.

I sighed. Yes indeed, this would take more than one conversation for us to embrace it.

It was over a week after my return when the first letter arrived from Gaspar, just as mine made way to him. Our carriers would have passed each other upon the road.

His dreams had eased since his return. Occasionally he would see Yeshua as an adult and he took this as his assurance that he would survive anything to be the teacher humanity needed. Then he too spoke of how his temple priests were still perplexed at Yeshua's words.

'I fear this will be something that may take months to embrace...'" he wrote.

"So true, my brother, so true," I said as I read this.

CHAPTER FORTY-THREE

The following years were simple and gentle. It took only weeks upon my return to settle back into my routine so that within months life seemed to be normal once more. The Kshatrapas returned to their homelands in the east, riding off upon camels and donkeys, with the bones of Mahesh tied across a saddle. My home ran business as usual with Daride in charge.

However it was a new normal. One does not have such an experience to return to their previous existence.

Yeshua's words continued to give us much to pray on and discuss. It changed how I viewed the old teachings and it changed how we all chose to counsel people. We had always encouraged people to seek the noble and right choices in their life. That was their path to being whole and complete in Mazda's eyes. That would invite paradise into their lives, if not now then when the awakening came to us.

Now though we knew the awakening was here: paradise was but a step away. There was no more waiting. We had chosen the awakening for our lifetime. Now we could choose to live in the wonder we had been promised for generations.

It was about embracing ourselves as gods. It was this point where we all stuttered and stumbled. Such a foreign concept: to acknowledge our innate ability to create. We had no sense of how we would do this or how it would manifest. We were the blind leading the blind.

"Until we can embrace this how can we teach it to others?" a priest finally said one day.

When he said this I realised it was not going to take many conversations or even several years. This was going to take a generation or two.

Our minds, hearts and lives had been shaped over generations. It only made sense that it would take that to reshape them.

I remembered the words I heard as I watched the first conjunction of Jupiter with Sharu.

"This is just the beginning…"

Now I truly understood what that meant.

We continued on as best we could. We told the story of our journey to all who would listen, knowing that within that was so much to share about our faith and the awakening. People listened with eyes wide and they walked away with not just renewed hope in Mazda but an entirely new hope as to how life could be.

Something within them shifted and as we saw it in the people we felt in ourselves as well. So many years had been spent watching and waiting for a predestined story to unfold. However Zarathustra had left out one part of what he had seen and that was what life would be like after the awakening had begun.

We knew it would be a life of abundance, free of suffering and conflict, but we all lived this life already. What had changed was that there simply was nothing to wait for. That became a bit of a challenge.

"What is next?" an acolyte asked me.

"We don't know until Yeshua grows older and speaks his teachings. In the meantime, let us just celebrate that the awakening has begun," I said to everyone.

So yes it was a wonderful time. There was no searching. No desperation or fear we would miss a message in the sky. Now all there was to do was enjoy our lives, remain upon a virtuous path and wait for Yeshua to speak.

Herod faded from our lives too. He never sent any soldiers to our lands and we knew that if he had intended to harm us we would never have survived travelling more than days away from Jerusalem. We heard of no other slaughters. Even when the soldiers rode through Judea to ask the Jewish astrologers of any news, not one person was harmed.

The astrologers all spoke the same story; we still await our king. They had heard of the massacre in Bethlehem and they knew why, but they also still doubted such a man would be born in such a place. So they had no concern that their messiah was killed.

"He will come from noble blood. He must," they all agreed.

But their noble blood was diluted through the ages. There was no clear lineage that anyone could totally and undeniably claim. Everyone could assert some connection to a noble name; even Joseph had been told he had ties to a Jewish king.

"Yahweh will declare him. Yahweh will let the elders know," was their final agreement and so they continued to wait for their pronouncement from god.

Any fears of Herod were truly gone when he died only a year after Yeshua's birth. Augustus divided Herod's region into three areas, with one area given to each of Herod's sons.

"If his insanity is hereditary then we can at least dilute it with this division. It will be easier to pick them off with an army only a third the size of their father's," Augustus reasoned.

When news reached us, we breathed a sigh of relief and the letters flowed fast between us. There was hope Joseph would return his family north and we might hear of this now. No letters came until several years had passed.

That scroll from the west though took over a year to get to us. It was crushed and creased into a flat strip of parchment. Joseph could not know where specifically to send it. He handed it to a messenger along with two of the gold coins we had gifted him.

"Just head to Babylonia. Give it to any temple you see there. It will find the right priest," he had said.

Joseph also added to not make any haste with its delivery. He knew he did not want it to seem urgent or important. That would mark the messenger for questioning by the soldiers who patrolled the roads. Instead the messenger knew to act as any traveller, pretending to be on his way to family or for their trade. He took his time and months later he crossed into Babylonia and entered the small town that marked our border.

"I need to find a temple," he said to someone who offered him wine.

"That is our temple there," answered the man and pointed to the magus' wood and mud brick home. The only difference between it and other homes was the huge star painted above the door.

He walked hesitantly towards this temple, looking it over as he did to make sure he wasn't being led to something else. The messenger stopped before the door and put his ear against it to see what he could hear. There was silence. He then gently knocked.

"Come in, dear one," he heard from behind the door.

The messenger pushed the door open and saw an elderly man standing, waiting for him.

"You are a magus?" the messenger asked.

"Indeed I am. Can I help you with something, my son?"

"I have been sent from Egypt with this."

The messenger stepped forward and handed the scroll to the magus. There was no wax seal. Joseph had no need of a seal - that was saved for the wealthy and nobility. Instead a simple string tied the paper in place.

When the magus saw this he smiled, wondering who could have sent this. He slid the string off the scroll which was already flattened from months in the messenger's satchel as well as the times it had lay hidden within his sleeve or the chest of his tunic.

The magus stroked the paper for a moment. "Egyptian papyrus. I have never seen or touched it before," he said softly.

The messenger could have left but he stayed in place, somehow knowing he should. He smiled as the magus was mesmerised by the scroll and then almost laughed as he watched his reaction to the words inside.

"Oh bless the stars and the moon! This is wonderful news!" cried the magus and then he looked up at the messenger. "I am glad you are still here. This scroll has much further to go. Shall you be willing to carry it further?"

"Of course ... but ... I need more payment."

The magus shuffled off to another room. "Of course ... of course..." he said waving his hand as he walked away. He returned within a moment and handed the messenger a gold coin.

"You need to head due east and find the temple of Malchiek and Balthasar. That is where this must finally be. Along the way stop at any town you see and make sure the priests there read it also before you continue onwards. They will provide you with food and shelter as you travel. As will I right now. Come let us eat!"

The next morning the magus farewelled the messenger directing him east to our temple. Then he copied the words of the original scroll along with his own message and sent two men from his town with them. One he sent north and the other south.

On the scroll he added this:

'Send this message along to any temple you know of within a day's ride. Tell them to send it on as well. We must let every magus in Babylon know of this news.'

So as the scroll arrived to each temple, it was sent onwards, but then two, three, even four copies spread out in all directions. Some temples received the same message several times but they did not care. They just let this show them that as many priests and temples as possible were hearing the news.

When the scroll arrived to me it had been opened, read, refolded and tied over twenty times in as many temples. Over one hundred men had held it in their hands and read the words.

'We are returning home to the north. Your servant, Joseph'

The writing was crude and simple. I imagined Joseph had searched to find someone who showed him what to write or paid them to scribe his words. Sitting here in my home, holding this tattered piece of papyrus, they were the grandest words we could have read.

Yeshua was still alive and returning to his homeland. I imagined him now; he would be walking and trying to make words.

These first years had been so quick and yet in that strange way it also felt an eternity since we rode away from Ben's farm. These words from Joseph, even though they were plain and brief, also told us so much more.

Our teacher has survived Herod. He had survived exile in a foreign land. He would survive his return.

His teachings would survive.

With the scroll in my hand I called out to every priest at the temple.

"Come! Come! I have wonderful news!"

CHAPTER FORTY-FOUR

It would be many years more until we heard any news of Yeshua again. We continued on with our study of those four words he gave us as a babe. Though our hearts and bah-ra'an were living differently now, it seemed some things still were the same.

My parents left me in quick succession. That did not surprise me. I remember watching them as a child and I simply could not imagine that at anytime had they ever been apart.

I used to love watching my mother help my father take off his over-coat when he arrived home from temple. It was so choreographed that they could have done it blindfolded. Each one knew the others every move so that not once did they ever bump each other or place a hand out of order. That coat would come off and my mother would hand it to a servant within seconds.

The same too at the dinner table: I would watch as my mother scooped more food upon his plate, not once interfering with the movement of his fork or knife. He would be talking to us and stabbing at the food, knowing it would be there.

So when my mother did not wake one morning, I saw my father was half-dead as well. No religion or work can replace that sort of connection with another. Malchiek had already decreased his hours at temple. The climb of its stairs had eluded him years ago and he required servants to carry him. Unfortunately in more recent times we would find him wandering through the temple not sure what he should be doing.

When he made the decision to remain at home more, my mother rejoiced.

"You can read to me. I so love when you do," she had said, though I imagine it was not the thought of books that made this a joy.

We laid my mother's body in the sitting room, as was custom, for one day. My father sat by her and looked at her face without anything distracting him.

"I feel she might have one last thing to say," he said quietly to me.

Her body was carried to temple for her last visit to the great fire and prayers. Then we put her to rest in the family crypt which was carved into the side of one of the mountains on the edge of town.

As we walked back home, my father smiled.

"She cried so much when I left you on the mountain when you were a boy." Then his smile dropped and he stopped in his tracks, turning to look back at the crypt. "We can't leave her there alone!"

Aluna grabbed my arm. "Oh heavens! What do we do?" she hissed.

I looked to my father and then back at the crypt, my mind racing. I had so many things I would have said to someone who gets so lost in their grief they lose reason but saying them to your parent is so different.

"She is safe I promise. Mazda would never let anything happen to her," was all I could think to say.

It was almost the same words he had yelled at my mother and sisters fifty years earlier as they fretted for me upon the mountain. Malchiek heard them like an echo within him. He lowered his head and slowly began to nod.

"Of course Mazda will care for her," he said and began to walk home once more.

One month later we were walking home from placing my father within the crypt beside my mother.

"Thank Mazda that neither of them are alone," whispered Aluna.

Death is always seen as a natural part of life when you are a priest. You bless babies, watch them grown and choose a vocation and a partner. They produce their own children who go on and begin their own lives.

Then you are part of the prayers as they grow weak and ill with old age. Our last rites were over the newly deceased body and then once more as they came to temple, wrapped tightly in their linen or silk shroud, smelling of incense and oils.

I had always accepted this cycle and progression without question. Even when my parents died, though I grieved as much as any of our family, I knew it was Mazda's plan for us. We had been given the gift of life by Mazda; so it was his to take back as well.

Now as I myself grew closer to this day I looked at death with a fresh eye and a heart that sometimes struggled with how much more it seemed to be around me.

First it was my parents and then the eldest of my sisters, Marit left us.

I sat and watched as her children cried over her body. "She could have stayed longer," I thought and immediately shocked myself to have considered this. I knew though that Marit had been long tired of life. She had struggled with health for many years and her death was the respite she had yearned for.

Then I began to hear of men my age who were leaving, including some priests. Death became something much closer to me. The elder priests dying had been to me like losing teachers and guides. They had been the ones to nurture us when myself and the other young ones had begun the dreams of the awakening. They were our foundation, upon which we opened the new era of humanity.

Now when those of my generation began to die I felt an ache within me. I was losing my brothers and it hurt as much as losing my sister. These had been the men who stood by me, who dreamed as Gaspar did and who knew the stars like Melchior did. They were the ones who had believed with me in the coming of a new prophet.

Our acolytes and younger priests were embracing all that we had shared with them, and I had faith they would carry on. Though part of me worried; would they stay true to what we had begun?

We had no word of Yeshua teaching yet. He would only have been around twenty when I had these thoughts. Most of us would be gone when he was truly speaking his words to the crowds. I prayed that the priests after us would hold him in their hearts as we did ours.

I really didn't need to worry.

Not a month went by that a priest from some remote village made way to either Melchior, Gaspar or myself.

"My elders told me to come and serve with you for some time," they would say when they arrived, handing me a letter from their temple elder.

They would come and tend the great fire. They would ask to see the scrolls I wrote when I returned from Bethlehem. I would let them have a day or two to do this, as well as settle into the temple dormitory.

Then I would invite them for dinner at my home. We would eat and make small talk and then when the sweets arrived with the dessert wines, I would turn to them and smile.

"Now, please, ask me what you really want to know!"

They would smile and look down as they worked up some courage. Or they would ask one small question to test the water. Some launched a barrage of questions at once. The questions all came down to the same few.

"What was it like to travel so far?"

"How did you keep your faith?"

"What tested you the most?"

"How were you so certain that Yeshua was the prophet of the awakening?"

There were many questions around these as well. I never tired of answering any of them because each time I spoke about our journey I relived it. Each time I relived it, its energy stayed alive. Each time I reflected upon it, my experience expanded.

Every priest who came to me and asked about the journey became a part of it through his questions. I know that as I spoke, they didn't just hear a story. They travelled with me through time to ride and see what I did.

It was not dwelling on the past. It was keeping the energy of it alive to carry on with a new generation. Each of these men would retell my stories and that in turn kept the journey going.

They travelled to the homes of Gaspar and Melchior as well, and so it continued on through them as well as anyone who was with us who spoke their story.

The words "this is just the beginning" came back again now.

There is never a real end to such an experience. Our bah-ra'an carries it with us always. Then as a group we carried it from generation to generation. It was as though our brotherhood had a bah-ra'an of its own; a soul that we all shared that called out to us all, that held our teachings and would not let our wisdom die.

When I had that epiphany late one night, I went to my desk and wrote to Gaspar and Melchior to tell them.

Gaspar actually laughed when he read it, while Melchior wept.

'There has always been an energy which connected us. I always thought it was Mazda and I know it was. But all men have that connection to the creator. For a group of men to unite with such faith, hope and love as we did, then this makes sense. The bah-ra'an of our brotherhood. That thing which bound us beyond that which even blood could have,' wrote Melchior.

Gaspar was less poetic.

'My priesthood is my life. It consumes me and feeds me. When I travelled with you my life became even more than what it was. It is wonderful that our souls can become even more than we think they are.'

I sat at my desk with both replies before me and I closed my eyes and called to my bah-ra'an. I felt it differently this time though. At first it was as always; that voice within me, that sense of something grand that washed through me.

Then I asked it to show me if there was a truth about our brother-hood bah-ra'an. I asked it to share with me if there was this collective soul amongst those of us who had called upon the awakening.

It was then I felt something that I will struggle to give you the words for. From the space of my soul and from the energy of my body I felt everything fall away. It was like when as a boy I stood before that grand tapestry at the old priest's home. The boundaries and limits of this world were no longer there. This time though I was not the lone soul feeling and experiencing this.

My bah-ra'an swelled up and burst through my personal world. I felt Gaspar, Melchior and every one of the priests who had been with us. We blended and melded into one, though I could still feel each one's identity within this oneness. I then felt every priest who had supported us from their temples and homes. Then the generations before us appeared and they too melded into this energy.

For a moment I felt I would lose myself forever within this mix of souls and experiences. It was then my own bah-ra'an called out to me, reminding that I could never be lost when I was with so much love.

I now truly understood my place. I knew why we had connected as a brotherhood to create this journey and create the new prophet. There was not one part of any of this that I questioned or doubted.

I saw the faces of thousands of priests, from the dawn of our religion to the new acolytes, and they all smiled with an intense love. I felt the thousands who were yet to come and knew we were all linked beyond space and time.

With a deep breath I opened my eyes and looked upon the parchments before me and the dozens of scrolls upon my shelves. I thought of the scrolls in the grand libraries and I knew with every fibre of my being that even when they were long dissolved and a new language may replace the words of our tongues, that their wisdom would never be lost.

In that moment I knew the love that our brotherhood shared and car-ried across the generations was beyond the simple wisdom of knowing information. Our connection through the love of spirit and with our passion for the birth of paradise upon Earth would never die.

This realisation was the greatest gift I could ever give myself. My bah-ra'an called out to me with a sweetness that I will call a caress without touch. The peace that I felt was like nothing I had ever known.

A small bird landed upon my open window sill and considered me, tilting its head from side to side. Then it sang a sweet song as it stretched out its wings. I looked upon the fledgling and saw the absolute beauty of all Mazda's design and I thanked him implicitly for allowing me to be a part of it all.

Not just that, but I thanked Mazda for allowing me the incredible part I had played in his creation. I could have been a farmer or a beggar, but he had allowed me to be his priest and a guardian of the awakening.

That was an honour that I would never forget across all my lifetimes.

CHAPTER FORTY-FIVE

There is a gentility that can come with old age if you allow it. Even with my responsibilities and the weight of what I had experienced I allowed it into my life.

I watched as new priests had to truly push themselves to listen to a villager who came for counselling and direction. I remembered when I first sat and listened as they came to speak to me. How I had had to force my focus onto their words while remembering to feel my essence as well. Now it was as effortless as a simple breath.

I could sit with someone now and not even have to hear their words so much. Their story did not matter. Instead I would feel what their heart was calling out for; happiness, clarity or some direction to step forward with. Then I would call to their bah-ra'an to come close.

In my later years there was little I would say to direct or provide solutions in the way of the human. Instead I would remind them of the glory of the creator that resided within them. After hearing those words from Yeshua there seemed little else to share with people that would be of any service to their life.

Some looked at me puzzled, others would sigh with deep relief as though I had lifted a disease from them. It would be the challenge for generations to come; to see beyond what was simply around them and to feel the grander elements of life at play in this world.

So to some that was a frustrating fairytale that provided no solace or solution. To others it was the freedom they craved.

I was almost upon my seventieth year when a man arrived on my doorstep. My butler came to me to announce his arrival without any name and I assumed he was yet another young priest sent to hear my story. Yet as I walked to the entry of my home to greet him I could feel this was someone else.

He didn't even need to say his name. His bright green eyes told me who he was exactly.

"Yeshua!" I cried out and held my arms out to him.

He said nothing and came to me so I could take him in my arms. There we both wept gently onto each other's shoulders.

When we finally pulled back I held onto his arms and looked into his face, while he continued to smile upon me.

"Where do we start?" was all I could say.

After Yeshua had bathed and had fresh clothes put upon him, we sat and ate the midday meal. I looked upon him, now fresh and clean, and saw his face was so clear and his eyes so present.

"This is truly a grand meal, Sire," he said as he reached for some goose.

"Do not call me Sire. I should call you that," I said.

"You know as well as I do that I am no grander than you," he replied.

"How can you say that?" I said and frowned.

Yeshua laughed. "My grand magus, I would not be here without you. You are to me as I am to you."

"Fine, then the names we were gifted by our fathers shall do," I laughed. "Do tell me all of what has been with you."

And so Yeshua spoke.

He told me of how Joseph had taken them to Egypt to escape Herod and their return to Nazareth upon Herod's death.

"Since I can remember my father told me stories of my birth. I heard about the messages from the angels, the journey to Bethlehem and all the people who cared for us there," Yeshua spoke softly then paused and the warmest smile broke upon his face. "Then he told me of you and your brothers. That was always my favourite part. He spoke of the dreams and how you arrived at Ben's farm with gifts.

"I would imagine you riding upon your camels, all that way, just to see me. All because of what you saw in the sky..." He said and his eyes glistened.

"Yes, because of what we saw in the sky," I replied.

"But I also know it was because of what you also felt in your hearts. Men of such wisdom must listen to something within as well, mustn't they?"

I nodded and felt a warmth fill my heart that made my chest feel like it would burst.

"I never tired of the story of you. I made my father tell me over and over again. Each time I heard it I could feel all of you watching over me, guiding me. I would pray to Yahweh that I would be as grand and wise as you believed me to be."

"Did Yahweh ever answer you?" I asked and my hand tightened on the glass I was holding.

Yeshua looked down for a moment and then he nodded. He looked up at me.

"He said I would be all you had hoped for, because you had gifted me with your journey. Yahweh has told me this many times."

"Is this all he has told you?" I asked knowing there was more before he even answered.

Yeshua nodded. "He has told me that I am Yahweh in a body as are all men and women." Then he paused and looked down. Without looking up he continued, "Now I just need to figure out how to share this with people. I will be a blasphemer to many, but to others I will give them all the answers they seek."

I nodded.

"It will take time ... and..." I faltered to find the right words. "And ... we may not ever find the way to do this in our lifetime ... but—we must begin it. No matter the outcome for us. We must begin it."

Yeshua looked up and I saw a resolve in his eyes. "Yes, Balthasar." He nodded. "That is what matters, that we begin it."

We rested after lunch as I wanted us to both stay awake into the night to watch the sky together. I stood and pointed out Jupiter, Sharu and Venus. Then I told him every movement of the dance they had played together; what had transpired with the priesthood at each stage and how our gathering had come about.

"Then came the day when we knew we would come to see you," I said.

"Gaspar told me this story also," he said with a laugh.

"Oh and you let me bore you with repeating it!" I declared.

"Not at all. I wanted to hear your version of it."

"Was it so different?" I asked.

Yeshua shook his head. "The words may have differed, but the story feels the same."

Yeshua had visited Gaspar just a week or so before me. There too he had sat and told of his childhood to my brother, who had let tears fall from his face as he listened.

"I know it was your dreams that saved my life," Yeshua said to him.

Gaspar could hardly speak to answer him. He was now in his final years and most things were an effort, some days even to talk.

"I was so scared we had failed you in our actions, despite all we had felt in our hearts and souls," he finally said. "You have no idea of the joy it is to sit with you here now as a man. I saw you so many times in my dreams as you are now. I know it is a gift from Mazda to see you as this so I may go to my death with the knowing that what I saw was your truth."

Gaspar had not sent word on to me of Yeshua's visit to him. He knew that Yeshua would reach me as quickly as any letter would. However once he had heard that Yeshua had made it to my temple I received what would be my last letter from Gaspar.

It was written in an unsteady hand that explained its brevity.

'My dear brother Balthasar,

I breathe deep and rejoice that my life was with the meaning that I prayed for as a child. I looked into Yeshua's eyes and saw the truth and confirmation of all we did. I will return to Mazda with the absolute knowing that we did indeed act as guardians of the grand awakening.

With love and honour

Your brother, Gaspar'

The next letter that I received from Gaspar's temple only months later was to inform me that he had died. It was a peaceful death. He had asked to be carried to lie before the great fire in his temple and there he took his last breath before the flames, surrounded by the men he had taught and led.

I sat at my desk, put my hands to face and sobbed like a child when I read the letter. I cried even more than at losing my parents. The loss of Gaspar though reached and tore at something deep within me. He had been my confidant and pillar, something beyond a friend or even a respected colleague.

I knew that our connection was beyond being part of a priesthood or even having a common purpose. We had chosen to work together, or perhaps Mazda had chosen us to be together to create all we had done along with Melchior.

Even though other priests of our time and the journey had died, to lose Gaspar now felt like the whole experience was beginning to dissolve. Part of me just was not ready for that.

CHAPTER FORTY-SIX

Yeshua stayed in my home for only a few days more. I heard how one day Joseph and Mary had thought him lost, only to find him speaking to some men in the town square about god and our place on Earth.

"I remember deciding to go for a walk when I was not even ten years old. I am still not sure what drove me to. Then I saw these men; to some they would seem to have been arguing but to me I saw them playing with words. They were discussing whether Yahweh had carved out their lives or whether he simply watched over us as we decided our path.

"It was the richest conversation I had ever heard and it intrigued me to see men outside the priesthood talking about their beliefs. So I walked up to them and they did not notice me at first which was good as I could listen more. Then I decided to join in.

"I said, 'What if we are created in Yahweh's image as he has told us, and he simply sets us free to have whatever experience we can. If our destinies were truly carved out and we are of his image as the testaments tell us, then we would all be upon the same path. Why would he choose prosperity for some and not others?

"They stopped and looked down at me. One of them told me to go home. Another asked if my father was a priest. Another declared I must simply be repeating what I had heard elsewhere. The fourth man squatted down before me and said, 'Speak more, child.'

"So I did. I took one deep breath and then the words just flowed. I spoke of things I had never been told of or even had read. I heard things come from my mouth that even made me want to stop and consider their meaning.

"By the time my mother found me a crowd had gathered. When I saw her walk towards me, thankfully smiling, I knew I had said enough. She excused herself and announced we needed to make way home. People called out to let me talk some more, but she said it was enough for one day.

"The next day, some of the men found out where we lived. They came and asked if I could speak more to them. I remember sitting behind my mother as she stood at the doorway with the men. She turned and looked at me without saying a word but I knew she was asking me if I wanted to speak with the men again.

"I stood and walked to the doorway. Part of me wanted to hesitate but I knew that could not be. I told my mother to let them in. Then I spoke again even more words that I did not know of before that day." Yeshua paused and reached for some tea that was before us.

"But you did stop speaking as such didn't you?" I asked.

"Yes, I had too," he replied. "It was not from any danger, though some priests did visit my father and told them I was a blasphemer. Each night as I lay in bed on the verge of sleep I had begun some other ... communications is probably the best word. An angel might appear at my bedside and tell me more of what I had spoken that day. Some nights I would hear Yahweh himself talk to me.

"When I was around twelve years of age he told me I needed to stop. When I asked why, expecting him to tell me I was doing it wrong, he assured me this was not the case.

"Instead I was told I needed time to be with myself, to know myself and hear my own voice."

I shuddered a bit, remembering the stories my father told me of the "hearers" who lost their way. Yeshua saw my reaction though.

"Yes, I too heard many stories of those who hear voices getting lost to them, so even though I knew this was the voice of Yahweh, I too was slightly fearful. But I took his heed and the next day when people came to the door we simply told them I had no more messages for them.

"That night the hugest angel I had ever seen arrived. His name is Raffa and he still comes to me sometimes. We spoke for hours, even into my sleep. This was over months of time. He taught me to know my inner voice from the voice of another energy, namely the eternal spirit of Yahweh. Most of all he reminded me to trust myself and that would stop me ever losing my way—and even if I did lose my way, well then I could call upon him or any of the angels to return me to my truth.

"So Balthasar, I am still upon my journey to know myself and to have my own experiences. I trust that spirit will guide me to teach when the time is perfect. And then it will also show me how it is to be done."

I nodded as he finished. Part of me wondered how differently my life would have been to have had that time just to listen to my own voice. I thought about sitting up in the mountain cave and almost wanted to laugh. It would have killed me to stop teaching or listening to the stars. Yes, my path had been just perfect as it was.

Yeshua though had much more that he needed to know of before he could step into his role as teacher once more. I understood that these years were being used to infuse him with wisdom and knowing. I was certain that was why he now visited with us, to share our wisdom and knowing. Then he would travel on and experience other priests and their teachings.

Imagine that; a teacher who had experienced everything he could, along with his innate divinity and wisdom gifted directly from the creator.

"You must go even further east and visit the Kshatrapas!" I declared.

Yeshua did head east but not without detouring north to visit Melchior and all the priests along the way.

At Melchior's he lay awake one night, after they had finished some time stargazing. He looked to the ceiling as the lamplight flickered upon it and suddenly the shadows and whips of light created shapes he could discern.

Yeshua saw the great caravan of ours moving west to see him. He looked at each animal and man one at a time and even though they were all rendered in sepia tones upon the ceiling, he could see each one as a separate being. He saw myself, then the other priests, followed by our servants and all others. Yeshua smiled and closed his eyes and called out to the spirit father Yahweh.

"I understand," he whispered.

In that moment, Yeshua had not just seen a group of men and animals travelling. He saw their very spirits united as one, each a separate flame of one great fire. Yeshua felt the heat of their love and the passion which drove them.

"Their story will remind others of their desire to birth a new era, to be reborn with spirit," he thought.

Yeshua turned down his lamp and the cinema above him was no more. He closed his eyes and slept soundly until dawn.

We heard word from Yeshua once he was deep within the lands you now refer to as India. The Kshatrapas had welcomed him to their homes with open arms and hearts. The ones who had returned from our journey had told and retold their story so much and so often that many there waited to hear from this new teacher.

Yeshua was taken to the place where Mahesh and the other pilgrims' ashes had been laid to rest. When Mahesh's bones had arrived they were burnt once more and ground into dust. The dust had then been scattered at the edge of a jungle.

"They say each year, at the time of the journey, a tiger comes and sits upon the ground where the dust was poured. They say the tiger is Mahesh coming to remind us of all that he did."

Yeshua was told this as they stood looking at the trees and just as the story finished he saw some orange and black move amongst the green. Then the grandest animal he had ever seen stepped from the trees right before them and sat, wrapping its tail around itself.

Behind Yeshua most of the men with him had run screaming back to the nearby village. Yeshua though stood in place.

"Master, you must—we must go! These animals eat us!" one of the remaining men begged as he began to step back.

Yeshua did not listen. There was no fear within him as he knew who this tiger was. He walked slowly towards the great cat, holding out one hand. When he was close enough he stroked the tiger's head.

"Thank you Mahesh," he said gently.

The tiger looked into his eyes then stood and walked back into the jungle. When Yeshua turned around the few men that had remained were fallen upon the ground calling out to any gods they could name, asking them to bless Yeshua.

"Oh please," laughed Yeshua as he walked past them. "Bless me yourselves by finding me some wine and food!"

CHAPTER FORTY-SEVEN

The story of Yeshua and the tiger was but one of the stories that made way back to me. Over the years I would receive many more and I will admit they kept me alive. I was well past the usual amount of years any man should live. Priests were renowned for living long due to our comfortable lives and a minimum of hard physical work. We simply did not get as worn out as a farmer or blacksmith.

I do believe though our longevity was also to do with our connection to spirit. We were born into or had chosen our life as a priest and that had inextricably tied our bah-ra'an to teaching the love and wisdom of Mazda. It just made sense that we would live lives as long as possible to gather and then share our wisdom for as long as possible.

Now this does not mean that some priests' lives did not end at younger ages; just they were few. We would even joke when a young priest took his final vows.

"Are you entirely sure? Because you will have many, many years to regret this!"

Even though we did say it as joke, I saw several men walk away from the great fire upon hearing it.

"I am not strong enough to make such a promise," one muttered and we never saw him again.

Longevity has its downfalls as well. You see loved ones pass away, the worst of all being your children or worse still your grandchildren. Some days I wondered if somehow I had cheated the very rules of a normal life simply due to my vocation.

My Elana walked with me until near the very end.

"My saviour, how could I leave you? Though some days the rest would be lovely," she laughed.

Now as I look back I know the real pull to remain as long as I could was to see what would become of Yeshua.

He visited me once more as he passed through Babylonia on the way back west and it would be the last time we would see each other, in person anyway. His hair was long as was his beard. Yeshua's face was plump and there was roundness to his belly but otherwise he was tall and lean.

"So much rice and these wonderful spicy stews that you must try some day," he had said as he patted his stomach. "Their wine though was terrible."

Yeshua told me of his time to the east, how everyone and not just the Kshatrapas had welcomed him.

"Once the story of who I was spread, they seemed to be waiting for me. There was never a meal I went without or a night without a bed," he recalled.

As Yeshua travelled he asked about their local religions and heard about the myriad of gods that they loved and adored.

"How do you tell these people that they have ten or twenty gods within themselves," he said and we both laughed.

"But then I understood it perfectly. Each God was a symbol of an aspect of life, of a part of each of us. A god for fertility and family. One for destruction and rebirth. Another for the part of us that connects to the earth.

"These people were all these gods as all these gods were parts of the one god. They had just broken it down to focus on what they needed in their lives at any given time.

"So I asked them: did they see that each god was a part of them - and some of them truly understood. Then they asked me to speak more and soon wherever I went I would have a crowd to listen. Though some threw rotten fruit at me too!"

We both laughed out loud at this.

"So you began to speak again?" I asked.

"Yes I did and it felt wonderful. It felt even stronger than it had when I was a child," Yeshua said smiling and then he paused for a moment.

"It felt so similar but it was also new. I truly know these years to myself had allowed me to be even closer to the wisdom I called upon when I spoke. I know it is not just age that allowed it.

"There felt like there was just so much more. And I also found something else that was wonderful; I listened to the people who had gathered. Many times they had as much wisdom and connection as I did. I learnt from their words as well or I heard my words back to me."

Yeshua put his hand to his heart as he went on. "I may have been marked at my birth for such things, but there are many who want to speak these truths and who know these truths as well as I do."

I slowly nodded. I knew the beauty of such camaraderie.

"Did you not want to stay and teach there?" I asked.

Yeshua smiled. "Yes I did. I felt so at home there. I even found someone I could have made my wife. They called me Eesa in their language and it pulled at something inside me like it was my true name.

"But spirit is calling me west once more. I know I must return to Judea. I know also that it won't be easy and there is a twist in my gut to even cross the river to go back there. I just know I must return and complete this life upon those lands."

When Yeshua left my home the next day I stood at my door and watched him walk through the village. I had offered him a camel but he had almost scoffed at the idea.

"Helpful, but also a responsibility I can do without. I prefer to walk. You see and hear so much more," he had said.

So he made way upon foot with a simple satchel upon his shoulder. In it was some dried bread, cheese and fruit. From his waist hung a small bladder for water or wine. I had handed him a small purse of gold, but he shook his head. Yeshua opened it and took out one coin before he handed the purse back to me.

"To remember you by," he had said and his eyes sparkled. "And in case I truly get into some trouble along the way."

I watched him walk now and you could almost imagine his satchel was filled with jewels and gold instead of just food.

"He doesn't walk like a simple man," I thought to myself.

That was because he was far from a simple man.

Over the following year or so the stories of Yeshua came to me. I heard his bold declarations that he was god. I heard the tales of his miracle healings. Some embraced his words and there came letters from those who followed him to support and teach with him.

I sat with the travellers who stopped in our homes and told me of all that was unfolding in Judea. They were heading east to spend time in the lands of India and Tibet after hearing of Yeshua's time there.

"He said we must stop and visit with the magi too," they all told me and I would smile every time.

Each one of them would arrive with eyes clear and sharp. There was clarity in their words and they reminded me of Yeshua as he headed east. These men would also pass by as they returned west and I would see in them what I saw in Yeshua as he made way home.

There would now be a calmness to them that was not just of maturity. They would head east with wide-eyed wonder and excitement as to the adventure ahead. On their return they would carry with them a knowing that slowed their actions and speech. It was an outward reflection of a very deep inner change, and I loved to see this in them.

I will admit that at first I imagined it was something to do with the lands they had visited. I know that many people still make way to these places in the quest to receive their enlightenment. However I had seen such change in men right here in Babylonia. I even thought about myself and how changed I was from that first counsel session I had sat in at in my youth. Then I compared that to who I was in my forties.

It was not just the lands of the east that did this to these men. It was the commitment to their spirit that allowed such a change. I imagine some of them could have gone to the temple schools in Egypt and done much the same.

They travelled east to emulate the time Yeshua, or Eesa, had gifted himself, and for the most part they gifted themselves. Some did choose to not return and live their life there and even fewer came back just as lost as when they had arrived. Not all journeys can be the same when all our heart and soul connections are so different.

I so loved to see the ones who sat in my homes as they travelled back west. I would ask them questions and revel in their answers. My favourite question to ask them was always this;

"What will you do with what you have learned during your travels?"

Some would stay silent for some time. Others would answer immediately. They would all smile as they answered with the same words.

"I will share it with whoever wants to know."

That made my heart swell with pride. Yeshua was not just a teacher of the new consciousness. He was also inspiring more teachers for the new humanity. These men were the beginning of a new priesthood. I knew they too would inspire even more to teach and share.

Yes this was just the beginning.

CHAPTER FORTY-EIGHT

My Elana left me that year. As she faded away gently on our bed I held her small hand in my hand.

"We will be together again in paradise soon my love," I said to her.

"This has been paradise, to live with you," she replied and closed her eyes for eternity.

That was the first time in my life that I had ever felt alone. I suddenly realised how big our home was and how few people around me had been there when I had left on my grand journey. I decided I needed to start bringing other things in my life to an end.

I called for assistance to make my last visit to the temple. I was carried up the stairs by four of my great-grandsons who were now priests. In fact there were ten priests now serving who were of my blood or married to my family. They along with the other priests gathered in the room of the great fire to hear me announce my official retirement.

"You have better things to do here than carry me up and down the stairs," I joked and many of them strained smiles.

I was given a grand party that was held at my home and I was gifted all sorts of things; walking canes made from wood of frankincense trees, jars of preserves from the west, sacks of incense, jars of oils, rolls of silks and so much more.

I looked upon them all, stacked in a corner of the room and wanted to laugh. I knew I did not have enough time left in me to use even half of these gifts, but my heart was warm with the love showed through them.

Even until my final years I would spend each night beneath the stars. It got harder to lift my head upwards so I had a special couch made that I could recline upon to watch with ease. I never fell asleep upon it once.

I could still hear them and see beyond them, but I always stopped to just admire their beauty too. Eighty years and more, yet I did not tire of their magnificence. These dazzling lights that Mazda put in place, with their dance amongst each other. One night I felt truly overcome as I recalled all they had been within my life.

I thought back to my lessons as a child. They had been such a wonderful time with my father. I recalled my dream in which the stars led me home and all that had triggered. Then most of all I would think about that year when Venus, Jupiter and Sharu changed our lives forever.

I did not cry but I was always overwhelmed at all they had allowed within my life. I even thought how it would be hard to believe in thousands of years. Would this all become a myth? Would it even be forgotten?

Part of me thanks you for reading this and keeping my bah-ra'an alive. Part of me also knows I need no recognition. What needed to be woken and revealed did so. How and who did this will be such a small part of the new era.

I lay back upon my couch and imagined thousands, even millions of people walking the Earth connected to their souls, with the beautiful knowing that they are god also.

I looked one last time at the stars and saw that each one of them was a promise from Mazda that this would be so.

I then closed my eyes for the final time as Balthasar the magus.

In loving memory of
David Strassler
1941 - 2011

Nobody would have waited for this
book with as much anticipation as you.
I know wherever you are that
you are reading it now.

Elana's Honey Cakes

I first channelled the story of Gaspar punching Balthasar over the secret honey cakes at an event in Sydney, Australia. Afterwards a woman who had been there came to me and said she had relatives who still made something very similar. I had a sense of exactly what the cakes would have been like and when this woman sent me a recipe I knew they were very close to what Balthasar described.

In modern times they are called "Melomakarona" in Greece and there are similar renditions through the Middle East and Egypt. In fact I even ate some while cruising on the Nile River.

This recipe seems the most simple and straight forward version I could find. I am sure it has a few things that Elana may not have used but I like to think it is pretty close to giving us the fun of trying her delicious cakes.

Ingredients

3 ½ cup flour
1 tsp baking powder
⅛ tsp salt
¼ cup orange juice
1 tsp orange zest
½ tsp bicarbonate soda
⅔ cup olive oil
6 tablespoon sugar
1 cup crushed walnuts

Recipe for Honey Syrup

1 cup honey
½ cup sugar
⅔ cup water
1 tsp lemon juice

- Put all ingredients into a saucepan over medium heat until boiling.

- Reduce heat and simmer for 5 minutes, keep warm.

Method

- Preheat oven to 180°C.

- Mix dry ingredients in a bowl.

- Blend juice, zest, oil and sugar well.

- Add flour mixture gradually to orange mixture, stir until combined.

- Roll dough into small balls.

- Transfer to greased baking sheet, press with the tines of a fork that was dipped in flour to flatten them a little.

- Bake for 20-25 minutes.

- Dip cookies into hot syrup, transfer to baking sheet, sprinkle with cinnamon and walnuts.

- Cool cookies completely before serving.

Enjoy!

Printed in the USA
CPSIA information can be obtained
at www.ICGtesting.com
LVHW020614121023
760848LV00012B/123